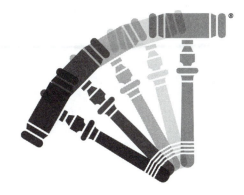

Casenote Legal Briefs

CONSTITUTIONAL LAW

Keyed to Courses Using

**Choper, Fallon, Kamisar, and Shiffrin's
Constitutional Law**

Eleventh Edition

Wolters Kluwer

Law & Business

Published by Wolters Kluwer Law & Business in New York.

Wolters Kluwer Law & Business serves customers worldwide with CCH, Aspen Publishers, and Kluwer Law International products.

No part of this publication may be reproduced or transmitted in any form or by any means, electronic or mechanical, including photocopy, recording, or any information storage and retrieval system, without permission in writing from the publisher. For information about permissions or to request permission online, visit us at *wolterskluwerlb.com* or a written request may be faxed to our permissions department at 212-771-0803.

To contact Customer Service, e-mail customer.service@wolterskluwer.com, call 1-800-234-1660, fax 1-800-901-9075, or mail correspondence to:

Wolters Kluwer Law & Business
Attn: Order Department
P.O. Box 990
Frederick, MD 21705

Printed in the United States of America.

1 2 3 4 5 6 7 8 9 0

ISBN 978-1-4548-0515-1

About Wolters Kluwer Law & Business

Wolters Kluwer Law & Business is a leading global provider of intelligent information and digital solutions for legal and business professionals in key specialty areas, and respected educational resources for professors and law students. Wolters Kluwer Law & Business connects legal and business professionals as well as those in the education market with timely, specialized authoritative content and information-enabled solutions to support success through productivity, accuracy and mobility.

Serving customers worldwide, Wolters Kluwer Law & Business products include those under the Aspen Publishers, CCH, Kluwer Law International, Loislaw, Best Case, ftwilliam.com and MediRegs family of products.

CCH products have been a trusted resource since 1913, and are highly regarded resources for legal, securities, antitrust and trade regulation, government contracting, banking, pension, payroll, employment and labor, and healthcare reimbursement and compliance professionals.

Aspen Publishers products provide essential information to attorneys, business professionals and law students. Written by preeminent authorities, the product line offers analytical and practical information in a range of specialty practice areas from securities law and intellectual property to mergers and acquisitions and pension/benefits. Aspen's trusted legal education resources provide professors and students with high-quality, up-to-date and effective resources for successful instruction and study in all areas of the law.

Kluwer Law International products provide the global business community with reliable international legal information in English. Legal practitioners, corporate counsel and business executives around the world rely on Kluwer Law journals, looseleafs, books, and electronic products for comprehensive information in many areas of international legal practice.

Loislaw is a comprehensive online legal research product providing legal content to law firm practitioners of various specializations. Loislaw provides attorneys with the ability to quickly and efficiently find the necessary legal information they need, when and where they need it, by facilitating access to primary law as well as state-specific law, records, forms and treatises.

Best Case Solutions is the leading bankruptcy software product to the bankruptcy industry. It provides software and workflow tools to flawlessly streamline petition preparation and the electronic filing process, while timely incorporating ever-changing court requirements.

ftwilliam.com offers employee benefits professionals the highest quality plan documents (retirement, welfare and non-qualified) and government forms (5500/PBGC, 1099 and IRS) software at highly competitive prices.

MediRegs products provide integrated health care compliance content and software solutions for professionals in healthcare, higher education and life sciences, including professionals in accounting, law and consulting.

Wolters Kluwer Law & Business, a division of Wolters Kluwer, is head-quartered in New York. Wolters Kluwer is a market-leading global information services company focused on professionals.

Format for the Casenote® Legal Brief

Nature of Case: This section identifies the form of action (e.g., breach of contract, negligence, battery), the type of proceeding (e.g., demurrer, appeal from trial court's jury instructions), or the relief sought (e.g., damages, injunction, criminal sanctions).

Party ID: Quick identification of the relationship between the parties.

Fact Summary: This is included to refresh your memory and can be used as a quick reminder of the facts.

Rule of Law: Summarizes the general principle of law that the case illustrates. It may be used for instant recall of the court's holding and for classroom discussion or home review.

Facts: This section contains all relevant facts of the case, including the contentions of the parties and the lower court holdings. It is written in a logical order to give the student a clear understanding of the case. The plaintiff and defendant are identified by their proper names throughout and are always labeled with a (P) or (D).

Palsgraf v. Long Island R.R. Co.

Injured bystander (P) v. Railroad company (D)

N.Y. Ct. App., 248 N.Y. 339, 162 N.E. 99 (1928).

NATURE OF CASE: Appeal from judgment affirming verdict for plaintiff seeking damages for personal injury.

FACT SUMMARY: Helen Palsgraf (P) was injured on R.R.'s (D) train platform when R.R.'s (D) guard helped a passenger aboard a moving train, causing his package to fall on the tracks. The package contained fireworks which exploded, creating a shock that tipped a scale onto Palsgraf (P).

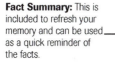

RULE OF LAW
The risk reasonably to be perceived defines the duty to be obeyed.

FACTS: Helen Palsgraf (P) purchased a ticket to Rockaway Beach from R.R. (D) and was waiting on the train platform. As she waited, two men ran to catch a train that was pulling out from the platform. The first man jumped aboard, but the second man, who appeared as if he might fall, was helped aboard by the guard on the train who had kept the door open so they could jump aboard. A guard on the platform also helped by pushing him onto the train. The man was carrying a package wrapped in newspaper. In the process, the man dropped his package, which fell on the tracks. The package contained fireworks and exploded. The shock of the explosion was apparently of great enough strength to tip over some scales at the other end of the platform, which fell on Palsgraf (P) and injured her. A jury awarded her damages, and R.R. (D) appealed.

ISSUE: Does the risk reasonably to be perceived define the duty to be obeyed?

HOLDING AND DECISION: (Cardozo, C.J.) Yes. The risk reasonably to be perceived defines the duty to be obeyed. If there is no foreseeable hazard to the injured party as the result of a seemingly innocent act, the act does not become a tort because it happened to be a wrong as to another. If the wrong was not willful, the plaintiff must show that the act as to her had such great and apparent possibilities of danger as to entitle her to protection. Negligence in the abstract is not enough upon which to base liability. Negligence is a relative concept, evolving out of the common law doctrine of trespass on the case. To establish liability, the defendant must owe a legal duty of reasonable care to the injured party. A cause of action in tort will lie where harm,

though unintended, could have been averted or avoided by observance of such a duty. The scope of the duty is limited by the range of danger that a reasonable person could foresee. In this case, there was nothing to suggest from the appearance of the parcel or otherwise that the parcel contained fireworks. The guard could not reasonably have had any warning of a threat to Palsgraf (P), and R.R. (D) therefore cannot be held liable. Judgment is reversed in favor of R.R. (D).

DISSENT: (Andrews, J.) The concept that there is no negligence unless R.R. (D) owes a legal duty to take care as to Palsgraf (P) herself is too narrow. Everyone owes to the world at large the duty of refraining from those acts that may unreasonably threaten the safety of others. If the guard's action was negligent as to those nearby, it was also negligent as to those outside what might be termed the "danger zone." For Palsgraf (P) to recover, R.R.'s (D) negligence must have been the proximate cause of her injury, a question of fact for the jury.

► ANALYSIS

The majority defined the limit of the defendant's liability in terms of the danger that a reasonable person in defendant's situation would have perceived. The dissent argued that the limitation should not be placed on liability, but rather on damages. Judge Andrews suggested that only injuries that would not have happened but for R.R.'s (D) negligence should be compensable. Both the majority and dissent recognized the policy-driven need to limit liability for negligent acts, seeking, in the words of Judge Andrews, to define a framework "that will be practical and in keeping with the general understanding of mankind." The Restatement (Second) of Torts has accepted Judge Cardozo's view.

▬

Quicknotes

FORESEEABILITY A reasonable expectation that change is the probable result of certain acts or omissions.

NEGLIGENCE Conduct falling below the standard of care that a reasonable person would demonstrate under similar conditions.

PROXIMATE CAUSE The natural sequence of events without which an injury would not have been sustained.

▬

Concurrence/Dissent: All concurrences and dissents are briefed whenever they are included by the casebook editor.

Analysis: This last paragraph gives you a broad understanding of where the case "fits in" with other cases in the section of the book and with the entire course. It is a hornbook-style discussion indicating whether the case is a majority or minority opinion and comparing the principal case with other cases in the casebook. It may also provide analysis from restatements, uniform codes, and law review articles. The analysis will prove to be invaluable to classroom discussion.

Issue: The issue is a concise question that brings out the essence of the opinion as it relates to the section of the casebook in which the case appears. Both substantive and procedural issues are included if relevant to the decision.

Holding and Decision: This section offers a clear and in-depth discussion of the rule of the case and the court's rationale. It is written in easy-to-understand language and answers the issue presented by applying the law to the facts of the case. When relevant, it includes a thorough discussion of the exceptions to the case as listed by the court, any major cites to the other cases on point, and the names of the judges who wrote the decisions.

Quicknotes: Conveniently defines legal terms found in the case and summarizes the nature of any statutes, codes, or rules referred to in the text.

Wolters Kluwer Law & Business is proud to offer *Casenote® Legal Briefs*—continuing thirty years of publishing America's best-selling legal briefs.

Casenote® Legal Briefs are designed to help you save time when briefing assigned cases. Organized under convenient headings, they show you how to abstract the basic facts and holdings from the text of the actual opinions handed down by the courts. Used as part of a rigorous study regimen, they can help you spend more time analyzing and critiquing points of law than on copying bits and pieces of judicial opinions into your notebook or outline.

Casenote® Legal Briefs should never be used as a substitute for assigned casebook readings. They work best when read as a follow-up to reviewing the underlying opinions themselves. Students who try to avoid reading and digesting the judicial opinions in their casebooks or online sources will end up shortchanging themselves in the long run. The ability to absorb, critique, and restate the dynamic and complex elements of case law decisions is crucial to your success in law school and beyond. It cannot be developed vicariously.

Casenote® Legal Briefs represents but one of the many offerings in Legal Education's Study Aid Timeline, which includes:

- *Casenote® Legal Briefs*
- *Emanuel Law Outlines*
- *Examples & Explanations* Series
- *Introduction to Law* Series
- Emanuel *Law in a Flash* Flash Cards
- Emanuel *CrunchTime* Series

Each of these series is designed to provide you with easy-to-understand explanations of complex points of law. Each volume offers guidance on the principles of legal analysis and, consulted regularly, will hone your ability to spot relevant issues. We have titles that will help you prepare for class, prepare for your exams, and enhance your general comprehension of the law along the way.

To find out more about Wolters Kluwer Law & Business's Study Aid publications, visit us online at *www.wolterskluwerlb.com* or email us at *legaledu@ wolterskluwer.com*. We'll be happy to assist you.

Get this Casenote® Legal Brief as an AspenLaw Studydesk eBook today!

By returning this form to Wolters Kluwer Law & Business, you will receive a complimentary eBook download of this Casenote® Legal Brief and AspenLaw Studydesk productivity software.* Learn more about AspenLaw Studydesk today at *www.wolterskluwerlb.com*.

Name	Phone ( )	
Address		Apt. No.
City	State	ZIP Code
Law School	Graduation Date Month _____ Year _____	

Cut out the UPC found on the lower left corner of the back cover of this book. Staple the UPC inside this box. Only the original UPC from the book cover will be accepted. (No photocopies or store stickers are allowed.)

Attach UPC inside this box.

Email (Print legibly or you may not get access!)
Title of this book (course subject)
ISBN of this book (10- or 13-digit number on the UPC)
Used with which casebook (provide author's name)

Mail the completed form to: Wolters Kluwer Law & Business
Legal Education Division
130 Turner Street, Bldg 3, 4th Floor
Waltham, MA 02453-8901

* Upon receipt of this completed form, you will be emailed a code for the digital download of this book in AspenLaw Studydesk eBook format and a free copy of the software application, which is required to read the eBook.

For a full list of eBook study aids available for AspenLaw Studydesk software and other resources that will help you with your law school studies, visit *www.wolterskluwerlb.com*.

Make a photocopy of this form and your UPC for your records.

For detailed information on the use of the information you provide on this form, please see the PRIVACY POLICY at *www.wolterskluwerlb.com*.

A. Decide on a Format and Stick to It

Structure is essential to a good brief. It enables you to arrange systematically the related parts that are scattered throughout most cases, thus making manageable and understandable what might otherwise seem to be an endless and unfathomable sea of information. There are, of course, an unlimited number of formats that can be utilized. However, it is best to find one that suits your needs and stick to it. Consistency breeds both efficiency and the security that when called upon you will know where to look in your brief for the information you are asked to give.

Any format, as long as it presents the essential elements of a case in an organized fashion, can be used. Experience, however, has led *Casenote® Legal Briefs* to develop and utilize the following format because of its logical flow and universal applicability.

NATURE OF CASE: This is a brief statement of the legal character and procedural status of the case (e.g., "Appeal of a burglary conviction").

There are many different alternatives open to a litigant dissatisfied with a court ruling. The key to determining which one has been used is to discover *who is asking this court for what.*

This first entry in the brief should be kept as *short as possible.* Use the court's terminology if you understand it. But since jurisdictions vary as to the titles of pleadings, the best entry is the one that addresses who wants what in this proceeding, not the one that sounds most like the court's language.

RULE OF LAW: A statement of the general principle of law that the case illustrates (e.g., "An acceptance that varies any term of the offer is considered a rejection and counteroffer").

Determining the rule of law of a case is a procedure similar to determining the issue of the case. Avoid being fooled by red herrings; there may be a few rules of law mentioned in the case excerpt, but usually only one is *the* rule with which the casebook editor is concerned. The techniques used to locate the issue, described below, may also be utilized to find the rule of law. Generally, your best guide is simply the chapter heading. It is a clue to the point the casebook editor seeks to make and should be kept in mind when reading every case in the respective section.

FACTS: A synopsis of only the essential facts of the case, i.e., those bearing upon or leading up to the issue.

The facts entry should be a short statement of the events and transactions that led one party to initiate legal proceedings against another in the first place. While some cases conveniently state the salient facts at the beginning of the decision, in other instances they will have to be culled from hiding places throughout the text, even from concurring and dissenting opinions. Some of the "facts" will often be in dispute and should be so noted. Conflicting evidence may be briefly pointed up. "Hard" facts must be included. Both must be *relevant* in order to be listed in the facts entry. It is impossible to tell what is relevant until the entire case is read, as the ultimate determination of the rights and liabilities of the parties may turn on something buried deep in the opinion.

Generally, the facts entry should not be longer than three to five *short* sentences.

It is often helpful to identify the role played by a party in a given context. For example, in a construction contract case the identification of a party as the "contractor" or "builder" alleviates the need to tell that that party was the one who was supposed to have built the house.

It is always helpful, and a good general practice, to identify the "plaintiff" and the "defendant." This may seem elementary and uncomplicated, but, especially in view of the creative editing practiced by some casebook editors, it is sometimes a difficult or even impossible task. Bear in mind that the *party presently* seeking something from this court may not be the plaintiff, and that sometimes only the cross-claim of a defendant is treated in the excerpt. Confusing or misaligning the parties can ruin your analysis and understanding of the case.

ISSUE: A statement of the general legal question answered by or illustrated in the case. For clarity, the issue is best put in the form of a question capable of a "yes" or "no" answer. In reality, the issue is simply the Rule of Law put in the form of a question (e.g., "May an offer be accepted by performance?").

The major problem presented in discerning what is *the* issue in the case is that an opinion usually purports to raise and answer several questions. However, except for rare cases, only one such question is really the issue in the case. Collateral issues not necessary to the resolution of the matter in controversy are handled by the court by language known as *"obiter dictum"* or merely *"dictum."* While dicta may be included later in the brief, they have no place under the issue heading.

To find the issue, ask *who wants what* and then go on to ask *why did that party succeed or fail in getting it.* Once this is determined, the "why" should be turned into a question.

The complexity of the issues in the cases will vary, but in all cases a single-sentence question should sum up the issue. *In a few cases,* there will be two, or even more rarely, three issues of equal importance to the resolution of the case. Each should be expressed in a single-sentence question.

Since many issues are resolved by a court in coming to a final disposition of a case, the casebook editor will reproduce the portion of the opinion containing the issue or issues most relevant to the area of law under scrutiny. A noted law professor gave this advice: "Close the book; look at the title on the cover." Chances are, if it is Property, you need not concern yourself with whether, for example, the federal government's treatment of the plaintiff's land really raises a federal question sufficient to support jurisdiction on this ground in federal court.

The same rule applies to chapter headings designating sub-areas within the subjects. They tip you off as to what the text is designed to teach. The cases are arranged in a casebook to show a progression or development of the law, so that the preceding cases may also help.

It is also most important to remember to *read the notes and questions* at the end of a case to determine what the editors wanted you to have gleaned from it.

HOLDING AND DECISION: This section should succinctly explain the rationale of the court in arriving at its decision. In capsulizing the "reasoning" of the court, it should always include an application of the general rule or rules of law to the specific facts of the case. Hidden justifications come to light in this entry: the reasons for the state of the law, the public policies, the biases and prejudices, those considerations that influence the justices' thinking and, ultimately, the outcome of the case. At the end, there should be a short indication of the disposition or procedural resolution of the case (e.g., "Decision of the trial court for Mr. Smith (P) reversed").

The foregoing format is designed to help you "digest" the reams of case material with which you will be faced in your law school career. Once mastered by practice, it will place at your fingertips the information the authors of your casebooks have sought to impart to you in case-by-case illustration and analysis.

B. Be as Economical as Possible in Briefing Cases

Once armed with a format that encourages succinctness, it is as important to be economical with regard to the time spent on the actual reading of the case as it is to be economical in the writing of the brief itself. This does not mean "skimming" a case. Rather, it means reading the case with an "eye" trained to recognize into which "section" of your brief a particular passage or line fits and having a system for quickly and precisely marking the case so that the passages fitting any one particular part of

the brief can be easily identified and brought together in a concise and accurate manner when the brief is actually written.

It is of no use to simply repeat everything in the opinion of the court; record only enough information to trigger your recollection of what the court said. Nevertheless, an accurate statement of the "law of the case," i.e., the legal principle applied to the facts, is absolutely essential to class preparation and to learning the law under the case method.

To that end, it is important to develop a "shorthand" that you can use to make marginal notations. These notations will tell you at a glance in which section of the brief you will be placing that particular passage or portion of the opinion.

Some students prefer to underline all the salient portions of the opinion (with a pencil or colored underliner marker), making marginal notations as they go along. Others prefer the color-coded method of underlining, utilizing different colors of markers to underline the salient portions of the case, each separate color being used to represent a different section of the brief. For example, blue underlining could be used for passages relating to the rule of law, yellow for those relating to the issue, and green for those relating to the holding and decision, etc. While it has its advocates, the color-coded method can be confusing and time-consuming (all that time spent on changing colored markers). Furthermore, it can interfere with the continuity and concentration many students deem essential to the reading of a case for maximum comprehension. In the end, however, it is a matter of personal preference and style. Just remember, whatever method you use, underlining must be used sparingly or its value is lost.

If you take the marginal notation route, an efficient and easy method is to go along underlining the key portions of the case and placing in the margin alongside them the following "markers" to indicate where a particular passage or line "belongs" in the brief you will write:

N   (NATURE OF CASE)
RL   (RULE OF LAW)
I   (ISSUE)
HL   (HOLDING AND DECISION, relates to
      the RULE OF LAW behind the decision)
HR   (HOLDING AND DECISION, gives the
      RATIONALE or reasoning behind the
      decision)
HA   (HOLDING AND DECISION, APPLIES
      the general principle(s) of law to the facts
      of the case to arrive at the decision)

Remember that a particular passage may well contain information necessary to more than one part of your brief, in which case you simply note that in the margin. If you are using the color-coded underlining method instead of marginal notation, simply make asterisks or checks in the margin next to the passage in question in the colors that indicate the additional sections of the brief where it might be utilized.

The economy of utilizing "shorthand" in marking cases for briefing can be maintained in the actual brief writing process itself by utilizing "law student shorthand" within the brief. There are many commonly used words and phrases for which abbreviations can be substituted in your briefs (and in your class notes also). You can develop abbreviations that are personal to you and which will save you a lot of time. A reference list of briefing abbreviations can be found on page xii of this book.

C. Use Both the Briefing Process and the Brief as a Learning Tool

Now that you have a format and the tools for briefing cases efficiently, the most important thing is to make the time spent in briefing profitable to you and to make the most advantageous use of the briefs you create. Of course, the briefs are invaluable for classroom reference when you are called upon to explain or analyze a particular

case. However, they are also useful in reviewing for exams. A quick glance at the fact summary should bring the case to mind, and a rereading of the rule of law should enable you to go over the underlying legal concept in your mind, how it was applied in that particular case, and how it might apply in other factual settings.

As to the value to be derived from engaging in the briefing process itself, there is an immediate benefit that arises from being forced to sift through the essential facts and reasoning from the court's opinion and to succinctly express them in your own words in your brief. The process ensures that you understand the case and the point that it illustrates, and that means you will be ready to absorb further analysis and information brought forth in class. It also ensures you will have something to say when called upon in class. The briefing process helps develop a mental agility for getting to the *gist* of a case and for identifying, expounding on, and applying the legal concepts and issues found there. The briefing process is the mental process on which you must rely in taking law school examinations; it is also the mental process upon which a lawyer relies in serving his clients and in making his living.

Abbreviations for Briefs

Table of Cases

Nature and Scope of Judicial Review

Quick Reference Rules of Law

Marbury v. Madison

Appointee (P) v. Secretary of State (D)

5 U.S. (1 Cranch) 137, 2 L.Ed. 60 (1803).

NATURE OF CASE: Petition before the Supreme Court for a writ of mandamus to compel a cabinet secretary to deliver a commission.

FACT SUMMARY: Congress authorized the Supreme Court to issue writs of mandamus, although the Constitution specifically limits the court's original jurisdiction to specific cases.

🏛 RULE OF LAW
The Supreme Court has the power, under the Supremacy Clause and Article VI, § 2 of the Constitution, to review acts of Congress that are repugnant to the Constitution and find them unconstitutional.

FACTS: Just before President Adams was to leave office, the Federalist Congress passed two acts which authorized the appointment of more federal judges and justices of the peace. Adams made the appointments, which Congress confirmed. The new "midnight" judges' commissions were signed by Adams and sealed by the Secretary of State. However, by the time anti-Federalist Jefferson took office, several of the commissions remained undelivered. Jefferson ordered his new Secretary of State, Madison (D), to withhold delivery pursuant to § 13 of the Judiciary Act of 1789, which authorized the Supreme Court to "issue writs of mandamus, in cases warranted by the principles and usages of law, to any court appointed, or persons holding office, under the authority of the United States." Marbury (P) and other frustrated "midnight" appointees petitioned the Supreme Court to compel Madison (D) to deliver the commissions.

ISSUE: Does the Supreme Court have the power, under the Supremacy Clause and Article VI, § 2 of the Constitution, to review acts of Congress that are repugnant to the Constitution and find them unconstitutional?

HOLDING AND DECISION: (Marshall, C.J.) Yes. The Supreme Court has the power, under the Supremacy Clause and Article VI, § 2 of the Constitution, to review acts of Congress that are repugnant to the Constitution and find them unconstitutional. The government of the United States is one of laws, not men. This appellation is meaningless if the laws furnish no remedy for the violation of a vested right. Clearly, Marbury (P) has a right to have his commission delivered. And furthermore, there is no political question problem here to bar the use of mandamus as a remedy. However, § 13 of the Judiciary Act is unconstitutional. The section gives the Supreme Court original jurisdiction to issue writs of mandamus. The Constitution, on the other hand, limits the Court's original jurisdiction to only designated cases (i.e., affecting ambassadors, other public ministers and consuls and those in which a state shall be a party); in all other cases, the Supreme Court has only appellate jurisdiction. The Constitution defines and limits the powers of the legislature. The legislature cannot alter the Constitution, which itself provides that it is the "Supreme law" of the land, by an ordinary act. To hold otherwise would render the Constitution only an absurd attempt to limit legislative power. If an act of the legislature is therefore repugnant to the Constitution, and void, does it, notwithstanding its invalidity, bind the courts and oblige them to give it effect? No. If a law be in opposition to the Constitution, the Court must determine which of these conflicting rules governs the case. The Constitution, if it is to have any meaning at all, must prevail. Article III, § 2 provides that the judicial power of the United States is extended to all cases arising under the Constitution. A case arising under the Constitution cannot be decided without examining the instrument under which it arises. Courts cannot be permitted to look into some parts of the Constitution and not others. Finally, the framers of the Constitution contemplated that instrument as a rule for the government of courts, as well as of the legislature. Why else are judges required to take an oath to uphold the Constitution? Thus, since the Supreme Court possesses the power to review acts of Congress, we find that § 13 of the Judiciary Act of 1789 is unconstitutional and that this Court lacks the authority, under the Constitution, to issue a writ of mandamus in this case.

▶ ANALYSIS

The power of the Court to declare acts of Congress repugnant to the Constitution is not exclusive; other branches of government are not absolved from their responsibility to assess the constitutionality of legislation governing their performance. Nor does *Marbury v. Madison* hold that the act before the Court for review, if found unconstitutional is void in all contexts. Since the Court is asked to pass on arguments presented by two adverse parties before it, its decision is limited to the facts of the case. However, there may be instances where a law is not only unconstitutional as applied but is void on its face.

▬▬

Quicknotes

WRIT OF MANDAMUS A court order issued commanding a public or private entity, or an official thereof, to perform a duty required by law.

▬▬

Martin v. Hunter's Lessee

Heir to land (P) v. Lessee (D)

14 U.S. (1 Wheat.) 304, 4 L.Ed. 97 (1816).

NATURE OF CASE: Appeal from an action of ejectment.

FACT SUMMARY: After the Supreme Court reversed a Virginia Court of Appeals ruling which had held that Martin (P) had lost title to land in favor of the state, the Virginia court ruled that insofar as the Federal Judiciary Act extended the Supreme Court's appellate jurisdiction to state courts, the Judiciary Act was unconstitutional.

RULE OF LAW
Federal courts may hear appeals brought from state court decisions.

FACTS: Martin (P), a British subject resident in England, inherited vast Virginia landholdings from his uncle, Lord Fairfax. In 1789, Virginia, pursuant to state laws confiscating land owned by British subjects, purported to grant a land patent to Hunter. Martin (P) sought to eject Hunter's lessee (D) from the land. The Virginia District Court ruled for Martin (P) on the basis of anti-confiscation clauses in the treaties of 1783 and 1794 with Great Britain. The Virginia Court of Appeals reversed on grounds that the 1796 act of compromise between the Fairfax claimants and the state settled the matter against Martin (P) and that the state's title had been perfected before the treaties. The Supreme Court, without discussing the compromise, reversed and remanded relying on the treaty of 1794. On remand, the Virginia court ruled that insofar as the Judiciary Act extended the Supreme Court's appellate jurisdiction to state courts, the Act was unconstitutional. Martin (P) appealed.

ISSUE: May federal courts hear appeals brought from state court decisions?

HOLDING AND DECISION: (Story, J.) Yes. Federal courts may hear appeals brought from state court decisions. The third article of the constitution grants appellate jurisdiction to the Supreme Court where it does not have original jurisdiction except in those instances where Congress has limited federal appellate jurisdiction. The framers anticipated federal courts would not have original jurisdiction over cases that arose in state court, but provided for appellate jurisdiction. Some argue that the federal courts cannot interfere with state sovereignty by taking jurisdiction over state cases, but the constitution provides in several other instances for state obligations and intrusions into state sovereignty. State judges are not entitled to independence from the federal judicial system but are in fact subject to it pursuant to the constitution. Federal appellate power over state cases is a necessity for uniformity because of the possibility of different state courts interpreting the same statute or treaty differently. The Supreme Court's job is not to inquire into the reasons the framers provided for federal appellate jurisdiction but to construe the constitution as written. The constitution expressly provides for federal appellate jurisdiction over cases arising in state courts. Reversed (judgment of the district court affirmed).

CONCURRENCE AND DISSENT: (Johnson, J.) The opinion is accurate; however, the Supreme Court is supreme over persons and cases but not over state tribunals.

ANALYSIS

As a historical note, Chief Justice Marshall disqualified himself in the first, remanded case, *Fairfax's Devisee v. Hunter's Lessee*, 7 Cranch 603 (1813), and in the case above. Marshall, as a member of the Virginia legislature, had negotiated the 1796 act of compromise while acting for the purchasers of the Fairfax estate. Marshall also had a great financial interest in the outcome because he and his brother had organized a syndicate which had purchased, from Martin (P), 160,000 acres of the land in question.

Quicknotes

FEDERAL JUDICIARY ACT § 34 The laws of the states shall be regarded as rules of decisions in trials at common law in the federal courts.

Nixon v. United States

Impeached judge (P) v. Federal government (D)

506 U.S. 224 (1993).

NATURE OF CASE: Appeal from holding that impeachment by Senate is nonjusticiable.

FACT SUMMARY: Nixon (P), a former U.S. District Court judge who was impeached by the Senate, brought suit claiming that the Constitution required the whole Senate, and not just a committee of senators, to take part in all impeachment proceedings.

 RULE OF LAW
The power of the Senate under the Impeachment Clause presents a nonjusticiable political question.

FACTS: U.S. District Court Chief Judge Nixon (P) was convicted by a jury of two counts of making false statements before a federal grand jury and sentenced to prison. The House of Representatives adopted three articles of impeachment for high crimes and misdemeanors and presented the articles to the Senate. The Senate voted to invoke its own Impeachment Rule XI, under which a committee of senators receives evidence and takes testimony and then presents the whole Senate with a complete transcript of the proceedings as well as a summarized report. After this occurred, final briefs were submitted to the full Senate, oral arguments were heard, and Nixon (P) gave a personal appeal. The Senate voted by more than the two-thirds required to impeach. Nixon (P) then filed suit, arguing that the Senate Impeachment Rule violated the constitutional grant of authority to "try" all impeachments because the whole Senate did not take part in the evidentiary hearings. The district court held that the claim was nonjusticiable, and the court of appeals for the District of Columbia Circuit affirmed. The Supreme Court granted certiorari.

ISSUE: Is the power of the Senate under the Impeachment Clause justiciable?

HOLDING AND DECISION: (Rehnquist, C.J.) No. The power of the Senate under the Impeachment Clause presents a nonjusticiable political question. The word "try" in the Impeachment Clause does not impose an identifiable textual limit on Senate authority to impeach. If courts were permitted to review actions of the Senate in order to determine if it had "tried" an impeached official, the Senate would not be functioning independently as mandated by the Constitution's use of the word "sole" in the Impeachment Clause's first sentence: "The Senate shall have the sole power to try all Impeachments." In addition, the constitutional system of checks and balances intended impeachment to be the only check on the Judicial Branch by the legislature. Furthermore, the court of appeals was correct in stating that judicial review of the impeach-

ment system would prevent finality and compromise the effectiveness of successors to those who have been impeached. Affirmed.

CONCURRENCE: (Stevens, J.) The hypotheticals mentioned by Justices White and Souter are highly improbable.

CONCURRENCE: (White, J.) The Court's judgment is correct because the Senate did, in effect, "try" Nixon (P). The Court should have, however, reached the merits of the case. Additionally, the Court wrongly interprets the political question doctrine. The framers explicitly provided responsibilities for impeachment proceedings to the House and the Senate. The word "sole" emphasizes the distinct obligations. Contrary to the majority's interpretation, the word "sole" does not prohibit judicial oversight of impeachment proceedings and the Court should not abandon its obligation. Further, the Court is quite capable of interpreting the term "try." The Impeachment Trial Clause sets minimal standards for the Senate but allows for great discretion. The Senate's use of a fact-finding committee is sufficient to "try" an impeachment case.

CONCURRENCE: (Souter, J.) There are scenarios imaginable where a comprehensive review of impeachment proceedings might be appropriate. Although based on the facts of this case the holding is correct, the political question doctrine should not serve to prevent review in all circumstances.

▶ ANALYSIS

There are several types of "political questions" that prevent the Court from reviewing an issue. Examples of when the doctrine may be invoked include: specific language of the Constitution, insufficient standards for resolving the issue at hand, or situations where another branch or authority is in the process of reviewing the issue. Although Justice Souter's concurrence was concerned with the outer limits of the political question doctrine, in reality its application is narrow and has not served to permit the abuses he suggested.

■▬■

Quicknotes

CERTIORARI A discretionary writ issued by a superior court to an inferior court in order to review the lower court's decisions; the Supreme Court's writ ordering such review.

■▬■

Ex parte McCardle

[Parties not identified in casebook excerpt.]

74 U.S. (7 Wall.) 506, 19 L.Ed. 264 (1869).

NATURE OF CASE: Appeal from denial of habeas corpus.

FACT SUMMARY: McCardle (D) appealed from a denial of habeas corpus to the Supreme Court, but Congress passed an act forbidding the court jurisdiction.

🏛 RULE OF LAW
Although the Supreme Court derives its appellate jurisdiction from the Constitution, the Constitution also gives Congress the express power to make exceptions to that appellate jurisdiction.

FACTS: After the Civil War, Congress imposed military government on many former Confederate States under authority of the Civil War Reconstruction Acts. McCardle (D), a Mississippi newspaper editor, was held in military custody on charges of publishing libelous and incendiary articles. McCardle (D) brought a habeas corpus writ based on a congressional act passed on February 5, 1867. The Act authorized federal courts to grant habeas corpus to persons held in violation of constitutional rights and also gave authority for appeals to the Supreme Court. The circuit court denied McCardle's (D) habeas corpus writ, but the Supreme Court sustained jurisdiction for an appeal on the merits. However, after arguments were heard, Congress passed an act on March 27, 1868, that repealed that much of the 1867 Act that allowed an appeal to the Supreme Court from the circuit court and the exercise by the Supreme Court of jurisdiction on any such appeals, past or present.

ISSUE: Although the Supreme Court derives its appellate jurisdiction from the Constitution, does the Constitution also give Congress the express power to make exceptions to that appellate jurisdiction?

HOLDING AND DECISION: (Chase, C.J.) Yes. Although the Supreme Court derives its appellate jurisdiction from the Constitution, the Constitution also gives Congress the express power to make exceptions to that appellate jurisdiction. The Court cannot inquire into congressional motives but only congressional constitutional power. Congress has passed a repealing act which deprives the court of jurisdiction. Only those cases appealed from circuit courts under the 1867 act fall within the act's purview. The only action left is for the court to dismiss the case for lack of jurisdiction. Appeal dismissed.

▶ ANALYSIS

McCardle is clearly an example of judicial restraint. The authority of Congress to control the jurisdiction of the Supreme Court is not unlimited. This was proved in *Marbury v. Madison*, 5 U.S. Cranch 137, 2 L.Ed. 60 (1803), where the Court, faced with an encroachment by Congress on its original jurisdiction as granted under the Constitution, merely declared the congressional act unconstitutional. But here, the Court backed away from confrontation with Congress due to current-day political crises that followed the Civil War. Thereafter, the Court sought to limit congressional power by the power of judicial review announced in *Marbury*. The Court held on several occasions that certain congressional attempts to delimit its jurisdiction were unconstitutional attempts to invade the judicial province. Such congressional actions were considered a violation of the separation of powers. Today, it is doubtful that *McCardle* would be sustained.

Quicknotes

HABEAS CORPUS A proceeding in which a defendant brings a writ to compel a judicial determination of whether he is lawfully being held in custody.

LIBEL A false or malicious publication subjecting a person to scorn, hatred or ridicule, or injuring him or her in relation to his or her occupation or business.

Maryland v. Baltimore Radio Show, Inc.

[Parties not identified in casebook excerpt.]

338 U.S. 912 (1950).

NATURE OF CASE: Denial of a petition for writ of certiorari.

FACT SUMMARY: [Justice Frankfurter on "The Rule of Four."]

RULE OF LAW
While an appeal may meet all technical requirements for a writ of certiorari, if fewer than four justices wish to hear the appeal, the writ will be denied.

FACTS: [Facts not stated in casebook excerpt. The case is a portion of an opinion by Justice Frankfurter regarding the denial of a petition for writ of certiorari.]

ISSUE: If an appeal meets all technical requirements for a writ of certiorari, may the writ be denied if fewer than four justices wish to hear the appeal?

HOLDING AND DECISION: (Frankfurter, J.) Yes. While an appeal may meet all technical requirements for a writ of certiorari, if fewer than four justices wish to hear the appeal, the writ will be denied. While a case may raise an important constitutional question, the record may be too unclear, making it more desirable for lower courts to further illuminate the matter. Practical considerations preclude the Supreme Court's indicating its reasons for denial of a writ. Different reasons may have moved different justices not to want to hear the case. Also, it would simply be too time consuming. It should be added that a justice's failure to note a dissent from a denial of a petition does not imply that only the justice who notes his dissent thought the petition should be granted.

▶ ANALYSIS

Certiorari is a discretionary matter with the Court. Under the "Rule of Four," four justices must vote to hear the case. When four justices so vote, the whole Court will hear the matter even though five justices did not feel the case was worthy of their time. Denial of a petition for writ of certiorari has nothing to do with the merits of the case. But summary disposition of an appeal—appeals are matters of right—is a disposition on the merits.

Quicknotes

CERTIORARI A discretionary writ issued by a superior court to an inferior court in order to review the lower court's decisions; the Supreme Court's writ ordering such review.

National Legislative Power

Quick Reference Rules of Law

McCulloch v. Maryland

Bank cashier (D) v. State (P)

17 U.S. (4 Wheat.) 316, 4 L.Ed. 579 (1819).

NATURE OF CASE: Action arising out of a violation of a state statute.

FACT SUMMARY: Maryland (P) taxed banks operating in the state without state authority. McCulloch (D) appealed the imposition of the tax against his bank branch.

RULE OF LAW

Congress may establish a bank because the Necessary and Proper Clause supplies it the discretion and power to choose and enact the means to perform the duties imposed upon it.

FACTS: A Maryland (P) statute prohibited any bank operating in the state without state authority from issuing bank notes without paying a 2% tax on the notes issued. The Bank of the United States operated a branch in Baltimore and issued bank notes. The state assessed the statutory penalty and McCulloch (D), the bank's cashier, appealed.

ISSUE: May Congress establish a bank?

HOLDING AND DECISION: (Marshall, C.J.) Yes. Congress may establish a bank because the Necessary and Proper Clause supplies it the discretion and power to choose and enact the means to perform the duties imposed upon it. This government is one of enumerated powers but the Constitution does not exclude incidental or implied powers. It does not require that everything be granted expressly and described in detail. To have so required would have entirely changed the character of the Constitution and made it into a legal code. The enumerated powers given to the government imply the ordinary means of execution. The power of creating a corporation may be implied as incidental to other powers or used as a means of executing them. The Necessary and Proper Clause gives Congress the power to make "all laws which shall be necessary and proper, for carrying into execution" the powers vested by the Constitution in the U.S. government. Maryland (P) argues that the word "necessary" limits the right to pass laws for the execution of the granted powers to those which are indispensable. However, in common usage "necessary" frequently means convenient, useful, essential. Considering the word's common usage, its usage in another part of the Constitution (Article I, § 10), and its inclusion among the powers given to Congress, rather than among the limitations upon Congress, it cannot be held to restrain Congress. The sound construction of the Constitution must allow Congress the discretion to choose the means to perform the duties imposed upon it. As long as the end is legitimate and within the scope of the Constitution, any means which are appropriate, which are plainly adapted to that end, and which are not prohibited by the Constitution but are consistent with its spirit, are constitutional. A bank is a convenient, useful, and essential instrument for handling national finances. Hence, it is within Congress's power to enact a law incorporating a U.S. bank. [Statutory tax invalidated on other grounds.]

ANALYSIS

Federalism is the basis of the Constitution's response to the problem of governing large geographical areas with diverse local needs. The success of federalism depends upon maintaining the balance between the need for the supremacy and sovereignty of the federal government and the interest in maintaining independent state government and curtailing national intrusion into intrastate affairs. The U.S. federal structure allocates powers between the nation and the states by enumerating the powers delegated to the national government and acknowledging the retention by the states of the remainder. The Articles of the Confederation followed a similar scheme. The Constitution expanded the enumerated national powers to remedy weaknesses of the Articles. The move from the Articles to the Constitution was a shift from a central government with fewer powers to one with more powers.

■■■

Quicknotes

NECESSARY AND PROPER CLAUSE Article I, § 8 of the United States Constitution; enables Congress to make all laws that may be "necessary and proper" to execute its other, enumerated powers.

■■■

Gibbons v. Ogden

Steamboat operator (P) v. Steamboat operator (D)

22 U.S. (9 Wheat.) 1, 6 L.Ed. 23 (1824).

NATURE OF CASE: Action for an injunction to restrain violation of state-granted monopoly navigation right.

FACT SUMMARY: Ogden (P) was given exclusive navigation rights on a water course between New York and New Jersey by New York. Gibbons (D) claimed a right to navigate the same water course under a federal licensing statute.

RULE OF LAW
The Commerce Clause gives Congress plenary power to regulate interstate commerce, including navigation within one state which affects other states.

FACTS: Livingston and Fulton received from the New York state legislature a grant of the exclusive right to navigate the waters of the state by steamboats for a number of years. From this monopoly Ogden (P) was assigned the right to navigate between New York City and New Jersey. Gibbons (D) was using in navigation between New York and New Jersey two steamboats licensed under federal law. Ogden (P) secured an injunction in a New York State court to prevent Gibbons (D) from violating his monopolistic right. Gibbons (D) appealed, arguing that the power of Congress to regulate commerce under the Commerce Clause, Article I, § 8, cl. 3 (which grants to Congress the power "to regulate commerce with the foreign nations and among the several states, and with the Indian tribes") is exclusive. Ogden (P) claimed that a concurrent power existed between the federal government and the states.

ISSUE: Does the Commerce Clause give Congress plenary power to regulate interstate commerce including navigation within one state which affects other states?

HOLDING AND DECISION: (Marshall, C.J.) Yes. The Commerce Clause gives Congress plenary power to regulate interstate commerce, including navigation within one state which affects other states. There are three main questions which must be addressed in determining the scope of Congress's power over commerce. First, what does the term "commerce" include? Commerce, undoubtedly is traffic, but it is something more—it is intercourse. It comprehends not only the buying and selling or the interchange of commodities but navigation as well. Second, to what extent does this power reach commerce within the separate states? While the completely internal commerce of a state is immune against federal regulation, the power of Congress does not stop at the jurisdictional lines of the several states. The power of Congress may be exercised within a state if a foreign voyage may commence or terminate at a port within that state. Congress thus may regulate all navigation which may affect more states than one. This power, like all others vested in Congress, is complete in itself, may be exercised to its utmost extent, and acknowledges no limitations other than are prescribed in the Constitution. Third, may the states severally exercise the same power within their respective jurisdictions? It has been suggested that the New York monopoly in question here is not inconsistent with Congress's power and thus should give way only to the extent required to give effect to the federal Coastal Act. However, unlike as in instances of state taxation and inspection laws, when a state proceeds to regulate interstate commerce, it is exercising the very power that is granted to Congress and is doing the very thing Congress is authorized to do. In the examples of taxation and inspection, the state derives its power from some residual power which remains with the state; its exercise of power is on subjects acknowledged to be within its control. This court, therefore, has the authority to inquire whether a particular state law collides with an act of Congress to regulate interstate commerce. Should a collision exist, it is immaterial that the state law was passed in virtue of a concurrent power. Accordingly, the grant of the monopolistic navigation right to Ogden (P), affecting as it did intercourse between New York and New Jersey, cannot stand in light of the federal Coastal Act. The injunction was improperly issued. Reversed.

ANALYSIS

Chief Justice Marshall's great opinion in *Gibbons*, by failing to clearly hold that Congress had exclusive power over interstate commerce, left unsettled the important question of whether the states, in the absence of federal regulation, retained any concurrent power. One commentator has suggested that this omission was deliberate since Marshall may have felt that there conceivably might be some state regulation which would have merely an incidental effect on interstate commerce. Also, by leaving the question open, Marshall hoped to enlarge the court's jurisdiction in future cases to balance state and federal regulation.

Quicknotes

COMMERCE CLAUSE Article 1, § 8, cl. 3 of the United States Constitution; grants Congress the power to regulate commerce with foreign countries and between the states.

PLENARY POWER The complete authority of a court to hear and determine cases pertaining to specified subject matter or particular parties.

The Lottery Case (Champion v. Ames)

[Parties not identified in casebook excerpt.]

188 U.S. 321 (1903).

NATURE OF CASE: Appeal from dismissal of a petition for a writ of habeas corpus after indictment for conspiracy to violate a lottery law.

FACT SUMMARY: The Federal Lottery Act prohibited transporting lottery tickets from one state to another.

🏛 RULE OF LAW

Under its power to regulate commerce, Congress may, for the purpose of guarding the morals of the people and protecting interstate commerce, prohibit the carrying of lottery tickets in interstate commerce.

FACTS: The Federal Lottery Act prohibited importing, mailing, or transporting lottery tickets from one state to another. A box of lottery tickets were shipped from Texas to California and the shipper was prosecuted under the Act. The shipper challenged the Act's constitutionality.

ISSUE: May Congress, under its commerce power, prohibit the transporting of lottery tickets in interstate commerce?

HOLDING AND DECISION: (Harlan, J.) Yes. Under its power to regulate commerce, Congress may, for the purpose of guarding the morals of the people and protecting interstate commerce, prohibit the carrying of lottery tickets in interstate commerce. The power to regulate commerce among the states has been expressly given to Congress. By this statute, Congress does not interfere with traffic or commerce carried on exclusively within the limits of a state. It is only regulating interstate commerce. As a state may, for the purpose of guarding the morals of its people, forbid all sales of lottery tickets within its limits, so can Congress. The Act is constitutional.

DISSENT: (Fuller, C.J.) The power to suppress lotteries belongs to the states and not to Congress. To hold that Congress has a general police power is to defeat the operation of the Tenth Amendment. The shipping of lottery tickets from state to state is not interstate commerce. Just as insurance policies create contractual relations and a means of enforcing a contract right and have been held not to be interstate commerce, so should it be with lottery tickets. Neither should a lottery ticket become an article of interstate commerce simply because it is placed in an envelope and mailed.

▶ ANALYSIS

Early twentieth century reformers seeking a constitutional basis for broader federal police measures were encouraged by the lottery decision. The decision is an example of one in which the court treats the commerce power as analogous to a federal police power, *The Lottery Case* precedent sustained a variety of early twentieth century laws excluding objects deemed harmful from interstate commerce. Examples include the Mann Act prohibiting the transportation of women for immoral purposes, a statute banning interstate transportation of adulterated or misbranded articles, and a statute banning interstate transportation of goods made in violation of state law or possession of which violated state law.

■══■

Quicknotes

COMMERCE POWER The power delegated to Congress by the Constitution to regulate interstate commerce.

FEDERAL LOTTERY ACT Legislation passed in 1895 that prohibited interstate transportation of lottery tickets on the grounds that lottery is an activity harmful to public morals. At issue was whether interstate commerce would be allowed to defeat state law.

HABEAS CORPUS A proceeding in which a defendant brings a writ to compel a judicial determination of whether he is lawfully being held in custody.

MANN ACT 18 U.S.C. § 2421 *et seq.* Prohibits transporting any person in interstate or foreign commerce for the purpose of engaging in prostitution or other sexual activity.

■══■

Houston, East & West Texas Ry. v. United States
(Shreveport Case)

Railroad (D) v. Federal government (P)

234 U.S. 342 (1914).

NATURE OF CASE: Appeal from an Interstate Commerce Commission (ICC) order setting certain railroad rates.

FACT SUMMARY: Houston, East & West Ry. (D) charged much higher rates between Shreveport, Louisiana, and points within Texas than it charged for transportation between points within Texas. The ICC ordered that the discriminatory rates be stopped. It set a maximum rate to be charged for transportation to and from Shreveport.

🏛 RULE OF LAW
Congress has control over interstate carriers in all matters having such a close and substantial relation to interstate commerce that it is necessary or proper to exercise the control for the effective government of that commerce.

FACTS: Houston, East & West Ry. (D) charged lower rates from Dallas and Houston eastward to intermediate points in Texas than from Shreveport westward to the same points. Shreveport competes with both of these cities for the trade of the intervening territory. The difference in rates charged was substantial and injuriously affected Shreveport commerce. Sixty cents carried traffic 160 miles eastward from Dallas, while the same amount would carry the same traffic only 55 miles into Texas from Shreveport. The ICC found that the interstate rates from Shreveport into Texas were unreasonable. It set a maximum for these rates which was the same as the rates fixed by the Railway Commission of Texas and charged for transportation for similar distances within the state. It ordered that the discriminatory rates from Shreveport be stopped and that no higher rates be charged from Shreveport to a point in Texas than was charged from that point to Shreveport.

ISSUE: Can Congress control the intrastate charges of an interstate carrier to prevent injurious discrimination against interstate traffic?

HOLDING AND DECISION: (Hughes, J.) Yes. Congressional power to regulate commerce embraces the right to control the operation of interstate carriers in all matters having such a close and substantial relation to interstate commerce that the control is necessary or proper for the effective government of that commerce. Examples of appropriate purposes of control would be the security of interstate traffic, the efficiency of interstate service, and the maintenance of conditions under which interstate commerce may be conducted fairly and without molestation

or hindrance. The fact that an interstate carrier also is an intrastate carrier does not derogate congressional authority over the former. Whenever the interstate and intrastate transactions of carriers are so related that the government of one involves the control of the other, it is Congress, and not the state, that can prescribe the dominant rule. Congress may, in the exercise of its paramount power, prevent carriers of both intrastate and interstate commerce from being used in their intrastate operations to the injury of interstate commerce. Here a carrier in interstate commerce is being used in a discriminatory manner to inflict injury on that commerce. This is sufficient ground for federal intervention, and it is immaterial that the discrimination arises from intrastate as compared to interstate rates. The order of the ICC is affirmed.

▶ ANALYSIS

In *Swift Co. v. U.S.*, 196 U.S. 375 (1905), the Court used the "current of commerce" theory in holding that an intrastate activity was controllable not because of its effect on commerce but because it could be viewed as part of the "current" of commerce. This language was used by Congress in drafting a 1921 act aimed at preventing unfair, discriminatory, or deceptive practices by meat packers in interstate commerce. It stated that a transaction would be considered to be in such commerce if the article is part of the current of commerce usual in the meatpacking industry. In *Stafford v. Wallace*, 258 U.S. 495 (1922), an attack on the act's constitutionality was rejected on the theory that the stockyards were but a throat through which the current of meat production flowed from one part of the country to another. However, the Court did add that only practices which affect commerce may be regulated.

■—■

Quicknotes

COMMERCE POWER The power delegated to Congress by the Constitution to regulate interstate commerce.

■—■

Hammer v. Dagenhart

U.S. Attorney General (D) v. Parent of child laborers (P)

247 U.S. 251 (1918).

NATURE OF CASE: Appeal from a decree enjoining enforcement of the Child Labor Act.

FACT SUMMARY: Congress passed a law prohibiting the shipment in interstate commerce of any products of any mills, mines, or factories which employed children.

🏛 RULE OF LAW
The making of goods and the mining of coal are not commerce, even if afterwards shipped or used in interstate commerce.

FACTS: Congress passed a law prohibiting the shipment in interstate commerce of any products of any mills, mines, or factories which employed children.

ISSUE: Is the making of goods and the mining of coal commerce if afterwards shipped or used in interstate commerce?

HOLDING AND DECISION: (Day, J.) No. The making of goods and the mining of coal are not commerce, even if afterwards shipped or used in interstate commerce. It is argued that the power of Congress to regulate commerce includes the power to prohibit the transportation of ordinary products in commerce. However, in cases such as *The Lottery Case*, the power to prohibit the carrying of lottery tickets is as to those particular objects the same as the exertion of the power to regulate. In those cases, the use of interstate commerce was necessary to the accomplishment of harmful results. Regulation over commerce could only be accomplished by prohibiting the use of interstate commerce to affect the evil intended. Here, the thing intended to be accomplished by this act is the denial of interstate commerce facilities to those employing children within the prohibited ages. The goods shipped are of themselves harmless. The production of articles intended for interstate commerce is a matter of local regulation. The making of goods and the refining of coal are not commerce, nor does the fact that these things are to be afterwards shipped or used in interstate commerce make their production a part thereof. It is also argued that congressional regulation is necessary because of the unfair advantage possessed by manufacturers in states which have less stringent child labor laws. However, Congress has no power to require states to exercise their police powers to prevent possible unfair competition. The act is unconstitutional and the decree enjoining its enforcement is affirmed.

DISSENT: (Holmes, J.) *The Lottery Case* and others following it establish that a law is not beyond Congress's commerce power merely because it prohibits certain transportation. There is no legal distinction between the evils sought to be controlled in those cases and the evil of premature and excessive child labor. The court has no right to substitute its judgment of which evils may be controlled.

▶ ANALYSIS

After the *Hammer* decision, Congress sought to regulate child labor through the taxing power. That law was invalidated in *Bailey v. Drexel Furnishing Co.*, 259 U.S. 20 (1922). Subsequently, Congress submitted a proposed constitutional amendment to the states which authorized a national child labor law. The amendment has not been ratified, but the need for it has largely disappeared in view of *U.S. v. Darby*, 312 U.S. 100 (1941), which overruled *Hammer*.

■■■■

Quicknotes

COMMERCE POWER The power delegated to Congress by the Constitution to regulate interstate commerce.

■■■■

United States v. Darby

Federal government (P) v. Manufacturer (D)

312 U.S. 100 (1941).

NATURE OF CASE: Criminal prosecution for violation of Fair Labor Standards Act.

FACT SUMMARY: Darby (D), a lumber manufacturer, shipped finished goods in interstate commerce. He was indicted for violation of the wage and hour provisions of the Fair Labor Standards Act.

🏛 RULE OF LAW
Congress has the power to regulate the hours and wages of workers who are engaged in the production of goods destined for interstate commerce and can prohibit the shipment in interstate commerce of goods manufactured in violation of the wage and hour provisions.

FACTS: Darby (D) was a Georgia manufacturer of finished lumber, and a large part of the lumber he produced was shipped in interstate commerce. The purpose of the Fair Labor Standards Act (the Act) was to prevent the shipment in interstate commerce of certain products produced under substandard labor conditions. The Act set up minimum wages and maximum hours and punished the shipment in interstate commerce of goods produced in violation of the wage/hour requirements and also punished the employment of persons in violation of those requirements. Darby (D) was indicted for both shipment of goods and employment of workers in violation of the Act. The trial court dismissed the indictment on the ground that the Act was an unconstitutional regulation of manufacturing within the states.

ISSUE: Does Congress have the power to regulate the hours and wages of workers who are engaged in the production of goods destined for interstate commerce and prohibit the shipment in interstate commerce of goods manufactured in violation of the wage and hour provisions of the Fair Labor Standards Act?

HOLDING AND DECISION: (Stone, J.) Yes. Congress has the power to regulate the hours and wages of workers who are engaged in the production of goods destined for interstate commerce and can prohibit the shipment in interstate commerce of goods manufactured in violation of the wage and hour provisions of the Fair Labor Standards Act. Both prohibitions are a constitutional exercise of Congress's commerce power. Although manufacturing itself is not interstate commerce, the shipment of goods across state lines is interstate commerce and the prohibition of such shipment is a regulation of commerce. Congress has plenary power to exclude from interstate commerce any article which it determines to be injurious to public welfare, subject only to the specific prohibitions of the Constitution. In the Fair Labor Standards Act, Congress has determined that the shipment of goods produced under substandard labor conditions is injurious to commerce and therefore has the power to prohibit the shipment of such goods, independent of the indirect effect of such prohibition on the states. The prohibition of employment of workers engaged in the production of goods for interstate commerce at substandard conditions is also sustainable, independent of the power to exclude the shipment of the goods so produced. The power over interstate commerce is not confined to the regulation of commerce among the states, but includes regulation of intrastate activities which so affect interstate commerce as to make regulation of them an appropriate means to the end of regulating interstate commerce. Here, Congress has determined that the employment of workers in substandard conditions is a form of unfair competition injurious to interstate commerce, since the goods so produced will be lower priced than the goods produced under adequate conditions. Such a form of competition would hasten the spread of substandard conditions and produce a dislocation of commerce and the destruction of many businesses. Since Congress has the power to suppress this form of unfair competition, and the Act is an appropriate means to that end, the wage/hour provisions are within Congress's power. It is irrelevant that only part of the goods produced will be shipped in interstate commerce. Congress has power to regulate the whole factory even though only a part of the products will have an effect on interstate commerce. Reversed.

▶ ANALYSIS

Darby is an example of the application of the affectation doctrine. It had long been the law that Congress had the power to exclude from interstate commerce harmful objects or immoral activities, such as mismarked goods or lottery tickets. This case extends the power to exclude articles produced under conditions that Congress considered harmful to the national welfare. Even though production of lumber was an entirely intrastate activity, it was a part of an economic process that led to the eventual sale of lumber across state limits, affecting interstate commerce. The federal commerce power extends to purely interstate transactions; the effect on commerce, not the location of the regulated act, is the basis for the exercise of the federal power. This case overruled the earlier case of *Hammer v. Dagenhart*, 247 U.S. 251 (1918), which held

Continued on next page.

unconstitutional an attempt by Congress to exclude articles made by child labor from interstate commerce.

■━■

Quicknotes

AFFECTATION DOCTRINE   Any activity, even if entirely intrastate, which in the aggregate has a substantial economic
effect on the stream of economic commerce may be regulated under the commerce clause.

COMMERCE POWER   The power delegated to Congress by
the Constitution to regulate interstate commerce.

■━■

Heart of Atlanta Motel, Inc. v. United States

Motel (P) v. Federal government (D)

379 U.S. 241 (1964).

NATURE OF CASE: Declaratory judgment action attacking the constitutionality of Title II of the Civil Rights Act of 1964.

FACT SUMMARY: The Heart of Atlanta Motel (P), which was located near a highway, advertised nationally, and derived most of its business from interstate travelers, claimed that its refusal to accept blacks was not within the scope of the federal Civil Rights Act.

🏛 RULE OF LAW
The power of Congress to promote interstate commerce also includes the power to regulate the local incidents thereof, including local activities in both the states of origin and destination, which might have a substantial and harmful effect upon that commerce.

FACTS: Title II of the Civil Rights Act of 1964, § 201(a), prohibits discrimination or segregation on the ground of race, color, religion, or national origin in any place of public accommodation which, as further defined in the Act, includes a motel having more than five rooms for rent. Only those motels affecting commerce were subject to injunctive action pursuant to the Act. The Heart of Atlanta Motel (P), with more than 216 rooms, was situated within ready access to interstate and state highways. Seventy-five percent of its registered guests were from out of state. Prior to the Act's enactment, the Motel (P) had followed a practice of refusing to rent to blacks.

ISSUE: Does the power of Congress to promote interstate commerce also include the power to regulate the local incidents thereof, including local activities in both the states of origin and destination, which might have a substantial and harmful effect upon that commerce?

HOLDING AND DECISION: (Clark, J.) Yes. The power of Congress to promote interstate commerce also includes the power to regulate the local incidents thereof, including local activities in both the states of origin and destination, which might have a substantial and harmful effect upon that commerce. The power of Congress over interstate travel permits it to regulate, by means of Title II, purely local activities in the states of origin and destination, so long as it can be shown that these local incidents might have a substantial and harmful effect upon interstate commerce. The congressional record is replete with testimony that millions of people of all races travel from state to state, that blacks particularly have been the subject of discrimination in transient accommodations, that often they have been unable to obtain accommodations, and that these conditions have become acute. There is also a qualitative effect in that the black traveler's pleasure and convenience have been threatened, thus discouraging travel. The Commerce Clause embraces all transportation whether or not commercial in character. That Congress was legislating against a moral problem does not make Title II less valid. Finally, the Act does not deprive the Motel (P) of liberty or property under the Fifth Amendment. Congress had a rational basis for finding that racial discrimination by motels affected commerce. The means it selected to eliminate that evil are reasonable and appropriate. Affirmed.

▶ ANALYSIS

In *Maryland v. Wirtz*, 392 U.S 183 (1968), the Court conclusively settled the issue of whether Congress's power under the Commerce Clause extends to purely local activities: "While Congress has in some instances left to the courts or to administrative agencies the task of determining whether commerce is affected in a particular instance, [Congress has the power] to declare that an entire class of activities affects commerce. The only question for the courts is then whether the class is 'within the reach of the federal power.' The contention that in Commerce Clause cases the courts have power to excise, as trivial, individual instances falling within a rationally defined class of activities has been put entirely to rest."

■=■

Quicknotes

CIVIL RIGHTS ACT OF 1964, 42 U.S.C. § 2000-2(a) § 703(a) Makes it an unlawful employment practice to hire or to discharge anyone on the basis of race, color, religion, sex, or national origin.

INJUNCTION A court order requiring a person to do or prohibiting that person from doing a specific act.

■=■

United States v. Morrison

Federal government (P) v. Students (D)

529 U.S. 598 (2000).

NATURE OF CASE: Suit alleging sexual assault in violation of the Violence Against Women Act.

FACT SUMMARY: Defendant was accused of sexually assaulting a freshman student at a Virginia university and the victim sued the defendant for civil damages under the Violence Against Women Act (VAWA). The defendant challenged the constitutionality of the civil damages portion of VAWA.

🏛 RULE OF LAW

Commerce Clause regulation of intrastate activity may only be upheld where the activity being regulated is economic in nature.

FACTS: Brzonkala (P), a student at Virginia Polytechnic Institute, complained that football-playing students Morrison (D) and Crawford (D) assaulted and repeatedly raped her. Virginia Tech's Judicial Committee found insufficient evidence to punish Crawford (D), but found Morrison (D) guilty of sexual assault and sentenced him to immediate suspension for two semesters. The school's vice president set this aside as excessive punishment. Brzonkala (P) then dropped out of the university and brought suit against the school and the male students (D) under the Violence Against Women Act, 42 U.S.C. § 13981, providing a federal cause of action of the crime of a crime of violence motivated by gender.

ISSUE: May Commerce Clause regulation of intrastate activity only be upheld where the activity being regulated is economic in nature?

HOLDING AND DECISION: (Rehnquist, C.J.) Yes. Commerce Clause regulation of intrastate activity may only be upheld where the activity being regulated is economic in nature. The Court considered whether either the Commerce Clause or the Fourteenth Amendment authorized Congress to create this new cause of action. There are three main categories of activity Congress may regulate under its Commerce Clause power: (1) the use of channels of interstate commerce; (2) regulation or protection of the instrumentalities of interstate commerce or persons or things in interstate commerce, though the threat may come from intrastate activities; and (3) the power to regulate those activities having a substantial relation to interstate commerce. Brzonkala (P) argued that § 13981 falls under the third category. In *Lopez*, this Court concluded that those cases in which federal regulation of intrastate activity (based on the activity's substantial effects on interstate commerce) has been sustained have included some type of economic endeavor. Gender motivated crimes of violence are not economic activities. While § 13981 is supported by numerous findings regarding the serious impact that gender-motivated violence has on victims and their families, the existence of congressional findings is not sufficient in itself to sustain the constitutionality of Commerce Clause legislation. Whether a particular activity affects interstate commerce sufficiently to come under the constitutional power of Congress to regulate is a judicial question. The Court also rejects the argument that Congress may regulate noneconomic, violent criminal conduct based solely on that conduct's aggregate effect on interstate commerce. The regulation and punishment of intrastate violence that is not directed at the instrumentalities of interstate commerce is reserved to the states. Brzonkala (P) also argued that § 5 of the Fourteenth Amendment authorized the statutory cause of action. This argument is based on the assertion that there is pervasive bias in various state justice systems against victims of gender-motivated violence. While sex discrimination is one of the objects of the Fourteenth Amendment, the amendment only prohibits state action.

CONCURRENCE: (Thomas, J.) The notion of a substantial effects test is inconsistent with Congress's powers and early Commerce Clause jurisprudence, perpetuating the federal government's (P) view that the Commerce Clause has no limits.

DISSENT: (Souter, J.) Congress has the power to legislate with regard to activities that in the aggregate have a substantial effect on interstate commerce. The fact of the substantial effect is a question for Congress in the first instance and not the courts. Here Congress assembled a mountain of data demonstrating the effects of violence against women on interstate commerce.

DISSENT: (Breyer, J.) Congress, in enacting the statute, followed procedures that work to protect the federalism issues at stake. After considering alternatives, Congress developed the federal law with the intent of compensating documented deficiencies in state legal systems, and tailored federal law to prevent its use in areas traditionally reserved to the states. This law represents the result of state and federal efforts to cooperate in order to resolve a national problem.

▶ ANALYSIS

The primary issue here is that the federal government is seeking to regulate areas traditionally regulated exclusively

Continued on next page.

by the states. The majority concludes that the regulation and punishment of intrastate violence that is not directed to the instrumentalities of interstate commerce is the exclusive jurisdiction of local government. What the dissent argues here is that Congress in this case has amassed substantial findings to demonstrate that such intrastate violence does have an effect on the instrumentalities of commerce.

■■■■

Quicknotes

COMMERCE CLAUSE   Article 1, § 8, cl. 3 of the United States Constitution, granting Congress the power to regulate commerce with foreign countries and between the states.

VIOLENCE AGAINST WOMEN ACT (VAWA)   Legislation passed in 1994 that provides harsh federal penalties for sexual assaults commonly perpetrated against women, and authorizes funding for training, counseling and treatment programs for victims of these specific forms of violence, including battered women's shelters and projects serving victims of domestic violence and child abuse.

■■■■

Steward Machine Co. v. Davis

Employer (P) v. Government (D)

301 U.S. 548 (1937).

NATURE OF CASE: Action challenging the constitutionality of the Social Security Act as applied to employers of eight or more.

FACT SUMMARY: The Social Security Act levies an excise tax on employers of eight or more. The proceeds go into the general treasury. However if a taxpayer has made contributions to a state unemployment fund, such contributions can be credited against the federal tax. Between 1929 and 1936 the United States suffered from extreme unemployment.

RULE OF LAW
A federal unemployment insurance tax statute which provides for credit for contributions made to state unemployment funds is valid because Congress enacted it primarily to safeguard its own treasury, the proceeds of the tax are not earmarked for a special group but go into the general treasury, and the act is directed to an end for which Congress and the states may lawfully cooperate.

FACTS: The Social Security Act imposes an excise tax on employers of eight or more based on the wages paid. The proceeds go into the general treasury. However if a taxpayer has made contributions to a state unemployment fund, such contributions can be credited against the federal tax, provided that the state law has been certified by the Social Security Board as satisfying certain minimum criteria. Between 1929 and 1936 there was an unprecedented number of unemployed in the United States, and the states were unable to give the requisite relief to the needy. Steward Machine Co. (P) paid a tax in accordance with the statute and filed a claim to recover the payment, asserting that the statute is unconstitutional.

ISSUE: Is a federal unemployment insurance tax statute which provides for credit for contributions made to state unemployment funds valid?

HOLDING AND DECISION: (Cardozo, J.) Yes. A federal unemployment insurance tax statute which provides for credit for contributions made to state unemployment funds is valid because Congress enacted it primarily to safeguard its own treasury, the proceeds of the tax are not earmarked for a special group but go into the general treasury, and the act is directed to an end for which Congress and the states may lawfully cooperate. First of all, in a crisis as extreme as the unemployment crisis, the use of the nation's moneys to relieve the unemployed and their dependents cannot be called a use for any purpose other than the promotion of the general welfare. By 1935,

when Congress enacted the Social Security Act, the unemployment situation had become so severe that the states were unable to continue to help those in need. There was need of help from the nation if people were not to starve. Before Congress enacted the Social Security Act, few states had passed unemployment laws. Many held back for fear that the toll placed on industry by such legislation would put them at an economic disadvantage as compared with neighboring states. The purpose of Congress's intervention in enacting the Social Security Act was to safeguard its own treasury, and, as an incident to that protection, to place the states upon a footing of equal opportunity as to unemployment insurance. Unlike the Child Labor Tax, the Federal Unemployment Tax will be abated upon the doing of an act that will satisfy the fiscal need subserved by the tax. Unlike the tax in *U.S. v. Butler*, 297 U.S. 1 (1936), the proceeds from the federal unemployment tax are not earmarked for a special group but go into the general treasury. Also, the state unemployment law, which is a condition of the credit, has had the state's approval (and could not be a law without such approval). Nor is the condition linked to an irrevocable agreement. The state may choose to repeal its unemployment law, thereby terminating the credit; further, the credit condition is not directed to achieve an unlawful end but an end, the relief of unemployment, for which the nation and states may lawfully cooperate. Lastly, the statute does not call for a surrender by the states of powers essential to their quasi-sovereign existence. The condition requiring that the state laws meet the Social Security Board's criteria is suitable to assure that those who look to the laws for protection receive that protection. "What is basic and essential may be assured by suitable conditions." The Social Security Act is constitutional.

ANALYSIS

Policy guidance via the spending power goes back to the beginning of the nation, as is pointed out in the majority opinion in *Steward*. The programs have increased considerably over the years, and there has been increasing opposition to narrow categorical grants-in-aid and advocacy of broader unrestricted grants to state and local governments. The Advisory Commission on Intergovernmental Relations was established in 1959. One of its major functions is the examination of the impact of national spending on the federal system. In its Annual Report for 1969 it stated, "unless state and local governments are permitted 'free,' albeit limited, access to the prime power

Continued on next page.

source—the Federal Income Tax—their positions within our federal systems are bound to deteriorate."

■═■

Quicknotes

SOCIAL SECURITY ACT Federal law creating the Social Security Administration, which is charged with the administration of a national program where contributions from employers and employees are held until the worker retires or is disabled, at which time they are paid out.

SPENDING POWER The power delegated to Congress by the Constitution to spend money in providing for the nation's welfare.

■═■

South Dakota v. Dole

State (P) v. Court (D)

483 U.S. 203 (1987).

NATURE OF CASE: Appeal from decisions upholding federal highway funding requirement.

FACT SUMMARY: Congress passed a law withholding federal highway funds to states with a minimum drinking age of less than 21 years. South Dakota (P) challenged the law because it allowed nineteen-year-olds to purchase alcohol.

🏛 RULE OF LAW
Congress may withhold federal highway funds to states with a minimum drinking age of less than 21 years.

FACTS: In 1984, Congress enacted 20 U.S.C. § 138, which directed the Secretary of Transportation to withhold 5% of federal highway funds to states with a drinking age of less than 21 years of age. South Dakota (P) permitted 19-year olds to purchase beer with 3.2% alcohol content. South Dakota (P) sought a declaration that the law was unconstitutional. The district and circuit courts upheld the law, and the Supreme Court granted review.

ISSUE: May Congress withhold federal highway funds to states with a minimum drinking age of less than 21 years?

HOLDING AND DECISION: (Rehnquist, C.J.) Yes. Congress may withhold federal highway funds to states with a minimum drinking age of less than 21 years. It is well recognized that Congress may use its spending power to induce cooperation by states in areas which it cannot necessarily regulate directly. Therefore, even if Congress could not directly legislate state drinking ages, it can use the threat of withheld funds to achieve its regulatory goal. South Dakota (P) argued that alcohol is a special case, as the Twenty-First Amendment specifically leaves the regulation of drinking to the states. However, this leads the analysis back to its point of origin, namely, that Congress can indirectly regulate through its spending power. That is all it has done here. Affirmed.

DISSENT: (O'Connor, J.) Section 158 cannot be justified as reasonably related to the federal highway system. It is an attempt to regulate alcoholic beverages, something Congress may not do.

▶ *ANALYSIS*

It is not uncommon for Congress to attempt to regulate "with a carrot" rather than by direct regulation. The present case is one such action. Probably the most controversial area where this has been subject to constitutional consideration is in the area of abortions. Cases such as *Maher v. Roe*, 432 U.S. 464 (1977), and *Rust v. Sullivan*, 500 U.S. 173 (1991), have established Congress's right in this area.

■━■

Quicknotes

SPENDING POWER The power delegated to Congress by the Constitution to spend money in providing for the nation's welfare.

TWENTY-FIRST AMENDMENT The Twenty-First Amendment to the United States Constitution prohibits the importation or possession of intoxicating liquors in any state or territory.

■━■

Garcia v. San Antonio Metropolitan Transit Authority

Employee (P) v. Transit authority (D)

469 U.S. 528 (1985).

NATURE OF CASE: Appeal from decision barring application of Fair Labor Standards Act to municipal mass transit system.

FACT SUMMARY: Garcia (P) appealed from a decision holding that the National League of Cities barred the application of the Fair Labor Standards Act to the San Antonio Metropolitan Transit Authority (D), a municipally owned and operated mass transit system, on the grounds that application in the present case would entrench on a "traditional governmental function."

🏛 RULE OF LAW
Sufficient restraints on the exercise of the commerce power to protect the states' sovereign interests are provided by procedural safeguards inherent in the structure of the federal system established by the Constitution and should not be provided by judicially created limitations on federal power.

FACTS: Garcia (P) appealed from a decision holding that National League of Cities barred the application of the Fair Labor Standards Act to the San Antonio Metropolitan Transit Authority (D), a municipally owned and operated mass transit system, on the grounds that application in the present case would entrench on a "traditional governmental function."

ISSUE: Are sufficient restraints on the exercise of the commerce power to protect the states' sovereign interests provided by procedural safeguards inherent in the structure of the federal system established by the Constitution?

HOLDING AND DECISION: (Blackmun, J.) Yes. Sufficient restraints on the exercise of the commerce power to protect the states' sovereign interests are provided by procedural safeguards inherent in the structure of the federal system established by the Constitution and should not be provided by judicially created limitations on federal power. In *National League of Cities*, this Court ruled that the Commerce Clause did not empower Congress to enforce wage and overtime standards of the Fair Labor Standards Act against the states in areas of "traditional governmental functions." Hodel summarized the four prerequisites for governmental immunity under *National League of Cities*, the third of which being that the challenged federal statute entrench on a "traditional governmental function." Since *National League of Cities*, this Court has been struggling to identify "traditional governmental functions." It has been difficult, if not impossible, to identify an organizing principle upon which this determination may be made. Failure to find a principled reason for distinguishing between

governmental and proprietary functions led them to rejection of a similar distinction in the tax field. Making immunity turn on a purely historical standard would prevent courts from accommodating changes in the historical functions of the states; a non-historical standard is likely to prove just as unworkable. Systems that purport to separate out important governmental functions are unfaithful to the role of the federalism system. The state must be free to engage in any activity allowed under the Constitution. Using a system defining important governmental functions invites an unelected federal judiciary to make judgments about appropriate state functions. The sovereignty of the states is limited by the Constitution itself: they retain sovereign authority to the extent that the Constitution has not divested them of their original powers. The principal means chosen by the founders to protect state sovereignty lies in the structure of the federal government itself. The states have a role in the selection of the executive and legislative branches of government. The effectiveness of the political process in protecting state interests is clearly evident from the course of federal legislation. Substantive restraints on the commerce power must be tailored to compensate for possible failings in the national political process. There is nothing in the Fair Labor Standards Act standards as applied to the San Antonio Metropolitan Transit Authority (D) that is destructive of state sovereignty or violative of any constitutional provision. The internal safeguards have performed as intended. *National League of Cities* is overruled.

DISSENT: (Powell, J.) Prior decisions embraced a balancing approach to determine if the application of the Commerce Clause powers intruded upon state sovereignty. The states do participate in the Electoral College but this does not mean the President serves as their protective representative fighting federal interference. Judicial enforcement of the Tenth Amendment is necessary to protect the federal-state balance intended by the Framers and made part of the Constitution. The Framers and Constitution anticipate state and local officials being in a better position to understand the needs of their constituents. This local accountability better preserves the federal system.

▶ ANALYSIS

Implicit in the opinions of the Court in the present case is that the judiciary is capable of balancing the particular federal and state interests at stake in any challenge to the exercise of the commerce power. Some commentators

Continued on next page.

have suggested that no judicial review of any congressional legislation challenged as violating state rights is necessary. See Choper, "The Scope of National Power Vis-á-Vis the States: The Dispensability of Judicial Review," 86 Yale L. J. 1552, 1556-57, 1621 (1977).

■■■

Quicknotes

COMMERCE POWER The power delegated to Congress by the Constitution to regulate interstate commerce.

TENTH AMENDMENT The Tenth Amendment to the United States Constitution reserves those powers therein, not expressly delegated to the federal government or prohibited to the states, to the states or to the people.

■■■

Printz v. United States

Law enforcement officer (P) v. Federal government (D)

521 U.S. 898 (1997).

NATURE OF CASE: Review of judgment dismissing constitutional challenge to federal legislation.

FACT SUMMARY: A provision in the Brady Handgun Violence Prevention Act which compelled local officials to enforce the Act was challenged as unconstitutional.

🏛 RULE OF LAW
The federal government may not compel the states to enact or administer a federal regulatory program.

FACTS: Congress enacted the Brady Handgun Violence Prevention Act. The law instituted a waiting period in the purchase of handguns. It also directed local law enforcement to conduct a background check on prospective handgun purchasers. This provision of the law was challenged by Printz (P) and other law enforcement officers (P) as unconstitutional. The Ninth Circuit upheld the law, and the Supreme Court granted review.

ISSUE: May the federal government compel the states to enact or administer a federal regulatory program?

HOLDING AND DECISION: (Scalia, J.) No. The federal government may not compel the states to enact or administer a federal regulatory program. Under our federal system of government, states are autonomous, sovereign entities, not mere instrumentalities of the federal government. The federal government may not recruit states to enforce its laws absent an express constitutional authorization for such command. Also, as a general matter, under the Constitution it is the responsibility of the president and the Executive Branch of government to enforce federal law. Congress cannot strip the president of this power. The present legislation tries to do this very thing. As there is no express constitutional grant of power to Congress to compel state compliance in its regulatory scheme at issue here, the measure is unconstitutional. Reversed.

CONCURRENCE: (O'Connor, J.) The Constitution does not permit Congress to compel the states to administer a federal regulatory program. Whether Congress may use its Commerce Clause powers to compel the states to perform ministerial reporting requirements is not decided today.

DISSENT: (Stevens, J.) If the Constitution empowers Congress to respond to a problem, there is nothing in the Constitution that forbids Congress to enlist state officers when necessary to make the response effective.

DISSENT: (Breyer, J.) Congress's approach in enforcing its law in this instance is hardly unique. The federal systems of many European nations involve local enforcement of federal law.

▶ ANALYSIS

One of the big issues of the 1990s has been federalism. States, reversing a trend of over half a century, have in the last decade been taking back some of the power that the federal government has assumed. The Tenth Amendment has come back from the dead, and the Court has shown a reluctance to give unlimited scope to the Commerce Clause as a basis for federal power. The present action is an example of the current emphasis on state's rights.

■━■

Quicknotes

BRADY ACT (THE BRADY HANDGUN VIOLENCE PREVENTION ACT) A law enacted by Congress in 1993 which would provide for a waiting period before the purchase of a handgun, and for the establishment of a national instant criminal background check system to be contacted by firearms dealers before the transfer of any firearm.

COMMERCE POWER The power delegated to Congress by the Constitution to regulate interstate commerce.

TENTH AMENDMENT The Tenth Amendment to the United States Constitution reserves those powers therein, not expressly delegated to the federal government or prohibited to the states, to the states or to the people.

■━■

Distribution of Federal Powers

Quick Reference Rules of Law

Youngstown Sheet & Tube Co. v. Sawyer (The Steel Seizure Case)

Steel company (P) v. Secretary of Commerce (D)

343 U.S. 579 (1952).

NATURE OF CASE: Suit for declaratory and injunctive relief from a presidential order.

FACT SUMMARY: Faced with an imminent steel strike during the Korean War, the President ordered governmental seizure of the steel companies to prevent the strike. The companies challenged his power to take such action as being without constitutional authority or prior congressional approval.

RULE OF LAW
The President, even relying on a concept of inherent powers, and in his capacity as Commander-in-Chief, may not make an order which usurps the lawmaking authority of Congress on the basis of a compelling need to protect national security.

FACTS: As a result of long, but unsuccessful, negotiations with various steel companies, the United Steelworkers of America served notice of intent to strike in April, 1952. Through the last months of the negotiating the President had utilized every available administrative remedy to effect a settlement and avert a strike. Congress had engaged in extensive debate on solutions but had passed no legislation on the issue. By order of the President, the Secretary of Commerce seized the steel companies so that steel production would not be interrupted during the Korean War. The steel companies sued in federal district court to have the seizure order declared invalid and to enjoin its enforcement. The government asserted that the President had "inherent power" to make the order and that it was "supported by the Constitution, historical precedent and court decisions." The district court granted a preliminary injunction; the Supreme Court granted direct review.

ISSUE: May the President, relying on a concept of inherent powers, and in his capacity as Commander-in-Chief, make an order which usurps the lawmaking authority of Congress on the basis of a compelling need to protect national security?

HOLDING AND DECISION: (Black, J.) No. The President, even relying on a concept of inherent powers, and in his capacity as Commander-in-Chief, may not make an order which usurps the lawmaking authority of Congress on the basis of a compelling need to protect national security. There is, admittedly, no express congressional authority for these seizures, and so, if any authority for the President's act can be found, it must come from the Constitution. In the absence of express authority for the President's act, it is argued that the power can be implied from the aggregate of his express powers granted by the

Constitution. This order cannot be justified by reliance on the President's role as Commander-in-Chief. Even though the term "theater of war" has enjoyed an expanding definition, it cannot embrace the taking of private property to prevent a strike. The President's powers in the area of legislation are limited to proposing new laws to Congress or vetoing laws which he deems inadvisable. This order is not executive implementation of a congressional act but a legislative act performed by the President. Only Congress may do what the President has attempted here. The Constitution is specific in vesting the lawmaking powers in Congress and we, therefore, affirm the district court's decision to enjoin the enforcement of this order.

CONCURRENCE: (Frankfurter, J.) This decision does not attempt to define the limits of presidential authority. The President cannot act in contravention of an express congressional act nor may he act where Congress has done nothing. Were this a case of a long history of congressional acquiescence to presidential practice our decision might be different, but no such showing has been made.

CONCURRENCE: (Jackson, J.) The power of the President to act can be viewed as three separate categories of circumstances. First, the President's power is at its maximum when he acts pursuant to express or implied congressional authority. Second, in the absence of a congressional grant of power, the President acts solely on the basis of his powers as specified in the Constitution. Third, when the President acts in contravention of congressional action, he may do so only where it can be shown that Congress has exceeded its constitutional powers and the President is acting in his own sphere of authority. It is in this last area where presidential acts are subject to the closest scrutiny. This order is clearly not in the first category. His act cannot be justified in the second category since Congress has limited seizure powers to specific instances not embracing this order. The constitutional grant of powers to the President is in specific terms that do not permit any loose aggregation to create powers not specified. There is little question that Congress could have authorized those seizures, and this very power denies the same authority to the President. Finally, the President's act is justified by arguing it is the result of powers accruing to his office by custom and practice of previous administrations. Present unconstitutional acts cannot be justified by the prior unconstitutional acts of others. Presidential

Continued on next page.

power may, in fact, enlarge due to congressional inaction, but the courts will not assist or approve this process.

DISSENT: (Vinson, C.J.) The President's seizure in this case is in accord with congressional intent to support the resistance of aggression in the world and is in further-ance of his duty to execute the laws of this nation. The executive is the only branch of government that may, by design, act swiftly to meet national emergencies. Congress and the courts typically support such actions as history reveals. This decision emasculates that necessary power and results in the President being no more than a messen-ger-boy for Congress.

▶ ANALYSIS

Justice Black's broad language was criticized by many scholars as being overly expansive for the case presented. However, other authorities pointed out that the broad arguments advanced by the government required a broad response. During oral argument before the Court, the gov-ernment counsel stated that while the Constitution imposed limits on congressional and judicial powers, no such limits were imposed on the presidency. While supple-mental briefs were filed modifying this position, the damage may already have been done. The Court was faced with a paucity of judicial precedents. The President and Congress have traditionally preferred political rather than judicial solutions to their conflicts. This practice avoids the limitations imposed on future actions by binding judicial precedents. And, as can be seen by the cases of *Marbury v. Madison*, 5 U.S. (1 Cranch) 137, 2 L.Ed. 60 (1803), and *United States v. Nixon*, 417 U.S. 683 (1974), the executive branch has not fared well when it has sub-mitted to judicial jurisdiction.

■■■■

Quicknotes

PRELIMINARY INJUNCTION A judicial mandate issued to require or restrain a party from certain conduct; used to preserve a trial's subject matter or to prevent threatened injury.

■■■■

United States v. Curtiss-Wright Export Corp.

Federal government (P) v. Export company (D)

299 U.S. 304 (1936).

NATURE OF CASE: Action to prosecute a company that violated an embargo authorized by Congress and proclaimed by the President.

FACT SUMMARY: Curtiss-Wright Export Corp. (D) challenged a joint resolution from Congress authorizing the President to prohibit the sale of arms to Bolivia and Paraguay as an unconstitutional delegation of legislative power.

🏛 RULE OF LAW
The constitutional powers of the federal government regarding foreign affairs are more expansive than those regarding domestic affairs.

FACTS: Congress passed a joint resolution authorizing the President to prohibit the sale of arms to Bolivia and Paraguay, who were involved in an armed conflict in Chaco. The President believed that such a prohibition would increase the chances of reestablishing peace in the region and declared an embargo. Curtiss-Wright Export Corp. (D) was indicted for violating the terms of the embargo, but the lower court found that the joint resolution was an unconstitutional delegation of legislative power. The United States (P) appealed the ruling.

ISSUE: Are the constitutional powers of the federal government regarding foreign affairs more expansive than those regarding domestic affairs?

HOLDING AND DECISION: (Sutherland, J.) Yes. The constitutional powers of the federal government regarding foreign affairs are more expansive than those regarding domestic affairs. The President's powers over international relations are not restricted by the Constitution to the same extent as those regarding domestic affairs. Although the Constitution's enumerated powers set strict limits on all branches of the federal government, these limits apply only to internal affairs. The President has exclusive and plenary power as the sole organ of the federal government in international relations. The President has the power to speak or listen as a representative of the country, and he alone negotiates treaties. Furthermore, the nature of foreign relations and the conditions of war necessitate that different rules apply under these conditions. Therefore, the lower court erred in finding that the resolution was an unconstitutional delegation. Reversed.

▶ ANALYSIS

Because the Constitution does not specifically assign powers regarding international affairs, the specifics have been worked out over time with the help of the President, Congress, and the Supreme Court. This case has received criticism because the Court seemed to indicate that the President's power is virtually limitless. While this is not entirely accurate, the balancing of the grey areas is continuously being negotiated.

Quicknotes

PLENARY POWER The complete authority of a court to hear and determine cases pertaining to specified subject matter or particular parties.

Campbell v. Clinton

Congressmen (P) v. President of the United States (D)

203 F.3d 19 (D.C. Cir. 2000).

NATURE OF CASE: Appeal from dismissal of suit.

FACT SUMMARY: Campbell (P) and other congressmen filed suit against President Clinton (D) alleging that he violated the War Powers Resolution [WPR] and the constitutional War Powers Clause when he ordered U.S. troop involvement in the NATO action in Yugoslavia. The court dismissed the suit for lack of standing.

🏛 RULE OF LAW
Members of Congress lack standing to claim the President has unconstitutionally involved U.S. troops in war when "war" is undefined.

FACTS: The War Powers Resolution (WPR) allows the President to engage U.S. troops in hostilities if imminently required and then submit a report to Congress within 48 hours. Congress then votes on a declaration of war and authorization of the action. If no declaration or authorization issues, the President is to cease the U.S. troop involvement. President Clinton (D) engaged U.S. troops in the NATO action in Yugoslavia and submitted a report to Congress two days later. Congress did not issue a declaration of war and did not authorize the action. It did, however, vote to fund the action and did not require the immediate cessation of U.S. troop involvement. The NATO action in the conflict in Yugoslavia continued for 79 days. Campbell (P) and several other congressmen sued President Clinton (D) alleging his order for continued troop involvement violated the WPR.

ISSUE: Do members of Congress lack standing to claim the President has unconstitutionally involved U.S. troops in war when "war" is undefined?

HOLDING AND DECISION: (Silberman, J.) Yes. Members of Congress lack standing to claim the President has unconstitutionally involved U.S. troops in war when "war" is undefined. Campbell (P) lacks standing. Affirmed.

CONCURRENCE: (Silberman, J.) The claims here are not justiciable and, therefore, no party has standing to bring them. Appellants claim that courts can define "war" but appellants have no constitutional support for their argument. Members of Congress lack standing to claim the President has unconstitutionally involved U.S. troops in war when "war" is undefined. The President has the power to involve U.S. troops in a war while Congress has the power to declare war. The two powers are not the same as declared in *The Prize Cases*, 67 U.S. 635 (1862). The Court held that the President need not wait for legislative authority to act in the face of foreign aggression and courts will not second-guess the level of force used. Judge Tatel ignores the *Prize* holding and questions the President's judgment for the appropriate level of force used. Here, the President stated that force was necessary in Yugoslavia.

CONCURRENCE: (Tatel, J.) The courts are able to develop the definition of "war" within the War Powers clause of the Constitution just as they are able to respond to other constitutional issues. In the *Prize* cases, the Court held that "war" depended upon the facts of the circumstances and refused to ignore the existence of actual war solely because a technical definition of the term could be agreed upon. The question here is whether the President had the authority to act as he did, which is not a political question but a judicial one. The courts have the final voice in constitutional issues, so some confusion resulting from multiple voices on a "foreign policy issue" is an acceptably small consequence.

▶ ANALYSIS

The Constitution does not allow the President to declare war or to involve the United States in war unchecked. The courts, however, are increasingly reluctant to second-guess presidential military action and often dismiss cases on procedural issues. Critics are concerned that Congress has been relegated to "implying consent" after presidential action and courts refuse oversight of the executive power, which leaves too much power in the hands of Presidents. The framers of the Constitution provided for all three branches of government to be involved when war is declared and the U.S. troops are engaged in conflict.

■=■

Boumediene v. Bush

Alien detainees (P) v. President of the United States (D)

553 U.S. 723 (2008).

NATURE OF CASE: Appeal from decisions holding that alien detainees designated as enemy combatants at the U.S. Naval Station at Guantanamo Bay, Cuba did not have the privilege of habeas corpus.

FACT SUMMARY: Aliens (P) designated as enemy combatants detained at Guantanamo Bay, Cuba, contended they had the constitutional privilege of habeas corpus, despite the procedures provided by the Detainee Treatment Act of 2005 (DTA) for review of the detainees' status, and that the Military Commissions Act of 2006 (MCA) operated as an unconstitutional suspension of the writ.

🏛 RULE OF LAW
Alien detainees designated as enemy combatants have the constitutional privilege of habeas corpus where procedures provided for review of their status are not an adequate and effective substitute for habeas corpus.

FACTS: [The United States government (D) captured aliens (P) abroad on the battlefields of Afghanistan or elsewhere and sent them to the U.S. Naval Station at Guantanamo Bay, Cuba. At the time, the United States District Court in Washington, D.C., had statutory habeas corpus jurisdiction to review the lawfulness of incarceration as enemy combatants. But then Congress passed the Military Commissions Act of 2006 (MCA), which stripped all U.S. courts of habeas jurisdiction over the detainees, and provided instead a limited review by the D.C. Circuit Court over decisions of the Combatant Status Review Tribunals (CSRTs) that the Department of Defense set up under the Detainee Treatment Act of 2005 (DTA). The Circuit Court's could review the cases only after CSRTs found detention to be warranted on the ground that the detainees were enemy combatants, and the Circuit Court cold only review with respect to whether the CSRTs had acted in accordance with applicable law. Some of the detainees (P) argued that the MCAs removal of habeas jurisdiction violated the Suspension Clause, which provides that habeas shall not be suspended unless public safety requires it in cases of rebellion or invasion. The government (D) argued that withdrawal of habeas did not violate the Suspension Clause, because the DTA provided enough judicial review as a substitute.]

ISSUE: Do alien detainees designated as enemy combatants have the constitutional privilege of habeas corpus where procedures provided for review of their status are not an adequate and effective substitute for habeas corpus?

HOLDING AND DECISION: (Kennedy, J.) Yes. Alien detainees designated as enemy combatants have the constitutional privilege of habeas corpus where procedures provided for review of their status are not an adequate and effective substitute for habeas corpus. MCA § 7 denies federal courts jurisdiction to hear habeas corpus actions pending at the time of its enactment. The issue is thus whether the statute is constitutional; if it is, the cases must be dismissed. The issue can further be parsed into two issues: whether the aliens (P) are barred from seeking the habeas writ or invoking the Suspension Clause's protections because of their status as designated enemy combatants or because of their geographic presence at Guantanamo. The writ's history as to the geographic question is not dispositive. At common law, the writ ran only to territories over which the Crown was sovereign, but while Guantanamo is subject to Cuba's de jure sovereignty, it is clear that the United States government (D) exercises de facto sovereignty over this territory. In prior cases, the Court has balanced practical considerations of military occupation with constitutional necessities. Those cases, however, did not adopt a formalistic, sovereignty-based test for determining the reach of the Suspension Clause, but instead turned on objective factors and practical concerns. Under the Government's (D) approach, it could lease territory from a third-party sovereign, exercise complete control over the territory, and govern the territory without legal constraints. The Constitution, however, cannot be contracted away in such a manner. The Constitution grants Congress and the President the power to acquire, dispose of, and govern territory, not the power to decide when and where its terms apply. Based on precedential cases, there are at least three factors that are relevant in determining the reach of the Suspension Clause: (1) the detainees' citizenship and status and the adequacy of the process through which that status was determined; (2) the nature of the sites where apprehension and then detention took place; and (3) the practical obstacles inherent in resolving the prisoner's entitlement to the writ. Application of this framework reveals, first, that the aliens' (P) status is in dispute: They are not American citizens, but deny they are enemy combatants; and although they have been afforded some process in CSRT proceedings, there has been no trial by military commission for violations of the laws of war. Second, while the sites of the aliens' (P) apprehension and detention, weigh against finding they have Suspension Clause rights, the Government (D) has absolute and indefinite control over the naval station. Third, although the Court is sensitive to the financial and administrative costs of holding the Suspension Clause

Continued on next page.

applicable in a case of military detention abroad, these factors are not dispositive because the Government (D) presents no credible arguments that the military mission at Guantanamo would be compromised if habeas courts had jurisdiction. For these reasons, the Suspension Clause applies with full effect at Guantanamo Bay. The aliens (P) thus are entitled to the privilege of habeas corpus to challenge the legality of their detention. The next issue that must be resolved, therefore, is whether the Suspension Clause has been complied with because the DTA review process provides an adequate substitute. Given its holding that the writ does not run to petitioners, the court of appeals found it unnecessary to consider whether there was an adequate substitute for habeas. This Court usually remands for consideration of questions not decided below, but departure from this rule is appropriate here as the costs of further delay substantially outweigh any benefits of remanding. The DTA's jurisdictional grant is quite limited, and was not intended by Congress to be coextensive with habeas corpus. It is uncontroversial that the habeas privilege entitles the prisoner to a meaningful opportunity to demonstrate that he is being held pursuant to "the erroneous application or interpretation" of relevant law, and the habeas court must have the power to order the conditional release of an individual unlawfully detained. The aliens (P) identify what they see as myriad deficiencies in the CSRTs, the most relevant being the constraints upon the detainee's ability to rebut the factual basis for the Government's (D) assertion that he is an enemy combatant. At the CSRT stage, the detainee has limited means to find or present evidence to challenge the Government's (D) case, does not have the assistance of counsel, and may not be aware of the most critical allegations that the Government (D) relied upon to order his detention. His opportunity to confront witnesses is likely to be more theoretical than real, given that there are no limits on the admission of hearsay. Even if the CSRTs satisfied due process, however, that would not end the inquiry, because, for the habeas writ, or its substitute, to function as an effective and meaningful remedy in this context, the court conducting the collateral proceeding must have some ability to correct any errors, to assess the sufficiency of the Government's (D) evidence, and to admit and consider relevant exculpatory evidence that was not introduced during the earlier proceeding. The DTA does not permit the court of appeals to conduct a proceeding meeting these requirements since the statute cannot be construed as permitting a detainee to present relevant exculpatory evidence that was not made part of the record in earlier proceedings. To hold that the aliens (P) at Guantanamo may, under the DTA, challenge the President's legal authority to detain them, contest the CSRT's findings of fact, supplement the record on review with exculpatory evidence, and request an order of release would come close to reinstating the § 2241 habeas corpus process Congress sought to deny them. The language of the statute, read in light of Congress's reasons for enacting it, cannot bear such an interpretation. Therefore, the aliens (P) have met their

burden of establishing that the DTA review process is, on its face, an inadequate substitute for habeas corpus and that there is no bar to the district court's entertaining their claims. A remaining question, nevertheless, is whether there are prudential barriers to habeas review under these circumstances. The Government (D) argues that the aliens (P) must seek review of their CSRT determinations in the court of appeals before they can proceed with their habeas corpus actions in the district court. In other contexts and for prudential reasons, this Court has required exhaustion of alternative remedies before a prisoner can seek federal habeas relief. The cases here involve detainees who have been held for years without judicial oversight, and there has been no showing that it would be excessively burdensome to respond to the habeas corpus actions. To require these detainees to pursue the limited structure of DTA review before proceeding with habeas actions would be to require additional months, if not years, of delay. This does not mean that a habeas court should intervene the moment an enemy combatant steps foot in a territory where the writ runs. Except in cases of undue delay, such as the present, federal courts should refrain from entertaining an enemy combatant's habeas petition at least until after the CSRT has had a chance to review his status. To reduce the burden habeas proceedings will place on the military, without impermissibly diluting the writ's protections, due consideration must be given to channeling future cases to a single district court and requiring that court to use its discretion to accommodate to the greatest extent possible the Government's (D) legitimate interest in protecting sources and intelligence gathering methods. Also, proper deference must be accorded to the political branches. Reversed and remanded to the court of appeals with instructions to remand to the district court.

DISSENT: (Roberts, C.J.) The majority has struck down as inadequate "the most generous set of procedural protections ever afforded aliens detained by this country," and replaced them with "a set of shapeless procedures to be defined by the federal court at some future date." The procedures under the DTA are a sufficient substitute for habeas review and adequately protect whatever constitutional rights aliens (P) captured abroad and detained as enemy combatants may enjoy. The undefined habeas process will most likely be like the DTA system it replaces, since the district courts will have to balance the need to review a prisoner's detention with the need to protect Americans from terrorism. The DTA system the political branches constructed adequately protects any constitutional rights aliens captured abroad and detained as enemy combatants may enjoy, and the cases should be dismissed on that ground. In addition, the Court should never have granted certiorari to hear the cases until the court of appeals had made its rulings on the nature and validity of the congressionally mandated proceedings in a given

Continued on next page.

alien's (P) case and until the alien detainees (P) had exhausted their remedies under the DTA. It is premature to decide that the aliens (P) have a right to habeas without first assessing whether the remedies under the DTA system vindicate their rights. If the CSRT procedures meet minimal due process requirements, and if an Article III court is available to ensure that these procedures are followed in future cases, there is no need to reach the Suspension Clause question. While the majority believes that requiring the aliens (P) to pursue DTA review before proceeding with their habeas actions will inject additional delay, there is no reason to believe that habeas review by the federal courts will proceed faster. On the contrary, it will take longer because it will precede review at the court of appeals—where review starts under the DTA system. The CSRTs mirror the procedural model of habeas for enemy combatants, which provide due process by military tribunals. The DTA also provides additional review in an Article III court that is authorized to decide whether the CSRT proceedings are consistent with the Constitution. The Court has already found that such review is sufficient to satisfy due process, even for citizens. At the CSRT stage, the detainees (P) are accorded significant access to classified materials, and have a Personal Representative. Then, at the court of appeals, they have full access to appellate counsel and the right to challenge the factual and legal bases of their detention. The only weak argument to all these procedural protections that the majority has is that detainees are unable to introduce at the appeal stage exculpatory evidence discovered after the conclusion of their CSRT proceedings. While this is true, a detainee who finds such evidence can have the court of appeals remand the case for a new CSRT determination, and the court of appeals can later review any new or reinstated decision in light of the supplemented record. In addition, the DTA provides for periodic review of any new evidence that may become available relating to the enemy combatant status of a detainee. This statutory scheme provides the enemy combatants held at Guantanamo greater procedural protections than have ever been afforded alleged enemy detainees—whether citizens or aliens—in our national history.

DISSENT: (Scalia, J.) In addition to the fact that, as pointed out by Chief Justice Roberts' dissent, the DTA provides the essential protections that habeas guarantees, there is an even more fundamental problems with the majority's opinion: "The writ of habeas corpus does not, and never has, run in favor of aliens abroad; the Suspension Clause thus has no application, and the Court's intervention in this military matter is entirely ultra vires." The country is at war with radical terrorists, and the majority's decision will make it more difficult for the Government (D) to fight terrorism and will "almost certainly cause more Americans to be killed." Such consequences are intolerable because they do not even protect a time-honored constitutional principle. It is already difficult enough for the military to determine in the

theater of battle who is an enemy combatant and who is not; the majority's decision makes it even more difficult by requiring military officials to appear before civilian courts to defend their decisions. With higher standards of proof, more enemies will be returned to battle. Providing classified information to detainees' defense counsel will only lead to its getting into enemy hands. Congress and the President have already determined that limiting the role of civilian courts in these matters is important to the war's success. Given that the Court must be especially deferential to Congress in military matters, and given that the majority concedes that common law is not dispositive of the issue, the majority has no basis on which to strike down the MCA, and should have left undisturbed the considered judgment of the coequal branches. In the past, alien combatants who have been on U.S. soil have not been accorded the habeas privilege.

▌ *ANALYSIS*

This decision held that the aliens (P) were entitled to seek the writ of habeas corpus, not that the writ would have to issue; that the DTA review procedures were an inadequate substitute for habeas corpus; that the aliens (P) did not need to exhaust the review procedures in the court of appeals before proceeding with their habeas actions in the district court; and that MCA § 7 was unconstitutional. Accordingly, both the DTA and the CSRT process remain intact. The case did not address whether the Government (D) had the authority in the first place to detain the aliens (P), and left that issue for decision in the district court. The Court expressly declined to decide whether the CSRT procedures satisfied due process.

■══■

Quicknotes

ALIEN An individual who is a citizen of a foreign country.

DUE PROCESS RIGHTS The constitutional mandate requiring the courts to protect and enforce individuals' rights and liberties consistent with prevailing principles of fairness and justice, and prohibiting the federal and state governments from such activities that deprive its citizens of a life, liberty or property interest.

HABEAS CORPUS A proceeding in which a defendant brings a writ to compel a judicial determination of whether he is lawfully being held in custody.

ULTRA VIRES An act undertaken by a corporation that is beyond the scope of its authority pursuant to law or its articles of incorporation.

■══■

INS v. Chadha

Government agency (D) v. Immigrant (P)

462 U.S. 919 (1983).

NATURE OF CASE: Action challenging the constitutionality of a deportation statute.

FACT SUMMARY: Chadha (P) challenged a resolution passed unilaterally by the House of Representatives that he did not meet the hardship requirements of the Immigration and Nationality Act of 1952 and should therefore be deported.

🏛 RULE OF LAW
A House of Congress may not act alone without review or presentment to overrule an Attorney General deportation decision because the Houses of Congress are subject to the bicameralism and presentment requirements of Article I of the Constitution.

FACTS: The Immigration and Nationality Act of 1952 authorized the Attorney General to suspend the deportation of a deportable alien if the alien met specified conditions and would suffer "extreme hardship" if deported. However, a federal statute authorized either House of Congress, by resolution, to invalidate the decision of the Attorney General. The Attorney General suspended the deportation of Chadha (P), but the House of Representatives accepted a conclusion by the House Committee that Chadha (P) did not meet the hardship requirements and passed a resolution that the deportation should not be suspended. The resolution was not submitted to the Senate or to the President. Chadha (P) brought suit challenging the constitutionality of the statute and the resolution. The lower courts ruled in his favor, and the Immigration and Naturalization Service (INS) (D) appealed.

ISSUE: May a House of Congress act alone without review or presentment to overrule an Attorney General deportation decision?

HOLDING AND DECISION: (Burger, C.J.) No. A House of Congress may not act alone without review or presentment to overrule an Attorney General deportation decision because the Houses of Congress are subject to the bicameralism and presentment requirements of Article I of the Constitution. The bicameral requirement, the Presentment Clauses, and the President's veto were intended to maintain checks on each branch of government and to protect the people from the improvident exercise of power by any one branch. The veto permitted by the statute at issue is a shortcut and a compromise of the Executive's power. The framers of the Constitution clearly ranked values other than expediency as more important. There is no support in the Constitution or the decisions of this Court that support the proposition that such

constitutional standards should be avoided because they are too cumbersome. Affirmed.

CONCURRENCE: (Powell, J.) The case can be decided on a narrower ground. Contrary to the Constitution, Congress has assumed a judicial function in deciding that Chadha (P) does not meet residence requirements. The Framers specifically provided in the Bill of Attainder Clause, Article I, § 9, clause 3, that trial by legislature lacks the necessary safeguards to prevent abuse of power.

DISSENT: (White, J.) In recent years the legislative veto has become increasingly common, suggesting that the alternatives have become less satisfactory. The concerns of presentation and bicameralism are both satisfied by the statute at issue here. The President's approval is found in the Attorney General's action in recommending to Congress that the deportation order for Chadha (P) be suspended. The House and the Senate can indicate their approval of the Executive's action by not passing a resolution of disapproval within the statutory period. Because the legislative veto is commonly found as a check upon rulemaking by administrative agencies and upon broad-based policy decisions of the Executive Branch, it is particularly unfortunate that the Court has chosen to strike down an entire class of statutes based on this one atypical case.

▶ *ANALYSIS*

Although the dissent asserted that this verdict would create a major shift in power by eliminating all legislative vetos, these fears have not been realized. Congress has been able to avoid this diminishment in power by being more careful and precise when drafting statutes. As a result, the balance of power between the branches remains relatively stable and unchanged, just as the framers intended.

■═■

Quicknotes

BICAMERAL REQUIREMENT In order for a bill to become a law, it must pass both houses of Congress (bicameralism), be presented to the President (presentment), and receive his approval by signature.

PRESENTMENT CLAUSE When a bill is presented to the President, he must act on it in its entirety and may not simultaneously veto some parts and approve other parts.

■═■

Clinton v. New York

President of the United States (P) v. State (D)

524 U.S. 417 (1998).

NATURE OF CASE: Challenge to the constitutionality of new presidential powers.

FACT SUMMARY: The Line Item Veto Act of 1996 allowed the president to cancel provisions that have been signed into law. Parties affected by President Clinton's (P) cancellation of a provision of the Balanced Budget Act of 1997 challenged the constitutionality of the Act.

RULE OF LAW
The cancellation provisions authorized by the Line Item Veto Act are not constitutional.

FACTS: President Clinton (P) used his authority under the Line Item Veto Act of 1996 to cancel a provision of the Balanced Budget Act of 1997. This forced New York (D) to repay certain funds to the federal government under the Medicaid program and removed a tax benefit to food processors acquired by farmers' cooperatives. New York (D) and several private organizations challenged the constitutionality of the Medicaid cancellation and the Snake River Potato Growers (a farmer's cooperative) (D) challenged the food processors provision.

ISSUE: Are the cancellation provisions authorized by the Line Item Veto Act constitutional?

HOLDING AND DECISION: (Stevens, J.) No. The cancellation provisions authorized by the Line Item Veto Act are not constitutional. The Line Item Veto Act gives the President (P) the power to "cancel in whole" three types of provisions that have already been signed into law: (1) any dollar amount of discretionary budget authority; (2) any item of new direct spending; or (3) any limited tax benefit. With respect to each cancellation, the President (P) must determine that it will (i) reduce the Federal budget deficit; (ii) not impair any essential government functions; and (iii) not harm the national interest. A cancellation takes effect upon receipt by Congress of the notification of the cancellation. However, a majority vote of both Houses is sufficient to make the cancellation null and void. Although the Constitution expressly authorizes the President (P) to veto a bill under Article I, § 7, it is silent on the subject of unilateral presidential action that repeals or amends parts of duly enacted statues as authorized under the Line Item Veto Act. Constitutional silence should be construed as express prohibition. If there is to be a new role for the president in the procedure to determine the final text of a law, such a change must come through the amendment procedures and not by legislation.

CONCURRENCE: (Kennedy, J.) Separation of powers was designed to protect liberty, because the concentration of power in any single branch is a threat to liberty.

DISSENT: (Breyer, J.) Given how complex our nation has become, Congress cannot divide bills into thousands or tens of thousands of separate appropriations bills, each of which the President (P) would have to veto or sign separately. Therefore, the Line Item Veto may help representative government work better.

CONCURRENCE AND DISSENT: (Scalia, J.) If the Line Item Veto Act authorized the President (P) to "decline to spend" any item of spending rather than "canceling" it, it would have been constitutional. Given that there is only a technical difference between the two actions and that it is no different from what Congress has permitted the President to do since the formation of the Union, the Line Item Veto does not offend Article I, § 7.

ANALYSIS

The majority did not comment on the wisdom of the Line Item Veto Act, because they found this step unnecessary given their finding that the Act was unconstitutional. Justice Kennedy did not let that stop him, since he felt that the Line Item Veto Act affected the separation of powers which in turn threatened liberty.

■=■

Quicknotes

LINE ITEM VETO ACT Act authorizes a governor to veto specified items in appropriation bills.

SEPARATION OF POWERS The system of checks and balances preventing one branch of government from infringing upon exercising the powers of another branch of government.

■=■

Morrison v. Olson

Independent council (P) v. Federal employees (D)

487 U.S. 654 (1988).

NATURE OF CASE: Appeal from reversal of denial of motion to quash subpoenas.

FACT SUMMARY: Morrison (P) appealed from a decision reversing a district court decision upholding the constitutionality of the independent counsel provisions of the Ethics in Government Act of 1978 and denying Olson's (D) motion to quash subpoenas, contending in part that those provisions were not violative of the Appointments Clause of the Constitution.

🏛 RULE OF LAW
The independent counsel provisions of the Ethics in Government Act are not violative of the Appointments Clause of the Constitution.

FACTS: The Ethics in Government Act of 1978 (the Act) allows for the appointment of an "independent counsel" to investigate and, if appropriate, prosecute certain high-ranking government officials for violations of criminal laws. The Attorney General conducts an initial investigation, and if circumstances warrant, applies to the Special Division, created by the Act, for appointment of independent counsel. The Special Division appoints independent counsel and defines the independent counsel's prosecutorial jurisdiction. Within this jurisdiction, the independent counsel is granted full power and independent authority to exercise all powers of the Department of Justice. The Act provides for congressional oversight of independent counsel's activities. The Attorney General sought the appointment of independent counsel, Morrison (P), to investigate the role of Olson (D) regarding a charge of perjury.

ISSUE: Are the independent counsel provisions of the Ethics in Government Act violative of the Appointments Clause of the Constitution?

HOLDING AND DECISION: (Rehnquist, C.J.) No. The independent counsel provisions of the Ethics in Government Act are not violative of the Appointments Clause of the Constitution. Since Morrison (P) is subject to removal by a higher executive branch official and since her office is restricted in jurisdiction, tenure and authorized duties, it is clear that she is an inferior officer and not a principal officer as the court of appeals concluded. Secondly, the Appointments Clause does not on its face provide for any limitation on interbranch appointments; rather, it seems to grant Congress considerable discretion as to where to vest the power to appoint inferior officials. While congressional power to provide for interbranch appointments is not unlimited, it is not impermissible in

this case for Congress to vest the power to appoint independent counsel in a specially created federal court (the Special Division). There is no actual incongruity in a court appointing prosecutorial officers where, as here, Special Division officers cannot participate in any matters handled by the appointed independent counsel. [The Court went on to conclude that these provisions did not violate Article Ill of the Constitution dealing with the separation of powers.] Reversed.

DISSENT: (Scalia, J.) The inarguable fact is that the President has sole discretion in conducting criminal prosecution and the law in question deprives the executive branch of its right to exercise sole discretion. This being so, the law violates separation of powers and thus should be invalidated.

▶ ANALYSIS

Other cases have upheld the federal court's power to appoint private attorneys to prosecute contempt of court orders, justifying the decision in part on the need for the Judiciary to have the power to independently vindicate its own authority. Justice Scalia, the author of the dissent, concurred in this judgment. See *Young v. United States ex rel Vuitton et Fils S.A.*, 481 U.S. 787 (1987).

■≡■

Quicknotes

APPOINTMENT POWER Power conferred upon the President pursuant to Article II, § 2, clause 2 of the United States Constitution to appoint ambassadors, public ministers and consuls, judges of the Supreme Court and all other officers of the United States with the advice and consent of the Senate.

INDEPENDENT COUNSEL An officer, whose appointment is authorized by the Ethics in Government Act, who is charged with the investigation of possible criminal activity by high level government officials.

MOTION TO QUASH To vacate, annul, void.

SEPARATION OF POWERS The system of checks and balances preventing one branch of government from infringing upon exercising the powers of another branch of government.

SUBPOENA A mandate issued by court to compel a witness to appear at trial.

■≡■

State Power to Regulate

Quick Reference Rules of Law

Cooley v. Board of Wardens

Shipowner (D) v. City agency (P)

53 U.S. (12 How.) 299, 13 L.Ed. 996 (1852).

NATURE OF CASE: Appeal from a decision imposing a fine for violation of a state pilotage law.

FACT SUMMARY: Cooley (D) argued that the Pennsylvania law requiring all ships using the port of Philadelphia to use a local pilot or face a fine was an unconstitutional interference with interstate commerce.

🏛 RULE OF LAW
It is constitutional for the states to regulate those areas of interstate commerce that are local in nature, as opposed to national, and not to demand a single uniform system or plan of regulation.

FACTS: Cooley (D) was fined for violating an 1803 Pennsylvania statute requiring all ships using the port of Philadelphia to engage a local pilot. He appealed the decision, arguing that the law was an unconstitutional interference with interstate commerce. The Board of Wardens (P) contended that the law was constitutional in light of a 1789 Act of Congress providing that "all pilots in the bays, inlets, rivers, harbors and ports of the United States shall continue to be regulated in conformity with the existing laws of the states, respectively, wherein such pilots may be, of with such laws as the state may respectively hereafter enact for the purpose, until further legislative provisions shall be made by the Congress."

ISSUE: Is it constitutional for the states to regulate those areas of interstate commerce that are local in nature, as opposed to national, and not to demand a single uniform system or plan of regulation?

HOLDING AND DECISION: (Curtis, J.) Yes. It is constitutional for the states to regulate those areas of interstate commerce that are local in nature, as opposed to national, and not to demand a single uniform system or plan of regulation. The Act of 1789 evidences Congress's intent that the regulation of pilots and pilotage should be left to the legislation of the states as a matter which is local and not national in nature. The mere grant to Congress of the power to regulate commerce did not deprive the states of power to regulate pilots, and although Congress has legislated on this subject, its legislation manifests an intention, with a single exception, not to regulate this subject, but to leave its regulation to the several states. Thus, the law in question is constitutional. Affirmed.

▶ ANALYSIS

As later cases have shown, it is not enough that a state law affecting interstate commerce relates to an area where local interest predominates over national interest. A state regulation will be held unconstitutional if, in addressing an essentially local concern, it discriminates against interstate commerce.

Quicknotes

COMMERCE CLAUSE Article, § 8, Clause 3 of the United States Constitution, granting Congress the power to regulate commerce with foreign countries and between the states.

Baldwin v. G.A.F. Seelig, Inc.

State agency (D) v. Milk dealer (P)

294 U.S. 511 (1935).

NATURE OF CASE: Action to enjoin enforcement of a state milk price support statute.

FACT SUMMARY: G.A.F. Seelig, Inc. (P), a New York milk dealer, sought to enjoin a New York statute establishing minimum producer-to-dealer prices on milk and prohibiting the sale in New York of milk purchased out of state at lower than the minimum price for a similar in-state purchase.

🏛 RULE OF LAW

It is a violation of the Commerce Clause for a state to regulate intrastate prices by prohibiting the importation of less expensive goods in interstate commerce.

FACTS: In addition to setting up minimum producer-to-dealer prices for the in-state sale of milk, a New York statute prohibited the sale in New York of milk bought out of state for lower prices. G.A.F. Seelig, Inc. (Seelig) (P), a New York milk dealer, bought milk in Vermont in 40-quart cans at prices below the minimums for similar in-state purchases. When New York then refused to license him to sell it, Seelig (P) brought an action seeking injunctive relief and charging an unconstitutional interference with interstate commerce. An injunction was granted as to the milk Seelig (P) wanted to sell in the original containers but not as to that milk which had been subsequently placed into bottles for sale in the New York market. The latter was deemed to have passed outside the stream of interstate commerce, thereby being subject to state regulation.

ISSUE: Can a state attempt to regulate intrastate prices by prohibiting the importation of less expensive goods in interstate commerce?

HOLDING AND DECISION: (Cardozo, J.) No. A state violates the Commerce Clause when it attempts to regulate intrastate prices by prohibiting the importation of less expensive goods in interstate commerce. Neither the power to tax nor the police power may be used by the state of destination with the aim and effect of establishing an economic barrier against competition with the products of another state or the labor of its residents. Such is a violation of the theory upon which the Constitution was framed that the peoples of the several states must sink or swim together and that the mutual jealousies of the states cannot be permitted to result in customs barriers and other economic retaliation. The form of the packages in such circumstances is immaterial, whether they are original or broken. The importer must be free from imposts framed for the very purpose of suppressing competition from without and leading inescapably to the suppression so intended. Thus, the injunction should extend to the milk in bottles, also. Affirmed in part; reversed in part.

▌ ANALYSIS

The underlying principle in this case is that one state may not, in its dealings with another, place itself in a position of economic isolation. Such a tenet is essential to maintenance of a union of states, which is why *Baldwin* is still recognized as authority.

■■■

Quicknotes

COMMERCE CLAUSE Article 1, § 8, Clause 3 of the United States Constitution, granting Congress the power to regulate commerce with foreign countries and between the states.

INJUNCTION A court order requiring a person to do or prohibiting that person from doing a specific act.

INTERFERENCE WITH INTERSTATE COMMERCE Interference with commercial dealings between two parties located in different states or located in one state and accomplished through a point in another state or a foreign country.

■■■

Dean Milk Co. v. Madison

Milk company (P) v. City (D)

340 U.S. 349 (1951).

NATURE OF CASE: Action challenging the constitutionality of a city ordinance.

FACT SUMMARY: Dean Milk Co. (P) challenged the constitutionality of a Madison (D) ordinance prohibiting the sale of milk as pasteurized unless it was processed and bottled at an approved plant within five miles of Madison's (D) central square.

RULE OF LAW
The Commerce Clause prohibits local health and safety regulations that have the effect of discriminating against interstate commerce if reasonable nondiscriminatory alternatives adequate to conserve legitimate local interests are available.

FACTS: Madison (D), a city in Wisconsin, passed an ordinance prohibiting the sale of any milk as pasteurized unless it had been processed and bottled at an approved pasteurization plant located within five miles of Madison's (D) central square. Dean Milk Co. (P), an Illinois-based concern selling milk in Illinois and Wisconsin, had pasteurization plants in Illinois 65 and 85 miles from Madison (D). The plants were licensed and inspected by Chicago health authorities and the milk labeled using the rating standards recommended by the U.S. Public Health Service. Dean Milk (P) brought suit challenging the ordinance as imposing an unconstitutional burden on interstate commerce.

ISSUE: Do local health and safety regulations violate the Commerce Clause if they discriminate against interstate commerce and there are reasonable nondiscriminatory alternatives available?

HOLDING AND DECISION: (Clark, J.) Yes. Local health and safety regulations that have the effect of discriminating against interstate commerce violate the Commerce Clause where reasonable nondiscriminatory alternatives adequate to conserve local interests are available. The ordinance at issue here clearly discriminates against interstate commerce, and other reasonable nondiscriminatory alternatives are available to protect the health of the people of Madison (D). For example, Madison (D) could inspect pasteurization plants beyond the five-mile limit now served and charge the expenses to those selling such milk in Madison (D). It could also prohibit the sale of milk not produced in conformity with standards as high as those it enforces. The existence of such alternatives renders this ordinance unconstitutional.

DISSENT: (Black, J.) The lower court found this was a good-faith attempt to safeguard public health and it has not been proved that the "alternatives" would not lower health standards.

ANALYSIS

There have been many instances where states or other localities have attempted to impose local standards more stringent than the uniform national standard for grading certain commodities. The courts have consistently found such a practice unconstitutional.

Quicknotes

COMMERCE CLAUSE Article 1, § 8, Clause 3 of the United States Constitution, granting Congress the power to regulate commerce with foreign countries and between the states.

Philadelphia v. New Jersey

Municipality (P) v. State (D)

437 U.S. 617 (1978).

NATURE OF CASE: Appeal of state court decision upholding state-imposed limitations on waste importation.

FACT SUMMARY: The State of New Jersey (D) enacted a statute banning the importation of waste products for disposal.

🏛 RULE OF LAW
A state may not enact bans on articles of commerce absent legitimate public welfare concerns.

FACTS: The State of New Jersey (D) enacted a ban on the importation of refuse into the state for disposal. The law was couched in environmentalist terms. Philadelphia (P) and other entities interested in disposing in New Jersey (D) challenged the constitutionality of the law. The New Jersey Supreme Court upheld the measure, and Philadelphia (P) appealed.

ISSUE: May a state enact bans on articles of commerce absent legitimate public welfare concerns?

HOLDING AND DECISION: (Stewart, J.) No. A state may not enact bans on articles of commerce absent legitimate public welfare concerns. Only when there is something apart from the external status of an article giving the reason for the prohibition of importation may the prohibition be legitimate. When the focus is on the out-of-state character of the article, the measure is protectionist. Whether the article is desirable or undesirable is irrelevant. Here, the only distinction made is between in-state and out-of-state waste. The public health is an issue, but public health cannot be advanced in a way which unnecessarily burdens interstate commerce. While New Jersey (D) could attack this problem by regulating more closely all waste, it cannot do so by enacting protectionist measures. Reversed.

DISSENT: (Rehnquist, J.) There is no difference between a state enacting legitimate quarantine laws and doing what New Jersey (D) did here.

▶ ANALYSIS

Generally speaking, health measures restricting interstate commerce fall into two categories. One is protectionism in health and safety clothing. This is illegitimate. The other is legitimate safety legislation incidentally affecting commerce, which are valid enactments. The law here was something different, a legitimate health measure which was accomplished by protectionist means.

■■

Quicknotes

INTERSTATE COMMERCE Commercial dealings between two parties located in different states or located in one state and accomplished through a point in another state or a foreign country; commercial dealings transacted between two states.

PROTECTIONIST MEASURES The imposition of tariffs or regulations that disadvantage foreign commodities for the economic benefit of domestic business.

■■

United Trash Haulers Ass'n v. Oneida-Herkimer Solid Waste Management Auth.

Private hauler of trash (P) v. County waste authority (D)

550 U.S. 330 (2007).

NATURE OF CASE: Suit challenging a county's "flow control" ordinance under the Dormant Commerce Clause.

FACT SUMMARY: A county's "flow control" ordinance required haulers of trash to deliver the trash to facilities owned and operated by a state-created public benefit corporation.

🏛 RULE OF LAW
An ordinance requiring that trash be delivered to a state-created public benefit corporation does not violate the Dormant Commerce Clause.

FACTS: [The Oneida-Herkimer Solid Waste Management Authority (WMA) (D) adopted a "flow control" ordinance requiring that all trash be delivered to a particular in-state waste processing facility. United Haulers Association (United Haulers) (P) sued the WMA (D), alleging that it could deliver trash to out-of-state facilities at lower costs than those required by the WMA's (D) ordinance. The trial court agreed with United Haulers' (P) Commerce Clause argument and enjoined the WMA (D) from enforcing the ordinance. The intermediate appellate court reversed, reasoning that the ordinance was permissible because it benefited a public entity instead of private businesses. United Haulers (P) petitioned the Supreme Court for further review.]

ISSUE: Does an ordinance requiring that trash be delivered to a state-created public benefit corporation violate the Dormant Commerce Clause?

HOLDING AND DECISION: (Roberts, C.J.) No. An ordinance requiring that trash be delivered to a state-created public benefit corporation does not violate the Dormant Commerce Clause. The distinction between private and public facilities is constitutionally significant because laws benefiting local government may serve several legitimate purposes instead of economic protectionism. To hold otherwise—that is, to treat public and private facilities equally under the Dormant Commerce Clause—would lead to much interference by federal courts in state and local affairs. Also worth noting is that the injury alleged by United Haulers (P)—more expensive waste disposal—will be borne by local citizens, not by citizens of other states. Typically, the Dormant Commerce Clause is enforced to prohibit shifting expenses out of state instead of keeping them at home. United Haulers' (P) proper remedy is therefore through the local political process, not through the federal courts. [Affirmed.]

CONCURRENCE IN PART: (Scalia, J.) The majority should not be balancing values; the Commerce Clause envisions that Congress will do that.

CONCURRENCE: (Thomas, J.) The Court has no policy role in regulating interstate commerce, which is why its negative Commerce Clause jurisprudence should be discarded.

DISSENT: (Alito, J.) Benefiting public facilities does not meaningfully distinguish this ordinance from the ordinance struck down in *C & A Carbone, Inc. v. Clarkstown*, 511 U.S. 383 (1994). The difference is merely formal because the waste facility in *Carbone* was "private" only in the most technical sense of the term: when that suit was filed, the facility's title was in the process of transferring to the town of Clarkstown. Further, the WMA's (D) ordinance here violates the market-participant doctrine, which prohibits local governments from discriminatorily regulating markets in which they participate. The ordinance here also fails to serve "legitimate goals unrelated to protectionism" because it clearly benefits local employees of the public facilities and local businesses who supply those facilities. Such preference is economic protectionism by any other name and thus deserves strict scrutiny. Finally, the fact that the WMA's (D) ordinance applies equally to in-state and out-of-state private businesses is not persuasive because caselaw squarely provides that such an equality of burdens cannot save legislation under the Dormant Commerce Clause.

▶ ANALYSIS

The Dormant Commerce Clause usually prohibits state and local regulations that impose relatively direct, overt burdens on interstate commerce. Here, the WMA's (D) ordinance clearly imposed direct, overt burdens on interstate commerce, but it did so for public benefit. That distinction with cases that bar interstate commerce to protect local private businesses saved the WMA's (D) ordinance under the Dormant Commerce Clause.

■■■

Quicknotes

INTERSTATE COMMERCE Commercial dealings between two parties located in different states or located in one state and accomplished through a point in another state or a foreign country; commercial dealings transacted between two states.

Continued on next page.

STRICT SCRUTINY The method by which courts determine the constitutionality of a law, when a law affects a fundamental right. Under the test, the legislature must have had a compelling interest to enact the law and measures prescribed by the law must be the least restrictive means possible to accomplish its goal.

■▬■

CTS Corp. v. Dynamics Corp.

Corporation (P) v. Acquiring corporation (D)

481 U.S. 69 (1987).

NATURE OF CASE: Appeal from ruling invalidating state corporate takeover law.

FACT SUMMARY: Dynamics Corp. (D) made a tender offer to acquire shares of CTS Corp. (P), an Indiana corporation, but Indiana law provided that a purchaser of "control shares" in a domestic corporation acquired voting rights only if approved by a majority of preexisting disinterested shareholders.

> 🏛 **RULE OF LAW**
> State laws regulating tender offers for the acquisition of controlling shares in domestic corporations do not burden interstate commerce or violate the Dormant Commerce Clause.

FACTS: An Indiana takeover law required a purchaser of controlling shares in an Indiana corporation with a significant number of shareholders resident in Indiana to submit to a vote of preexisting disinterested shareholders to determine whether its shares would be voting or nonvoting. Dynamics Corp. (D) made such a tender offer to acquire a controlling interest in CTS Corp. (P) but wanted to benefit from direct transfer of the voting interest in the shares it acquired. It therefore challenged the constitutionality of Indiana's statute under the Dormant Commerce Clause, alleging it burdened interstate commerce. The court of appeals agreed, holding that the state regulation hindered tender offers. The Supreme Court granted certiorari.

ISSUE: Do state laws which regulate tender offers for the acquisition of controlling shares in domestic corporations burden interstate commerce or violate the Dormant Commerce Clause?

HOLDING AND DECISION: (Powell, J.) No. State laws which regulate tender offers for the acquisition of controlling shares in domestic corporations do not burden interstate commerce or violate the Dormant Commerce Clause. The free market system of this country operates through national stock exchanges, which trade the securities of corporations which are creatures of state law. If these corporations listed on national exchanges could not be organized under the laws of specific states, the primary national mechanism for raising capital would disintegrate. Further, states such as Indiana have interests in avoiding the potentially coercive effects of tender offers in preventing their corporate forms from becoming shields for unfair business practices and in insuring its investors an effective voice in corporate affairs. These interests are protected by affording shareholders at the time a takeover offer is made a collective opportunity to decide whether any resulting change in voting control of the corporation would be desirable. Reversed.

CONCURRENCE: (Scalia, J.) Nothing in the Constitution says that the protection of "entrenched management" is any less important than a "putative local benefit" in the protection of "entrenched shareholders." Therefore, if a state's corporation law does not discriminate against out-of-state interests, it survives scrutiny under the Commerce Clause whether it promotes shareholder welfare or industrial stagnation.

DISSENT: (White, J.) CTS (P) stock is traded on a national exchange and is owned by people from all over the country. Thus, Indiana's direct regulation of the purchase and sale of shares of stock in interstate commerce by potentially refusing Dynamics Corp. (D) or other purchasers voting rights in the acquired corporation violates the Commerce Clause.

▶ *ANALYSIS*

Compare *Edgar v. MITE Corp.*, 457 U.S. 624 (1982), which considered an Illinois law that vested its Secretary of State with discretion to decide the substantive fairness of tender offers, and to deny registration if he concluded the offer was unfair or would work a fraud or deceit on the stockholders. In *Edgar v. MITE Corp.*, Justice White, the dissenter here, wrote the majority opinion which held the Illinois law violative of the Commerce Clause. White opined that the law had an extraterritorial effect, harmed interstate commerce by preventing shareholders from selling their shares at a premium, and reduced the incentive on incumbent management to perform well by shielding them from outside takeover attempts.

Quicknotes

DORMANT COMMERCE CLAUSE The regulatory effect of the commerce clause on state activity affecting interstate commerce, where Congress itself has not acted to control the activity; a provision inferred from, but not expressly present in, the language of the Commerce Clause.

INTERSTATE COMMERCE Commercial dealings between two parties located in different states or located in one state and accomplished through a point in another state or a foreign country; commercial dealings transacted between two states.

TENDER OFFER An offer made by one corporation to the shareholders of a target corporation to purchase their shares subject to number, time, and price specifications.

Kassel v. Consolidated Freightways Corp.

State (D) v. Common carrier (P)

450 U.S. 662 (1981).

NATURE OF CASE: Appeal from decision holding that an Iowa statute unconstitutionally burdens interstate commerce.

FACT SUMMARY: Consolidated Freightways Corp. (P) challenged the constitutionality of an Iowa statute which prohibited the use of certain large trucks within the state boundaries.

🏛 RULE OF LAW

A state safety regulation will be unconstitutional if its asserted safety purpose is outweighed by its degree of interference with interstate commerce.

FACTS: The state of Iowa passed a statute restricting the length of vehicles that may use its highways. The state law sets a general length limit of 55 feet for most vehicles, and 60 feet for trucks pulling two trailers ("doubles"). Iowa is the only state in the western or midwestern United States to outlaw the use of 65-foot doubles. Consolidated Freightways Corp. (P), one of the largest common carriers in the country, alleged that the Iowa statute unconstitutionally burdens interstate commerce. The district court and the court of appeals found the statute unconstitutional and Kassel (D), on behalf of the state, appealed.

ISSUE: Will a state safety regulation be held to be unconstitutional if its asserted safety purpose is outweighed by the degree of interference with interstate commerce?

HOLDING AND DECISION: (Powell, J.) Yes. A state safety regulation will be unconstitutional if its asserted safety purpose is outweighed by its degree of interference with interstate commerce. While bona fide state safety regulations are entitled to a strong presumption of validity, the asserted safety purpose must be weighed against the degree of interference with interstate commerce. Less deference will be given to the findings of state legislators where the local regulation has a disproportionate effect on out-of-state residents and businesses. Here, the State of Iowa failed to present any persuasive evidence that 65-foot doubles are less safe than 55-foot single trailers. Consolidated Freightways Corp. (P) demonstrated that Iowa's law substantially burdens interstate commerce by compelling trucking companies either to route 65-foot doubles around Iowa or use the smaller trucks allowed by the state statute. Thus, the Iowa statute is in violation of the Commerce Clause. Affirmed.

CONCURRENCE: (Brennan, J.) In ruling on the constitutionality of state safety regulations, the burdens imposed on commerce must be balanced against the regulatory purposes identified by the state legislators.

Protectionist legislation is unconstitutional under the Commerce Clause, even if its purpose is to promote safety, rather than economic purposes.

DISSENT: (Rehnquist, J.) A sensitive consideration must be made when weighing the safety purposes of a statute against the burden on interstate commerce. A state safety regulation is invalid if its asserted safety justification is merely a pretext for discrimination against interstate commerce. The Iowa statute is a valid highway safety regulation and is entitled to the strongest presumption of validity.

▶ ANALYSIS

Traditionally, states have been free to pass public safety regulations restricting the use of highways and railway facilities. However, state safety regulations have been struck down when only a marginal increase in safety causes a substantial burden on interstate commerce. This case simply follows this rationale.

Quicknotes

INTERSTATE COMMERCE Commercial dealings between two parties located in different states or located in one state and accomplished through a point in another state or a foreign country; commercial dealings transacted between two states.

PROTECTIONISM In commercial law, government trade policy which imposes customs duties upon imported, foreign commodities for the purpose of encouraging enrichment of domestic manufacturers of similar products.

West Lynn Creamery, Inc. v. Healy

Milk dealer (P) v. State (D)

512 U.S. 186 (1994).

NATURE OF CASE: Review of judicial rejection of legal challenge to agricultural assessment.

FACT SUMMARY: A law assessing a fee on all milk sold in Massachusetts (D), the funds of which were disbursed solely to local producers, was challenged as unconstitutional.

RULE OF LAW

An assessment scheme that levies a tax on all distribution of a good but disburses its assets only to local producers is unconstitutional.

FACTS: The legislature in Massachusetts (D), perceiving a need to protect local dairy producers, enacted an assessment system wherein a certain levy was placed on all dairy products sold in Massachusetts (D), the proceeds of which were disbursed only to Massachusetts (D) producers. The system was challenged by West Lynn Creamery, Inc. (P), a milk dealer who purchased out-of-state milk, as unconstitutional. The state courts rejected the challenge, and the Supreme Court granted review.

ISSUE: Is an assessment scheme that levies on all distribution of a good but disburses its assets to local producers unconstitutional?

HOLDING AND DECISION: (Stevens, J.) Yes. An assessment scheme that levies on all distribution of a good but disburses its assets only to local producers of the distributed goods is unconstitutional. A state may not enact a tariff on out-of-state goods; to do so is a clear violation of the Commerce Clause. The system at issue here, although taking two steps to achieve its goal, is a de facto tariff. While all producers pay equally into the fund, the assets go only to local producers. This is, in effect, a tariff. The fact that Massachusetts (D) could validly enact either a local subsidy or a nondiscriminatory tax is irrelevant; coupled, the two measures constitute a tariff and cannot stand, as the assessment is clear discrimination against interstate commerce. Reversed.

CONCURRENCE: (Scalia, J.) The Court's opinion unnecessarily broadens the scope of the Dormant Commerce Clause. Unless a law facially discriminates against interstate commerce or falls within a precedent of this Court, it should survive Commerce Clause scrutiny. Massachusetts (D) law should be invalidated because it is indistinguishable from an otherwise nondiscriminatory tax from which in-state members are exempted, a method of taxation that has been held unconstitutional by this Court.

DISSENT: (Rehnquist, C.J.) The law of Massachusetts (D) represents this sort of subsidy of a domestic industry that has heretofore been approved under the Commerce Clause.

ANALYSIS

The Commerce Clause, in its dormant expression, operates on two levels. If a law directly discriminates against commerce from another state, it is per se invalid. If it only incidentally burdens interstate commerce, a court must look to the benefits of the law versus its burdens. The law at issue here was of the former type.

Quicknotes

COMMERCE CLAUSE Article 1, § 8, Clause 3 of the United States Constitution, granting Congress the power to regulate commerce with foreign countries and between the states.

DORMANT COMMERCE CLAUSE The regulatory effect of the commerce clause on state activity affecting interstate commerce, where Congress itself has not acted to control the activity; a provision inferred from, but not expressly present in, the language of the Commerce Clause.

TARIFF Duty or tax imposed on articles imported into the United States.

Reeves, Inc. v. Stake

Cement buyer (P) v. State (D)

447 U.S. 429 (1980).

NATURE OF CASE: Appeal from denial of relief from a state commerce policy.

FACT SUMMARY: Reeves, Inc. (P) contended South Dakota's (D) policy of preferring in-state customers for its state cement production violated the Commerce Clause.

🏛 RULE OF LAW
State activity as a market participant is not subject to Commerce Clause regulation.

FACTS: South Dakota (D) adopted a policy that during a cement shortage its cement manufacturing plant would give preference to in-state buyers. Reeves, Inc. (P), an out-of-state buyer, contested the policy as unduly burdensome on interstate commerce. South Dakota (D) defended the policy, arguing its activities as a market participant rather than a market regulator were not subject to Commerce Clause regulation. The trial and appellate courts upheld the policy, and the Supreme Court granted certiorari.

ISSUE: Is state activity as a market participant subject to Commerce Clause regulation?

HOLDING AND DECISION: (Blackmun, J.) No. State activity as a market participant is not subject to Commerce Clause regulation. There is no constitutional barrier to states acting as any other free market participant. When so acting, a state may take any necessary steps to protect its market position. Thus it can discriminate against out-of-state buyers without violating the Commerce Clause. Affirmed.

DISSENT: (Powell, J.) The government cannot impede the flow of interstate commerce when it becomes involved in private market activity. South Dakota (D) is a state involved in private commerce and could make political rather than marketplace decisions with market regulation as the result. The state's preference for in-state customers and barrier to interstate cement trade is a violation of the Commerce Clause.

▶ ANALYSIS

The present case addresses the issue yet leaves it unresolved whether a subsidy program aimed at aiding small businesses in competition with outsiders is subject to Commerce Clause analysis and regulation. Some commen-tators argue such subsidies are protected as the sovereign power of the state is being exercised through the collective wealth of the state to protect its own.

Quicknotes

COMMERCE CLAUSE Article 1, § 8, Clause 3 of the United States Constitution, granting Congress the power to regulate commerce with foreign countries and between the states.

MARKET PARTICIPANT DOCTRINE Allows states acting as market participants (i.e., businesses) to be exempted from the dormant clause.

United Building & Construction Trades Council v. Mayor of Camden

Trade council (P) v. City (P)

465 U.S. 208 (1984).

NATURE OF CASE: Appeal from judgment upholding constitutionality of a municipal ordinance.

FACT SUMMARY: The New Jersey Supreme Court held that the Privileges and Immunities Clause did not apply to ordinances that discriminate on the basis of municipal rather than state citizenship.

🏛 RULE OF LAW

The Privileges and Immunities Clause applies to discrimination based on municipal residence as well as state citizenship.

FACTS: The City of Camden (D), New Jersey, enacted an ordinance that required that at least 40% of the employees of contractors and subcontractors working on city construction projects be Camden (D) residents. United Building & Construction Trades Council (United) (P) sued, contending the ordinance violated the Privileges and Immunities Clause. The Supreme Court of New Jersey held that the Privileges and Immunities Clause did not apply in cases such as this one where the discrimination is based on municipal residence rather than state citizenship. United (P) appealed.

ISSUE: Does the Privileges and Immunities Clause apply to municipal ordinances that discriminate on the basis of municipal residence?

HOLDING AND DECISION: (Rehnquist, J.) Yes. The Privileges and Immunities Clause applies to discrimination based on municipal residence as well as state citizenship. A municipality is merely a political subdivision of a state. Its power is directly derived from the state. Therefore, that which is unconstitutional when done by a state directly is equally unconstitutional when done by a political subdivision of a state. Under the ordinance, a New Jersey citizen who resides outside of Camden (D) and a citizen of another state do not enjoy the same privileges as a resident of Camden (D). The pursuit of a livelihood is a fundamental privilege protected by the Clause, and therefore the statute violates the Clause. Reversed and remanded.

DISSENT: (Blackmun, J.) The framers of the Constitution intended for the states to handle potential discrimination based on municipal residence. The Privileges and Immunities Clause thus does not apply to such discrimination. Several states have already prohibited municipal residence discrimination so the theory has been put into practice.

▶ ANALYSIS

In this case, the Court pointed out the distinction between a Commerce Clause analysis and a Privileges and Immunities Clause analysis. Under the Commerce Clause, Camden (D) could have been considered a market participant and, therefore, able to discriminate against out-of-state businesses. Yet, even though the ordinance may have been valid under the Commerce Clause, it was invalid under the Privileges and Immunities Clause where the market participant-market regulator distinction is inapplicable.

■▬■

Quicknotes

PRIVILEGED AND IMMUNITIES CLAUSE OF ARTICLE IV, § 2 A provision in the Fourteenth Amendment to the United States Constitution recognizing that any individual born in any of the United States is entitled to both state and national citizenship and guaranteeing such citizens the privileges and immunities thereof.

■▬■

Complete Auto Transit, Inc. v. Brady

Contract motor carrier (P) v. State (D)

430 U.S. 274 (1977).

NATURE OF CASE: Appeal from a decision upholding the constitutionality of a state privilege tax.

FACT SUMMARY: Complete Auto Transit, Inc. (P), a contract motor carrier of interstate commerce, brought this action to challenge the constitutionality of a Mississippi privilege tax for the privilege of doing business within the state.

🏛 RULE OF LAW
A tax on the privilege of engaging in an activity within a state may be applied to an activity that is part of interstate commerce.

FACTS: Mississippi imposed privilege taxes for the privilege of doing business within the state measured by a percent of gross income. General Motors shipped fully assembled vehicles by rail from other states to Jackson, Mississippi, destined for Mississippi dealers. Complete Auto Transit, Inc. (Complete Auto) (P), a contract motor carrier, hauled them from Jackson to the dealers. The court upheld the application of the tax to Complete Auto's (P) Mississippi business and gross income. Complete Auto (P) appealed, contending that its transportation was but one part of an interstate movement, and that the taxes were unconstitutional as applied to operations in interstate commerce. The Mississippi Supreme Court concluded that the tax did not discriminate against interstate commerce and was valid. Complete Auto (P) appealed.

ISSUE: May a tax on the privilege of engaging in an activity within a state be applied to an activity which is part of interstate commerce?

HOLDING AND DECISION: (Blackmun, J.) Yes. A tax on the privilege of engaging in an activity within a state may be applied to an activity that is part of interstate commerce. Complete Auto's (P) attack is based solely on decisions of this Court holding that a tax on the privilege of engaging in an activity may not be applied to an activity that is part of interstate commerce. However, under the present state of the law, this so-called *Spector* rule [*Spector Motor Service v. O'Connor*, 340 U.S. 602 (1951)], as it has come to be known, has no relationship to economic realities. If Mississippi had called its tax one on "net income" or on the "going concern value" of Complete Auto's (P) business, the *Spector* rule could not invalidate it. There is no economic consequence that follows necessarily from the use of the particular words, "privilege of doing business," and a focus on that formalism merely obscures the question whether the tax produces a forbidden effect. Accordingly, it is held that a tax on the privilege of engaging in an activity within a state may be applied to an activity which is part of interstate commerce. Affirmed and the rule of *Spector* rejected.

► ANALYSIS

Complete Auto recognized that a state has a significant interest in exacting from interstate commerce its fair share of the cost of state government. Not all tax burdens impermissibly impede interstate commerce. The Commerce Clause balance tips against the tax only when it unfairly burdens commerce by exacting more than a just share from the interstate activity. See *Dept. of Rev. v. Assn. of Washington Stevedoring Cos.*, 435 U.S. 734 (1978).

Quicknotes

INTERSTATE COMMERCE Commercial dealings between two parties located in different states or located in one state and accomplished through a point in another state or a foreign country; commercial dealings transacted between two states.

PRIVILEGE TAX A tax associated with operating a business of occupation for which a license or franchise is required.

Substantive Protection of Economic Interests

Quick Reference Rules of Law

Lochner v. New York

Employer (D) v. State (P)

198 U.S. 45 (1905).

NATURE OF CASE: Appeal from conviction for violation of a labor law.

FACT SUMMARY: A state labor law prohibited employment in bakeries for more than 60 hours a week or more than 10 hours a day. Lochner (D) permitted an employee in his bakery to work over 60 hours in one week.

🏛 RULE OF LAW
An act must have a direct relation, as a means to an end, to an appropriate and legitimate state objective to be a fair, reasonable, and appropriate use of a state's police power.

FACTS: Lochner (D) was fined for violating a state labor law. The law prohibited employment in bakeries for more than 60 hours a week or more than 10 hours a day. Lochner (D) permitted an employee to work in his bakery for more than 60 hours in one week.

ISSUE: Must an act have a direct relation, as a means to an end, to an appropriate and legitimate state objective to be a fair, reasonable, and appropriate use of a state's police power?

HOLDING AND DECISION: (Peckham, J.) Yes. An act must have a direct relation, as a means to an end, to an appropriate and legitimate state objective to be a fair, reasonable, and appropriate use of a state's police power. The general right to make a contract in relation to one's business is part of the liberty of the individual protected by the Fourteenth Amendment. The right to purchase or sell labor is part of the liberty protected by this amendment. However, the states do possess certain police powers relating to the safety, health, morals, and general welfare of the public. If the contract is one which the state in the exercise of its police power has the right to prohibit, the Fourteenth Amendment will not prevent the state's prohibition. When, as here, the state acts to limit the right to labor or the right to contract, it is necessary to determine whether the rights of the state or the individual shall prevail. The Fourteenth Amendment limits the state's exercise of its police power, otherwise the states would have unbounded power once they stated that legislation was to conserve the health, morals, or safety of its people. It is not sufficient to assert that the act relates to public health. Rather, it must have a more direct relation, as a means to an end, to an appropriate state goal, before an act can interfere with an individual's right to contract in relation to his labor. In this case, there is no reasonable foundation for holding the act to be necessary to the health of the public or of bakery officials. Statutes such as this one are mere meddlesome interferences with the rights of the individual. They are invalid unless there is some fair ground to say that there is material danger to the public health or to the employees' health if the labor hours are not curtailed. It cannot be said that the production of healthy bread depends upon the hours that the employees work. Nor is the trade of a baker an unhealthy one to the degree which would authorize the legislature to interfere with the rights to labor and of free contract. Lochner's (D) conviction is reversed.

DISSENT: (Harlan, J.) Whether or not this is wise legislation is not a question for this Court. It is impossible to say that there is not substantial or real relation between the statute and the state's legitimate goals. This decision brings under the Court's supervision matters which supposedly belonged exclusively to state legislatures.

DISSENT: (Holmes, J.) The word liberty in the Fourteenth Amendment should not invalidate a statute unless it can be said that a reasonable person would say that the statute infringes fundamental principles of our people and our law. A reasonable person might think this statute valid. Citizens' liberty is regulated by many state laws which have been held to be valid, e.g., the Sunday laws, the lottery laws, laws requiring vaccination.

▶ ANALYSIS

From the *Lochner* decision in 1905 to the 1930s the Court invalidated a considerable number of laws on substantive due process grounds, such as laws fixing minimum wages, maximum hours, and prices and laws regulating business activities. The modern Court claims to have rejected the *Lochner* doctrine. It has withdrawn careful scrutiny in most economic areas but has maintained and increased intervention with respect to a variety of noneconomic liberties. However, not only economic regulations were struck down under *Lochner*. That doctrine formed the basis for absorbing rights such as those in the First Amendment into the Fourteenth Amendment concept of liberty. *Lochner* also helped justify on behalf of other noneconomic rights such as the right to teach in a foreign language [*Meyer v. Nebraska*, 262 U.S. 390 (1923)]. *Meyers* was to be relied upon in the birth control decision, *Griswold v. Connecticut*, 381 U.S. 479 (1965).

Continued on next page.

Quicknotes

FOURTEENTH AMENDMENT 42 U.S.C. § 1983 Defamation by state officials in connection with a discharge implies a violation of a liberty interest protected by the due process requirements of the United States Constitution.

RIGHT TO CONTRACT Article 4, § 10 of the United States Constitution guarantees the right to contract and prohibits any state from passing any law that impairs this right, or impairs the obligations tendered by contractual agreement.

■═■

Nebbia v. New York

Store owner (D) v. State (P)

291 U.S. 502 (1934).

NATURE OF CASE: Appeal from conviction for violation of an order of the Milk Board.

FACT SUMMARY: The state Milk Board fixed nine cents as the price to be charged for a quart of milk. Nebbia (D) sold two quarts of milk and a loaf of bread for eighteen cents.

RULE OF LAW
Upon proper occasion and by appropriate measures, a state may regulate a business in any of its aspects, including fixing prices.

FACTS: In 1933, the New York Legislature established a Milk Control Board (the Board). The Board was given the power to fix minimum and maximum retail prices to be charged by stores to consumers. The Board fixed the price of a quart of milk at nine cents. Nebbia (D), a grocery store proprietor, charged eighteen cents for two quarts of milk and a five-cent loaf of bread. The law establishing the Board was based on a legislative finding that, "Milk is an essential item of diet. Failure of producers to receive a reasonable return threatens a relaxation of vigilance against contamination. The production of milk is a paramount industry of the state, and largely affects the health and prosperity of its people."

ISSUE: Upon proper occasion and by appropriate measures, may a state regulate a business in any of its aspects, including fixing prices?

HOLDING AND DECISION: (Roberts, J.) Yes. Upon proper occasion and by appropriate measures, a state may regulate a business in any of its aspects, including fixing prices. The general rule is that both the use of property and the making of contracts shall be free from government interference. However, neither property rights nor contract rights are absolute. Equally fundamental with the private interest is the public's to regulate it in the common interest. The Fifth and Fourteenth Amendments do not prohibit governmental regulation for the public welfare. They guarantee merely that regulation shall be consistent with due process. The guarantee of due process demands only that the law shall not be unreasonable, arbitrary, or capricious, and that the means selected shall have a real and substantial relation to the object sought to be attained. If an industry is subject to regulation in the public interest, its prices may be regulated. An industry which is "affected with a public industry" is one which is subject to police powers. A state is free to adopt whatever economic policy may be reasonably deemed to promote the public welfare. The courts are without authority to override such policies. If the laws passed have a rational relation to a legitimate purpose and are neither arbitrary nor discriminatory, the requirements of due process are satisfied. Price control may fulfill these requirements as well as any other type of regulation. The New York law creating the Milk Control Board and giving it power to fix prices does not conflict with the due process guarantees and is constitutionally valid. Nebbia's (D) conviction is affirmed.

DISSENT: (McReynolds, J.) The Legislative Committee pointed out as the cause of decreased consumption of milk the consumer's reduced buying power. Higher store prices will not enlarge this power, nor will they increase production. This statute arbitrarily interferes with citizens' liberty since the means adopted do not reasonably relate to the end sought, the promotion of the public welfare.

ANALYSIS

The early attitude of the Court had been that the states could regulate selling prices only for industries affecting the public interest. Regulation of prices and rates charged by public utilities, dairies, grain elevators, etc., were upheld, but regulation of the prices of theater tickets or ice were not. *Nebbia* held that price control regulation was to be treated the same as other police powers and a rational relation to a legitimate goal was all that was necessary. The dissent, representing the Court's earlier position, does not want to treat the legislation with the deference exercised by the majority. In its judgment, the method adopted by New York does not rationally relate to its goal. *Nebbia* represents the modern position of the Court, which is to presume the propriety of the legislation.

Quicknotes

DUE PROCESS CLAUSE Clause found in the Fifth and Fourteenth Amendments to the United States Constitution providing that no person shall be deprived of "life, liberty, or property, without due process of law."

Kelo v. New London

Homeowner (P) v. City (D)

545 U.S. 469 (2005).

NATURE OF CASE: Appeal from judgment for defendant city in condemnation suit.

FACT SUMMARY: New London, Connecticut (D) condemned the private residences of Kelo (P) and others in order to use their property as part of a planned economic development.

🏛 RULE OF LAW
Governmental economic development constitutes a "public use" under the Fifth Amendment's eminent domain.

FACTS: New London, Connecticut (D) revitalized the New London Development Corp. (NLDC) to propose plans for economic development after decades of decline. Pfizer, a pharmaceutical company, also announced plans to build a $300 million facility next to Fort Trumball in the New London (D) area. The NLDC operated as a private entity but its plans intended to benefit the city's growth. New London (D) authorized NLDC to purchase or condemn property in its name for the purpose of its approved development plan. Kelo (P) owned property in the Fort Trumball development area and refused to sell. New London (D) initiated condemnation proceedings although Kelo's (P) property was not blighted or otherwise deteriorating. Kelo (P) filed suit in state court against New London (D) claiming that the condemnation violated the taking clause's "public use" restriction. The Connecticut Supreme Court held for New London (D) and Kelo (P) appealed to the United States Supreme Court.

ISSUE: Does governmental economic development constitute a "public use" under the Fifth Amendment's eminent domain?

HOLDING AND DECISION: (Stevens, J.) Yes. Governmental economic development constitutes a "public use" under the Fifth Amendment's eminent domain. The government cannot transfer private property from one private entity to another even if the first is adequately compensated. The government can, however, take private property from one private entity with just compensation for "public use." This particular case does not fit in either scenario. New London (D) cannot offer a pretextual "public use" if the true benefit is to a definable class of private individuals, but no such class can be identified here. It is true that the planned development will not be completely open to the public and the stores will not act as common carriers to the public, but such a literal definition of "public use" is not required. The precedent in *Berman*, 348 U.S. 26 (1954), and *Midkiff*, 467 U.S. 229 (1984), support a

broad interpretation of "public use." Kelo (P) requests a bright-line rule for "public use" that would not include economic development. It is longstanding tradition of government to promote economic development and that development may be better served by using a private entity rather than government agencies. A bright-line rule cannot issue because legislatures need flexibility when determining appropriate action for the economic development of its cities. States are free to further restrict "public use" requirements beyond those of the federal government's and many have already done so. Affirmed.

CONCURRENCE: (Kennedy, J.) A party may make a claim of pretextual "public use" taking that actually benefits a private entity. A presumption exists that the government acted reasonably in its taking, but courts should review all claims to the contrary by looking closely at the facts of the case. A city may take property with the public only incidentally benefiting. Here, no facts existed to show that Pfizer alone would benefit from New London (D) condemning Kelo's (P) property.

DISSENT: (O'Connor, J.) The Court's decision eliminates "for public use" from the takings clause because it allows for incidental public benefit from ordinary private use of property. The government simply cannot condemn private property when the condemnation is to benefit another private person or entity. The Court's reliance on *Berman* and *Midkiff* is misplaced because those cases actually underscore the public use versus private benefit. Both cases involved takings that directly benefited the public. Those properties were blighted and causing harm to the public in their current use. When private property is being used in its ordinary, non-harmful fashion, it cannot be taken to benefit another private user. It is nearly impossible to isolate the true motives behind a governmental taking, so the government can now condemn with near impunity. The government can also always seek to improve a property's use if the private owner is not making the most productive or attractive use of it. The facts of today's case do not justify the holding.

DISSENT: (Thomas, J.) The Court adopts the overly broad "public use" definitions of *Berman* and *Midkiff* without reasoned analysis. A legislature's determination of what constitutes "public use" is not entitled to such blind deference. The original intent of the Public Use Clause was to provide full legal rights to the public for the use of any condemned property. The Court should return to the original intent. Further, the property most likely to be taken

Continued on next page.

under this new definition will be that of poor communities lacking political power and likely using their property at less than its most productive use. These communities should be protected rather than exploited.

▶ ANALYSIS

This case caused a firestorm of fury throughout the United States. Multiple states quickly passed legislation tightening the state eminent domain laws to restrict the ability of governmental entities to take private property for anything less than blatantly public purposes. A small but vocal group of citizens began a petition to condemn Judge Breyer's private vacation residence so that the property may be put to a "better" use for the public.

■≡■

Quicknotes

CONDEMNATION The taking of private property for public use so long as just compensation is paid therefor.

EMINENT DOMAIN The governmental power to take private property for public use so long as just compensation is paid therefore.

PUBLIC USE Basis for governmental taking of property pursuant to its power of eminent domain so that property taken may be utilized for the benefit of the public at large.

■≡■

Protection of Individual Rights:
Due Process, the Bill of Rights, and
Nontextual Constitutional Rights

Quick Reference Rules of Law

Griswold v. Connecticut

Executive (D) v. State (P)

381 U.S. 479 (1965).

NATURE OF CASE: Appeal from conviction for violating state laws prohibiting the counseling of married persons to take contraceptives.

FACT SUMMARY: Doctor (D) and layman (D) were prosecuted for advising married persons on the means of preventing conception.

🏛 RULE OF LAW

The right to marital privacy, although not explicitly stated in the Bill of Rights, is under the penumbra formed by certain other explicit guarantees, and as such, is protected against state regulation which sweeps unnecessarily broad.

FACTS: Griswold (D), the Executive Director of the Planned Parenthood League of Connecticut, and Dr. Buxton (D) were convicted under a Connecticut law which made counseling of married persons to take contraceptives a criminal offense.

ISSUE: Is the right to marital privacy, although not explicitly stated in the Bill of Rights, under the penumbra formed by certain other explicit guarantees, and as such, is it protected against state regulation which sweeps unnecessarily broad?

HOLDING AND DECISION: (Douglas, J.) Yes. The right to marital privacy, although not explicitly stated in the Bill of Rights, is under the penumbra formed by certain other explicit guarantees, and as such, is protected against state regulation which sweeps unnecessarily broad. The various guarantees which create penumbras, or zones, of privacy include the First Amendment's right of association, the Third Amendment's prohibition against the peacetime quartering of soldiers, the Fourth Amendment's prohibition against unreasonable searches and seizures, the Fifth Amendment's Self-Incrimination Clause, and the Ninth Amendment's reservation to the people of non-enumerated rights. The Connecticut (P) law, by forbidding the use of contraceptives rather than regulating their manner or sale, seeks to achieve its goals by means having a maximum destructive impact upon that relationship. Reversed.

CONCURRENCE: (Goldberg, J.) The Ninth Amendment, while not constituting an independent source of rights, suggests that the list of rights in the first eight amendments is not exhaustive. This right is a "fundamental" one which cannot be infringed on the state's slender justification in protecting marital fidelity.

CONCURRENCE: (Harlan, J.) The Court, instead of focusing on "specific provisions" of the Bill of Rights, should have instead relied on the Due Process Clause in finding this law violative of basic values "implicit in the concept of ordered liberty."

CONCURRENCE: (White, J.) The Due Process Clause should be the test in determining whether such laws are reasonably necessary for the effectuation of a legitimate and substantial state interest and are not arbitrary or capricious in application. Here, the causal connection between married persons engaging in extramarital sex and contraceptives is too tenuous.

DISSENT: (Black, J.) While the law is offensive, neither the Ninth Amendment nor the Due Process Clause invalidates it. Both lead the Court into imposing its own notions as to what are wise or unwise laws. What constitutes "fundamental" values is indeterminable. Keeping the Constitution "in tune with the times" is accomplished only through the amendment process. Similarly, the Due Process Clause is too imprecise and lends itself to subjective interpretation.

DISSENT: (Stewart, J.) The Due Process Clause is not the "guide" because there was no claim here that the statute is unconstitutionally vague or that the defendants were denied any of the elements of procedural due process at their trial. The Ninth Amendment simply restricts the federal government to a government of express and limited powers. Finally, the Constitution is silent on the "right to privacy."

▶ ANALYSIS

Although the theory of "substantive due process" has declined as a means to review state economic regulation—at least since 1937—the Court, as here, has freely applied strict scrutiny to state laws affecting social areas.

Quicknotes

DUE PROCESS CLAUSE Clause found in the Fifth and Fourteenth Amendments to the United States Constitution providing that no person shall be deprived of "life, liberty, or property, without due process of law."

NINTH AMENDMENT The Ninth Amendment to the United States Constitution providing that the enumeration of any rights contained therein are not to be construed as denying or disparaging other rights retained by the people.

Continued on next page.

PENUMBRA A doctrine whereby authority of the federal government is implied pursuant to the Necessary and Proper Clause; one implied power may be inferred from the conferring of another implied power.

■≡■

Roe v. Wade

Unmarried woman (P) v. State (D)

410 U.S. 113 (1973).

NATURE OF CASE: Challenge to state laws making it a crime to procure an abortion except by medical advice to save the life of the mother.

FACT SUMMARY: Roe (P), a single woman, wished to have her pregnancy terminated by an abortion.

🏛 RULE OF LAW
The right of privacy found in the Fourteenth Amendment's concept of personal liberty and restrictions upon state action is broad enough to encompass a woman's decision whether or not to terminate her pregnancy.

FACTS: The Texas abortion laws challenged here were typical of those adopted by most states. The challengers were Roe (P), a single, pregnant woman, a childless couple with the wife not pregnant (J and M Doe), and a licensed physician with two criminal charges pending (Halford). Only Roe (P) was found to be entitled to maintain the action. Although her 1970 pregnancy had been terminated, her case was not found moot since pregnancy "truly could be capable of repetition, yet evading review."

ISSUE: Does the constitutional right of privacy include a woman's right to choose to terminate her pregnancy?

HOLDING AND DECISION: (Blackmun, J.) Yes. While the Constitution does not explicitly mention any right of privacy, such a right has been recognized. This right of privacy, whether founded in the Fourteenth Amendment's concept of personal liberty and restrictions upon state action, as this Court feels it is, or in the Ninth Amendment's reservation of rights to the people, is broad enough to encompass a woman's decision to terminate her pregnancy. A statute regulating a fundamental right, such as the right to privacy, may be justified only by a compelling state interest, and such statutes must be narrowly drawn. Here, Texas (D) argues that the fetus is a person within the meaning of the Fourteenth Amendment whose right to life is guaranteed by that amendment. However, there are no decisions indicating such a definition for "fetus." The unborn have never been recognized in the law as persons in the whole sense. Texas (D) may not, by adopting one theory of life, override the rights of the pregnant woman that are at stake. However, neither are the woman's rights to privacy absolute. The state does have a legitimate interest in preserving the health of the pregnant woman and in protecting the potentiality of life. Each of these interests grows in substantiality as the woman approaches term, and, at a point, each becomes compelling. During the first trimester, mortality in abortion is less than mortality in childbirth. After that point, in promoting its interest in the mother's health, the state may regulate the abortion procedure in ways related to maternal health (i.e., licensing of physicians, facilities, etc.). Prior to viability, the physician, in consultation with the pregnant woman, is free to decide that a pregnancy should be terminated without interference by the state. Subsequent to viability, the state, in promoting its interest in the potentiality of life, may regulate, and even proscribe abortion, except where necessary to save the mother's life. Because the Texas (D) statute makes no distinction between abortions performed in early pregnancy and those performed later, it sweeps too broadly and is, therefore, invalid.

CONCURRENCE: (Stewart, J.) The Texas (D) statute invaded the "liberty" protected by the Fourteenth Amendment Due Process Clause. Justice Stewart suggests that substantive due process has been resurrected.

CONCURRENCE: (Douglas, J.) A woman's right to an abortion arises from the periphery of the Bill of Rights. This decision has nothing to do with substantive due process.

DISSENT: (White, J.) This issue, for the most part, should be left with the people. There is nothing in the language or history of the Constitution to support the Court's opinion. "The Texas (D) statute is not constitutionally infirm because it denies abortions to those who seek to serve only their own convenience rather than to protect their life or health."

DISSENT: (Rehnquist, J.) The test to be applied is whether the abortion law has a rational relation to a valid state objective. Here, the Court applies the compelling state interest test. The application of this test requires the Court to examine the legislative policies and pass on the wisdom of those policies, a task better left to the legislature.

▶ ANALYSIS

Doe v. Bolton, 410 U.S. 179 (1973), was the companion case to *Roe v. Wade*. The Georgia laws attacked in *Doe* were more modern than the Texas (D) laws. They allowed a physician to perform an abortion when the mother's life was in danger, or the fetus would likely be born with birth defects, or the pregnancy had resulted from rape. The Court held that a physician could consider all attendant circumstances in deciding whether an abortion should be performed. No longer could only the three situations specified be considered. The Court also struck down the

Continued on next page.

requirements of prior approval for an abortion by the hospital staff committee and of confirmation by two physicians. They concluded that the attending physician's judgment was sufficient. Lastly, the Court struck down the requirement that the woman be a Georgia resident.

■═■

Quicknotes

FOURTEENTH AMENDMENT 42 U.S.C. § 1983 Defamation by state officials in connection with a discharge implies a violation of a liberty interest protected by the due process requirements of the U.S. Constitution.

FUNDAMENTAL RIGHT A liberty that is either expressly or impliedly provided for in the United States Constitution, the deprivation or burdening of which is subject to a heightened standard of review.

■═■

Planned Parenthood of Southeastern Pennsylvania v. Casey

Clinic (P) v. State (D)

505 U.S. 833 (1992).

NATURE OF CASE: Appeal of order upholding abortion statutes, except a husband-notification Eighth Amendment provision.

FACT SUMMARY: Planned Parenthood of Southeastern Pennsylvania (P) facially challenged the constitutionality of Pennsylvania's (D) abortion law.

RULE OF LAW
A law is unconstitutional as an undue burden on a woman's right to an abortion before fetal viability if the law places a substantial obstacle in the path of a woman seeking to exercise her right.

FACTS: The Pennsylvania Abortion Control Act (the Act) required (a) a doctor to provide a woman seeking an abortion with information designed to persuade her against abortion and imposed a waiting period of at least 24 hours between provision of the information and the abortion; (b) a minor to obtain consent of one parent or a judge's order before having an abortion; (c) a married woman to sign a statement averring that her husband had been notified, her husband was not the father, her husband forcibly had impregnated her, or that she would be physically harmed if she notified her husband; and (d) a public report on every abortion, detailing information on the facility, physician, patient, and steps taken to comply with the Act. The name of the patient was confidential. It provided the first three provisions would not apply in a "medical emergency," i.e., a condition a doctor determines to require immediate abortion to avert death or serious risk of substantial, irreversible impairment of a major bodily function. Five clinics (P), including Planned Parenthood of Southeastern Pennsylvania (P), and five doctors (P) sued Pennsylvania (D), including Governor Casey (D), claiming the Act was unconstitutional on its face. The district court held the entire Act invalid under *Roe v. Wade*, 410 U.S. 113 (1973). The court of appeals reversed, upholding the entire Act except the husband-notification requirement. Planned Parenthood et al. (P) appealed.

ISSUE: Is a law unconstitutional as an undue burden on a woman's right to an abortion before fetal viability if the law places a substantial obstacle in the path of a woman's exercise of her right?

HOLDING AND DECISION: (O'Connor, J.) Yes. A law is unconstitutional as an undue burden on a woman's right to an abortion before fetal viability when it places a substantial obstacle in the path of a woman seeking to exercise her right. For two decades people have organized lives relying on the availability of abortion. The

Court rarely resolves a controversy as intensely divisive as in *Roe*. Such a decision only should be overturned if it proves unworkable or if new information arises which renders the decision unjustified in the present. *Roe* is neither unworkable nor based on outdated assumptions. Medical technology has altered the age of viability, but that does not affect the validity of viability as a dividing line. Viability is the point at which a fetus can be said to be an independent life, so that the state's interest in protecting it then outweighs the mother's decisionmaking interest. The Court and the nation would be seriously damaged if the Court were to overturn *Roe* simply on the basis of a philosophical disagreement with the 1973 Court, or as a surrender to political pressure. The liberty rights of women and the personal, intimate nature of childbearing sharply limit state power to insist a woman carry a child to term or accept the state's vision of her role in society. Thus, the integrity of the Court, stare decisis, and substantive due process require the central principle of *Roe* to be reaffirmed: a state may not prevent a woman from making the ultimate decision to terminate her pregnancy before viability. *Roe* also recognized the state interest in maternal health and in protecting potential life. Application of the rigid trimester framework often ignored state interests, leading to striking down abortion regulations which in no real sense deprived women of the ultimate decision. Therefore, the trimester framework must be rejected and undue burden analysis put in its place. Here, the information requirement is not an undue burden. Truthful, nonmisleading information on the nature of abortion procedure, health risks, and consequences to the fetus is reasonable to ensure informed choice, one which might cause a woman to choose childbirth. The 24-hour waiting period does not create a health risk and reasonably furthers the state interest in protecting the unborn. Requiring a period of reflection to make an informed decision is reasonable. A waiting period may increase cost and risk of delay, but on a facial challenge it cannot be called a substantial obstacle. Prior cases establish that a state may require parental consent before abortions by minors, provided there is a judicial bypass procedure. On its face, the statute's definition of "medical emergency" is not too narrow. The reporting requirement is reasonably directed to the preservation of maternal health, providing a vital element of medical research, and the statute protects patient confidentiality. The husband-notification requirement imposes an undue burden on abortion rights of the abused women who fear for their safety and the safety of their children and are likely to

Continued on next page.

be deterred from procuring an abortion as surely as if the state outlawed abortion. A husband has a strong interest in his wife's pregnancy, but before birth it is a biological fact that regulation of the fetus has a far greater impact on the woman. The husband-notification requirement is unconstitutional, and the rest of the statute is valid. Affirmed.

CONCURRENCE AND DISSENT: (Stevens, J.)

A burden is "undue" if it is too severe or lacks legitimate justification. The information, waiting period, and parental consent requirements, as well as the husband-notification requirement, are invalid. The Court's opinion implicitly reaffirms its holding that a fetus is not a "person" within the meaning of the Fourteenth Amendment. The state interest in protecting potential life is legitimate but not grounded in the Constitution. A woman has constitutional liberty rights to bodily integrity and to decide personal and private matters. So, the state may promote a preference for childbirth, but decisional autonomy must limit the state's power to interject into a woman's most personal deliberations its own views of what is best. Pennsylvania's law goes too far by requiring a doctor to provide information designed to persuade a woman to opt against abortion, just as she is weighing her personal choice. In contrast, the requirement of informing a woman of the nature and risks of abortion and childbirth enhances decisionmaking. The 24-hour waiting period illegitimately rests on assumptions that a decision to terminate pregnancy is wrong, and that a woman is unable to make decisions. There is no legitimate reason to require a woman who has agonized over her decision to leave the hospital and return another day.

CONCURRENCE AND DISSENT: (Blackmun, J.)

The Court correctly reaffirms a woman's right to abortion. However, that right should remain fundamental, and any state-imposed burden upon it should be subjected to the strictest judicial scrutiny. Categorizing a woman's right to abortion as merely a "liberty interest" is not sufficient. In striking down the husband-notification requirement, the Court sets up a framework for evaluating abortion regulations in the social context of women facing issues of reproductive choice. The Court failed to strike down the information, waiting period, parental consent, and reporting requirements on their face, but the Court's standard at least allows future courts to hold that in practice such regulations are undue burdens. The reporting requirement does not further maternal health. Fearing harassment, many doctors will stop performing abortions if their names appear on public reports. However, none of these requirements would survive under the strict-scrutiny standard of review. The trimester framework should be maintained. No other approach better protects a woman's fundamental right while accommodating legitimate state interests. The Court's cases do not create a list of personal liberties: they are a principled account of how these rights are grounded in a general right of privacy.

CONCURRENCE AND DISSENT: (Rehnquist, C.J.)

Roe was wrongly decided, has led to a confusing body of law, and should be overturned. The Court's decision, replacing *Roe*'s strict scrutiny standard and trimester framework with a new, unworkable undue burden test, cannot be justified by stare decisis. Authentic principles of stare decisis do not require erroneous decisions to be maintained. The Court's integrity is enhanced when it repudiates wrong decisions. Americans have grown accustomed to *Roe*, but that should not prevent the Court from correcting a wrong decision. The Fourteenth Amendment concept of liberty does not incorporate any all-encompassing right of privacy. Unlike marriage, procreation, and contraception, abortion terminates potential life and must be analyzed differently. Historic traditions of the American people, critical to an understanding of fundamental rights, do not support a right to abortion. A woman's interest in having an abortion is liberty protected by due process, but states may regulate abortion in ways rationally related to a legitimate state interest. All provisions of the Pennsylvania law do so and are constitutional. The husband-notification requirement is reasonably related to promoting state interests in protecting the husband's interests, potential life, and the integrity of marriage.

CONCURRENCE AND DISSENT: (Scalia, J.)

The limits on abortion should be decided democratically. The Constitution is silent on abortion, and American traditions have allowed it to be proscribed. Applying the rational basis test, the Pennsylvania law should be upheld in its entirety. *Roe* was wrongly decided. It begged the question by assuming a fetus is merely potential human life. The whole argument of abortion opponents is that the state seeks to protect human life. *Roe* also failed to produce a settled body of law. *Roe* did not resolve the deeply divisive issue of abortion. It made compromise impossible and elevated the issue to a national level where it has proven infinitely more difficult to resolve. Here, the Court claims to rely on stare decisis but throws out *Roe*'s trimester framework. The new undue burden standard is meaningless in application, giving a district judge freedom to strike down almost any abortion restriction he does not like. The Court's suggestion that public opposition to an erroneous decision mitigates against overturning it is appalling.

▶ ANALYSIS

The Court also affirmed *Roe*'s holding that after viability the state may regulate, or even proscribe, abortion, except where it is necessary to preserve the life or health of the mother. This is only the second time in modern Supreme Court jurisprudence that an opinion has been jointly authored. Justice Kennedy's portion of the opinion

Continued on next page.

addresses the importance of public faith in and acceptance of the Court's work by opening with the statement:
"Liberty finds no refuge in a jurisprudence of doubt."
Justice O'Connor expounds on the essential nature of a
woman's right to an abortion, while Justice Souter performs the stare decisis analysis, concluding that there is
no reason to reverse the essential holding of *Roe*. It
appears that the instant case marks the first time the
Court has downgraded a fundamental right to a protected
liberty and by so doing removed from the usual strict
scrutiny standard of review.

Quicknotes

FUNDAMENTAL RIGHT A liberty that is either expressly or
impliedly provided for in the United States Constitution,
the deprivation or burdening of which is subject to a
heightened standard of review.

LEGITIMATE STATE INTEREST Under a rational basis standard of review, a court will not strike down a statute as
unconstitutional if it bears a reasonable relationship to
the furtherance of a legitimate governmental objective.

STARE DECISIS Doctrine whereby courts follow legal precedent unless there is good cause for departure.

SUBSTANTIVE DUE PROCESS A constitutional safeguard
limiting the power of the state, irrespective of how fair
its procedures may be; substantive limits placed on the
power of the state.

UNDUE BURDEN Unlawfully oppressive or troublesome.

Gonzales v. Carhart

Attorney General (D) v. Abortion doctor (P)

550 U.S. 124 (2007).

NATURE OF CASE: Facial due-process challenge to the federal Partial-Birth Abortion Ban Act.

FACT SUMMARY: Congress passed a statute that criminalized doctors' performance of partial-birth abortions.

🏛 RULE OF LAW

The Partial-Birth Abortion Ban Act does not place a substantial obstacle to late-term, but pre-viability, abortions.

FACTS: In 2003, Congress enacted the Partial-Birth Abortion Ban Act (the Act), which criminalized doctors' performance of partial-birth abortions. The Act explicitly and precisely defined "partial-birth abortion," in part as an abortion following the "deliver[y] [of] a living fetus." [Carhart (P), a doctor who performed partial-birth abortions, filed suit for injunctive relief to prohibit the Act from being applied against him. The trial court granted the injunction, and the intermediate appellate court affirmed.] The Government (D) sought further review in the Supreme Court.

ISSUE: Does the Partial-Birth Abortion Ban Act place a substantial obstacle to late-term, but pre-viability, abortions?

HOLDING AND DECISION: (Kennedy, J.) No. The Partial-Birth Abortion Ban Act does not place a substantial obstacle to late-term, but pre-viability, abortions. The Act can be construed as not prohibiting the standard form of partial-birth abortion invalidated in *Stenberg v. Carhart*, 530 U.S. 914 (2000), and the Act therefore is not facially invalid on that basis. Further, instead of placing a substantial obstacle to a partial-birth abortion, the Act simply respects human life—an objective that lies within the legislative power. The Act advances that objective by ensuring that women will be fully informed about the methods of abortion to which they consent. Moreover, Congress can legitimately legislate even in the face of the medical uncertainty on whether such a prohibition on one form of abortion subjects women "to significant health risks." Such uncertainty does not support a facial challenge to the Act. The proper way to attack the Act would be through an as-applied challenge that would permit review of a more precise factual scenario. [Reversed.]

DISSENT: (Ginsburg, J.) This decision mocks *Casey*, 505 U.S. 833 (1992), and *Stenberg*, and it flies in the face of medical approval of abortion procedures. The Act does subject women to significant health risks by forcing them to choose less safe methods of abortion, and, in the process,

the statute does not save even one fetus because the Act merely criminalizes a method of abortion, not abortion itself. As the Court suggests, the real basis for today's decision is "moral concerns" for what the majority sees as emotionally fragile women. This rationale circumvents the concerns for stare decisis that have supported our prior decisions in this area. Today's decision is actually only a veiled attempt to undermine, in a piecemeal fashion, a woman's established right to an abortion.

▶ *ANALYSIS*

The right to an abortion announced in *Roe v. Wade*, 410 U.S. 113 (1973), remains intact after *Gonzales v. Carhart*. That right is now more difficult to exercise, though, and, as Justice Ginsburg suggests in dissent, the federal statute's omission of safeguards for women's health is at best problematic under the Court's prior abortion decisions.

Quicknotes

DUE PROCESS The constitutional mandate requiring the courts to protect and enforce individuals' rights and liberties consistent with prevailing principles of fairness and justice and prohibiting the federal and state governments from such activities that deprive its citizens of life, liberty, or property interest.

INJUNCTION A court order requiring a person to do, or prohibiting that person from doing, a specific act.

INJUNCTIVE RELIEF A court order issued as a remedy, requiring a person to do, or prohibiting that person from doing, a specific act.

STARE DECISIS Doctrine whereby courts follow legal precedent unless there is good cause for departure.

Michael H. v. Gerald D.

Biological father (P) v. Husband of mother (D)

491 U.S. 110 (1989).

NATURE OF CASE: Appeal from denial of claim of paternity and visitation rights.

FACT SUMMARY: Michael H. (P) wanted paternity and visitation rights to a child he fathered with Gerald D.'s (D) wife during an affair.

🏛 RULE OF LAW
A father has no constitutionally protected fundamental liberty interest in a relationship with a child conceived with another man's wife.

FACTS: Michael H. (P) had an affair with Gerald D.'s (D) wife, and they had a little girl. Gerald D. (D) was listed as the father on the birth certificate but both Gerald D. (D) and Michael H. (P) claimed the child as his own. Nevertheless, blood tests revealed that it was virtually certain Michael H. (P) was the true father. Until the girl was three, Gerald D.'s (D) wife lived off and on with Michael H. (P), as well as with her husband and a third man. Michael H. (P) sued under California law for parental and visitation rights, but California denied these rights to a father who had a child by a married woman who had a husband who was neither impotent nor sterile. Consequently, Michael H. (P) lost on his claim in the California courts and appealed to the Supreme Court.

ISSUE: Does a father have a constitutionally protected fundamental liberty interest in a relationship with a child conceived with another man's wife?

HOLDING AND DECISION: (Scalia, J.) No. A father does not have a constitutionally protected fundamental liberty interest in a relationship with a child conceived with another man's wife. To be protected by the Due Process Clause, an interest denominated as both a "liberty" and "fundamental" must be one traditionally protected by U.S. society. Further, analysis of the interest must operate at the most specific level protecting, or denying protection to, the asserted rights. Here, under U.S. historic practices, only the marital family has been a protected unit, and a natural father has been generally denied the power—even in modern times—to assert parental rights over a child born into a woman's existing marriage with another man. Affirmed.

CONCURRENCE: (O'Connor, J.) A single mode of historical analysis, i.e., the limitation of relevant traditions to the "most specific level" available, should not be imposed; other levels of generality should be considered so as not to foreclose the unanticipated.

DISSENT: (Brennan, J.) "Tradition" does not provide a discernible or objective boundary around the Constitution because what is "deeply rooted" in this country is arguable, as are the contents and significance of any such "tradition." Further, the majority defines "parenthood" here at an overly refined level of specificity. "Parenthood," whether by a natural unmarried adulterous father or otherwise, is a fundamental liberty interest protected by the Due Process Clause. California's conclusive presumption of paternity is outmoded in a world in which blood tests can prove the identity of natural fathers and illegitimacy is no longer scorned.

▶ ANALYSIS

Some commentators have criticized both the majority and dissenting opinions in this case as "over-abstracting" relevant traditions. Justice Scalia "abstracted away" the fact that despite the unorthodox father-child interaction between Michael H. (P) and his little girl, there did exist a bona fide, continuing relationship based on natural parenthood. Justice Brennan, on the other hand, "abstracted away" the fact that despite Michael H.'s (P) natural parenting of his child, he still had engaged in an adulterous affair, and adultery would be relevant—among other considerations—in determining Michael H.'s (P) rights, if any, to custody or visitation. See Tribe & Dorf, "Levels of Generality in the Definitions of Rights," 57 U. Chi. L. Rev. 1057, 1092-1093 (1990).

Quicknotes

DUE PROCESS CLAUSE Clause found in the Fifth and Fourteenth Amendments to the United States Constitution providing that no person shall be deprived of "life, liberty, or property, without due process of law."

Washington v. Glucksberg

State (D) v. Terminally ill patients (D)

521 U.S. 702 (1997).

NATURE OF CASE: Review of order striking down state assisted-suicide ban.

FACT SUMMARY: A Washington (D) state law prohibiting physician-assisted suicide was challenged as a violation of due process.

🏛 RULE OF LAW
State law prohibiting physician-assisted suicide is not a violation of due process.

FACTS: The state of Washington (D) had a statute expressly prohibiting physician-assisted suicide, categorizing it as murder. This statute was challenged by four physicians (P) and three terminally ill patients (P) who advocated the right of a patient to choose to have a physician administer life-ending treatment. The district court held that the law constituted a violation of due process under the Fourteenth Amendment, and held the law unconstitutional. A Ninth Circuit panel reversed, but the court, en banc, reversed the panel and affirmed the district court. The Supreme Court granted review.

ISSUE: Does state law prohibiting physician-assisted suicide constitute a violation of due process?

HOLDING AND DECISION: (Rehnquist, C.J.) No. State law prohibiting physician-assisted suicide is not a violation of due process. It has long been the rule that the Fourteenth Amendment not only guarantees procedural fairness but also incorporates a substantive element such that certain "fundamental" liberties are to be held beyond the reach of the state to proscribe. However, this Court has always been very reticent to find an unenumerated right in the Fourteenth Amendment guarantee of due process, as the declaration of such rights borders on judicial lawmaking. Therefore, such rights will be found only with the greatest caution. In deciding whether a right is so fundamental as to be protected by the Fourteenth Amendment, it must be a right deeply rooted in our nation's historical concept of ordered liberty, and the liberty interest involved must be carefully defined. Here, the question is whether one has the right to choose the time and manner of one's death, or put more bluntly, whether there is a right to die. An examination of this nation's legal and cultural traditions militates strongly against a holding that such a right exists. Anglo-American tradition has long disfavored suicide. At one time suicide itself was a criminal offense so severe that the suicide's property was confiscated to the state. While most if not all states have abandoned such a draconian approach, this has not been due to any increasing tolerance of suicide, but rather a realization that a

suicide's family should not be penalized for the crime. All but one state (Oregon, which changed its law recently through an initiative) continue to outlaw all assisting of suicides, which demonstrates that there is no historical tradition of a right to die. This being so, the right to die is not a fundamental interest as the term is defined for Fourteenth Amendment purposes. Therefore, a state law prohibiting suicide assistance need only be rationally related to a legitimate state purpose. While physician-assisted suicide is a matter of great current debate, there can be no disputing the conclusion that a state has a legitimate interest in doing whatever it can to discourage suicide. Washington's (D) interests include the concern that voluntary euthanasia may progress down a slippery slope to coercion, that it would corrupt the traditional role of medicine, and that legal assisted suicide would be disproportionately used against the poor and disaffected. Whether these concerns are true is a matter of debate, but it is a matter for political resolution, not judicial decree. Reversed.

CONCURRENCE: (O'Connor, J.) There is no reason to think that the political process will not strike a proper balance between the competing interests at work here. There clearly is no generalized right to assisted suicide, but a mentally competent person who is experiencing great suffering may have a constitutionally cognizable interest in obtaining relief.

CONCURRENCE: (Stevens, J.) The present case was a facial challenge to Washington's (D) assisted suicide law, and as such, must fail. However, there may be some future case where a state proscription on assisted suicide will be so egregious as to be open to challenge.

CONCURRENCE: (Souter, J.) The proper analysis is whether, in light of the liberty interest being claimed, a state law can be seen as arbitrary or purposeless. Here, the state interests are sufficiently serious to defeat such a claim.

CONCURRENCE: (Ginsburg, J.) [Justice Ginsburg by reference incorporated the analysis of the Justice O'Connor concurrence.]

CONCURRENCE: (Breyer, J.) The Court has framed the right involved here incorrectly. The right involved is not the right to die, but the right to die with dignity. However, as physicians are free to alleviate suffering at a nonlethal level, this right is not categorically abridged by a ban on assisted suicide. There may be cases

Continued on next page.

in the future, however, when a specific application of such a ban might violate this right.

▶ *ANALYSIS*

One of the more controversial social issues in recent years has been the so-called right to die. Since everyone dies, the issue is more properly cast as whether one has the right to control the circumstances of one's death. It had been hoped that the prior case, *Cruzan v. Director, Missouri Dep't of Health*, 497 U.S. 261 (1990), would answer this question. It did not do so, but merely held that states may require clear and convincing proof that an incompetent, comatose family member would desire termination of life support systems prior to withdrawing such treatment. The Court in *Glucksberg* appears to have answered the question in the negative in this case. However, there was sufficient equivocation in some of the concurrences to lead to the conclusion that the issue might be reopened some day.

■■■■

Quicknotes

DUE PROCESS CLAUSE   Clause found in the Fifth and Fourteenth Amendments to the United States Constitution providing that no person shall be deprived of "life, liberty, or property, without due process of law."

FOURTEENTH AMENDMENT 42 U.S.C. § 1983   Defamation by state officials in connection with a discharge implies a violation of a liberty interest protected by the due process requirements of the U.S. Constitution.

FUNDAMENTAL RIGHT   A liberty that is either expressly or impliedly provided for in the United States Constitution, the deprivation or burdening of which is subject to a heightened standard of review.

LIBERTY INTEREST   A right conferred by the Due Process Clauses of the state and federal constitutions.

RIGHT TO DIE   Proposed legislation which would decriminalize doctor-assisted suicide that has been rejected by federal courts but is being pursued through continuing ballot initiatives at the state level. Some states have passed so-called "Death with Dignity" acts (e.g., Oregon), but they are being challenged in appeals.

■■■■

Bowers v. Hardwick

State (D) v. Homosexual (P)

478 U.S. 186 (1986).

NATURE OF CASE: Appeal from decision finding state sodomy statute unconstitutional.

FACT SUMMARY: Bowers (D) and other state officials appealed from a court of appeals decision finding the Georgia sodomy statute unconstitutional in that it violated Hardwick's (P) fundamental rights, since it applied to consensual, homosexual sodomy.

RULE OF LAW
The Constitution does not grant a fundamental right to engage in consensual homosexual sodomy.

FACTS: Hardwick (P), a gay man, was charged with violating a state law criminalizing sodomy. After a preliminary hearing, the District Attorney decided not to present the matter to the grand jury unless further evidence developed. Hardwick (P) brought suit, challenging the constitutionality of the statute in that it criminalized consensual sodomy. He claimed the law as administered by the state placed him in imminent danger of arrest and was unconstitutional on a number of grounds. The district court dismissed the claim for failing to state a claim, relying heavily on the Supreme Court decision in *Doe v. Commonwealth's Attorney for the City of Richmond*, 425 U.S. 901 (1976), which summarily affirmed a case involving a similar Virginia sodomy statute. The court of appeals reversed, finding that the statute violated Hardwick's (P) fundamental rights because the homosexual activity was a private and intimate association beyond the reach of state regulation. From this decision, Bowers (D) and other state officials appealed.

ISSUE: Does the Constitution grant a fundamental right to engage in consensual homosexual sodomy?

HOLDING AND DECISION: (White, J.) No. The Constitution does not grant a fundamental right to engage in consensual homosexual sodomy. None of the fundamental rights announced in previous cases bears any resemblance to the claimed constitutional right to engage in sodomy asserted in the present case. Fundamental liberties identified by this Court and deserving of heightened judicial scrutiny have either been liberties implicit in the concept of ordered liberty or liberties deeply rooted in this nation's history and traditions. Neither of these formulations would extend the liberty sought in the present case. Great restraint should be used when expanding the contours of constitutional due process. The fact that the conduct in question occurred in the privacy of the home does not necessarily shield it from regulation, as can be seen in statutes punishing a number of other victimless

and/or sex crimes. The conduct at issue is not a fundamental right, and the state has provided a rational basis for the statute. Reversed.

CONCURRENCE: (Burger, C.J.) This is a question not of personal preference but of the legislative authority of the state, and nothing in the Constitution forbids the state statute at issue.

CONCURRENCE: (Powell, J.) Hardwick (P) may be protected under the Eighth Amendment, but he has not been tried, sentenced, or convicted, and has not raised any Eighth Amendment issues.

DISSENT: (Blackmun, J.) The state in the present case is legislating particular forms of private, consensual sexual conduct. The Court's obsession with homosexual activity is difficult to justify, since the statute's language encompasses non-homosexual conduct. The Court fails to comprehend the magnitude of the liberty interest at stake in this case.

DISSENT: (Stevens, J.) The essential liberty to choose how to conduct private sexual conduct surely encompasses the right to engage in nonreproductive, sexual conduct that others may find offensive or immoral. The state cannot justify the selective application of the statute in question, given the conceded unconstitutionality of the statute as applied to non-homosexual conduct. Hardwick (P) at this stage of the litigation has stated a constitutional claim sufficient to withstand a motion to dismiss.

▶ ANALYSIS

Also plaintiffs in the original action were a "Doe" couple, who had alleged that they wished to engage in the proscribed activity and were chilled and deterred by the existence of the statute and Hardwick's (P) arrest. The district court dismissed their claim for lack of standing, as the selective enforcement of the law left them in no immediate danger, and this judgment was upheld by the court of appeals. The "Doe" couple did not challenge this holding in the present case.

■=■

Quicknotes

EIGHTH AMENDMENT The Eighth Amendment to the federal constitution prohibits the imposition of excessive bail, fines, and cruel and unusual punishment.

■=■

Lawrence v. Texas

Sodomy convict (D) v. State (P)

539 U.S. 558 (2003).

NATURE OF CASE: Appeal from a criminal conviction.

FACT SUMMARY: When Lawrence (D) and his male partner, both adults, were prosecuted and convicted for consensual sodomy in their own private dwelling, they argued the unconstitutionality of the statute.

🏛 **RULE OF LAW**
Legislation that makes consensual sodomy between adults in their own dwelling criminal violates due process.

FACTS: Two Houston, Texas, police officers were dispatched to a private residence in response to a reported weapons disturbance. They entered an apartment where Lawrence (D) resided. The right of the police to enter was not an issue. The officers observed Lawrence (D) and another man engaging in sodomy. Both men were arrested, charged, and convicted before a justice of the peace of the statutory crime of "deviate sexual intercourse, namely anal sex, with a member of the same sex." Each defendant entered a plea of nolo contendere and was fined $200. Both men were adults at the time of the alleged offense. Their conduct was in private and consensual. Lawrence (D) and his partner appealed to the Supreme Court, arguing the Texas statute to be unconstitutional.

ISSUE: Does legislation that makes consensual sodomy between adults in their own dwelling criminal violate due process?

HOLDING AND DECISION: (Kennedy, J.) Yes. Legislation that makes consensual sodomy between adults in their own dwelling criminal violates due process. Liberty protects the person from unwarranted government intrusions into a dwelling or other private places. In our tradition the state is not omnipresent in the home. Furthermore, freedom extends beyond spatial bounds. Liberty presumes an "autonomy of self" that includes freedom of thought, belief, expression, "and certain intimate conduct." This case involves liberty of the person both in its spatial and more transcendent dimensions. The penalties and purposes of the Texas statute in the instant case have far-reaching consequences, touching upon the most private human conduct, sexual behavior, and in the most private of places, the home. The statute seeks to control a personal relationship that, whether or not entitled to formal recognition in the law, is within the liberty of persons to choose without being punished as criminals. This Court acknowledges that adults may choose to enter into private relationships in the confines of their own homes and their own private lives and still retain their dignity as free persons. When sexuality finds expression in intimate conduct with another person, the conduct can be but one element in a personal bond that is more enduring. The liberty protected by the Constitution allows homosexual persons the right to make this choice. Here, two adults who, with full and mutual consent from each other, engaged in sexual practices common to a homosexual lifestyle. They are entitled to respect in their private lives. The state cannot demean their existence or control their destiny by making their private sexual conduct a crime. Reversed.

CONCURRENCE: (O'Connor, J.) Rather than relying on the substantive component of the Fourteenth Amendment's Due Process Clause, as the Court does, I base my conclusion of unconstitutionality on the Fourteenth Amendment's Equal Protection Clause.

DISSENT: (Scalia, J.) Homosexual sodomy is not a right "deeply rooted in our Nation's history and tradition." Constitutional entitlements do not spring into existence because some states choose to lessen or eliminate sanctions on criminal behavior. Today's opinion is the product of a Court that has largely signed on to the so-called homosexual agenda.

DISSENT: (Thomas, J.) The instant Texas statute is "uncommonly silly" and should be repealed, nevertheless, no general constitutional right of privacy was violated in this situation.

▶ **ANALYSIS**

In *Lawrence*, the Supreme Court noted that of the 13 states with laws prohibiting sodomy, only 4 have enforced their legislation. In those states in which sodomy was still proscribed, whether for same-sex or heterosexual conduct, there was a pattern of nonenforcement with respect to consenting adults acting in private. Even Texas admitted in 1994 that as of that date it had not prosecuted anyone under those circumstances.

Quicknotes

DUE PROCESS The constitutional mandate requiring the courts to protect and enforce individuals' rights and liberties consistent with prevailing principles of fairness and justice and prohibiting the federal and state governments from such activities that deprive its citizens of life, liberty, or property interest.

District of Columbia v. Heller

Federal district/city (D) v. Handgun registration applicant (P)

554 U.S. 570 (2008).

NATURE OF CASE: Appeal from reversal of dismissal of a constitutional challenge to a city's gun regulations.

FACT SUMMARY: The District of Columbia (the District) (D) contended that its general ban on the possession and registration of handguns, its prohibition on the possession of usable handguns in the home, and its requirement that lawfully owned firearms (such as long guns) be kept unloaded and disassembled or bound by a trigger lock or similar device in a residence, did not violate the Second Amendment.

🏛 RULE OF LAW
The Second Amendment protects an individual's right to possess a firearm unconnected with service in a militia, and to use that arm for traditionally lawful purposes, such as self-defense within the home.

FACTS: [The District of Columbia (the District) (D) bans handgun possession by making it a crime to carry an unregistered firearm and prohibiting the registration of handguns and requires residents to keep lawfully owned firearms (such as long guns) unloaded and disassembled or bound by a trigger lock or similar device. Heller (P), a District (D) special policeman, applied to register a handgun he wished to keep at home, but the District (D) refused. He filed suit seeking, on Second Amendment grounds, to enjoin the city from enforcing the bar on handgun registration, the licensing requirement insofar as it prohibits carrying an unlicensed firearm in the home, and the trigger-lock requirement insofar as it prohibits the use of functional firearms in the home. The district court dismissed the suit, but the court of appeals reversed, holding that the Second Amendment protects an individual's right to possess firearms and that the city's total ban on handguns, as well as its requirement that firearms in the home be kept nonfunctional even when necessary for self-defense, violated that right. The Supreme Court granted certiorari.]

ISSUE: Does the Second Amendment protect an individual's right to possess a firearm unconnected with service in a militia, and to use that arm for traditionally lawful purposes, such as self-defense within the home?

HOLDING AND DECISION: (Scalia, J.) Yes. The Second Amendment protects an individual's right to possess a firearm unconnected with service in a militia, and to use that arm for traditionally lawful purposes, such as self-defense within the home. The District (D) argues that

the Second Amendment protects only the right to possess and carry a firearm in connection with militia service, whereas Heller (P) claims that the right to carry a firearm is unconnected with militia service and protects use for traditionally lawful purposes, such as self-defense within the home. The Amendment is divided into its prefatory clause and operative clause. The prefatory clause announces a purpose, but does not limit or expand the scope of the second part, the operative clause. The operative clause's text and history demonstrate that it connotes an individual right to keep and bear arms. The first salient feature of the operative clause is that it codifies a "right of the people." Based on other provisions of the Constitution, this right is an individual, rather than collective, right. This contrasts markedly with the phrase "militia" in the prefatory clause, which identifies a class that is a subset of "the people." That subset was comprised of able bodied males of a certain age. Thus, reading the Second Amendment as protecting only the right to "keep and bear Arms" in an organized militia therefore fits poorly with the operative clause's description of the holder of that right as "the people." The right protected by the Amendment is therefore exercised individually and belongs to all Americans. The terms "Arms" refers to weapons not specifically designed for military use but that could assist with self defense. To "keep and bear Arms" means to possess and carry weapons for the purpose of being armed and ready. The meaning in no way connotes participation in a structured military organization. Contrary to the dissent's opinion, no dictionary has ever adopted a definition of "bear arms" that connotes the carrying of arms only in the service of an organized militia. Under such an idiomatic interpretation, the Second Amendment would protect only the right to be a soldier and wage war. The Amendment's historical background confirms that it was intended to protect the individual right to possess and carry weapons in case of confrontation. The Second Amendment codified existing rights—which had nothing to do with service in the militia and permitted Englishmen to never be disarmed. The prefatory clause comports with this interpretation of the operative clause. The "militia" comprised all males physically capable of acting in concert for the common defense. Congress had the power to create an army, but the militia was already in existence. The power to organize it was the power to order it, not to create it. This interpretation is supported by analogous arms-bearing rights in state constitutions that preceded and immediately followed the Second Amendment. The next step is to

Continued on next page.

determine whether any of the Court's precedents foreclose the conclusions reached thus far. None of the Court's precedents refute the individual-rights interpretation or limit the right to keep and bear arms to militia purposes. Instead, some of those cases limit the type of weapon to which the right applies to those used by the militia, i.e., those in common use for lawful purposes. Like most rights, the Second Amendment right is not unlimited. It is not a right to keep and carry any weapon whatsoever in any manner whatsoever and for whatever purpose: For example, concealed weapons prohibitions have been upheld under the Amendment or state analogues. The Court's opinion should not be taken to cast doubt on longstanding prohibitions on the possession of firearms by felons and the mentally ill, or laws forbidding the carrying of firearms in sensitive places such as schools and government buildings, or laws imposing conditions and qualifications on the commercial sale of arms. The Court's precedent, holding that the sorts of weapons protected are those "in common use at the time," finds support in the historical tradition of prohibiting the carrying of dangerous and unusual weapons. Applying these principles to the case at bar requires the conclusion that the handgun ban and the trigger-lock requirement (as applied to self-defense) violate the Second Amendment. The District's (D) total ban on handgun possession in the home amounts to a prohibition on an entire class of "arms" that Americans overwhelmingly choose for the lawful purpose of self-defense. Under any of the standards of scrutiny the Court has applied to enumerated constitutional rights, this prohibition—in the place where the importance of the lawful defense of self, family, and property is most acute—would fail constitutional muster. Similarly, the requirement that any lawful firearm in the home be disassembled or bound by a trigger lock makes it impossible for citizens to use arms for the core lawful purpose of self-defense and is hence unconstitutional. Because Heller (P) conceded at oral argument that the District (D) licensing law is permissible if it is not enforced arbitrarily and capriciously, the Court assumes that a license will satisfy his prayer for relief and does not address the licensing requirement. Assuming he is not disqualified from exercising Second Amendment rights, the District (D) must permit Heller (P) to register his handgun and must issue him a license to carry it in the home. Affirmed.

DISSENT: (Stevens, J.) The issue presented by this case is not whether the right protected by the Second Amendment is an individual right, but rather, what the scope of that right is, and whether the Amendment protects the right to possess and use weapons for nonmilitary purposes. The Amendment's history indicates that it was intended to protect state militias, not to enshrine the common-law right of self-defense. The Court's precedent, requiring that the possession of a weapon have a reasonable relationship to the preservation of a militia, is the most natural reading of the Amendment's text and the

interpretation most faithful to history. The Amendment's preamble makes clear that it is intended to preserve the militia. The majority overlooks that the Framers used "the people" to refer back to the object announced in the preamble. Those words mean that it is the collective action of individuals having a duty to serve in the militia that the text directly protects. The words "To keep and bear Arms" refer to the unitary right to possess arms if needed for military purposes and to use them in conjunction with military activities. Different language would have been used to protect nonmilitary use and possession of weapons. Contrary to the majority's position, there is no language in the Amendment that is intended to protect the right of law-abiding citizens to protect themselves in their homes.

DISSENT: (Breyer, J.) The District's (D) regulation of handguns and weapons is consistent with the Second Amendment, even if interpreted as protecting citizens' interest in self-defense, because it focuses upon the presence of handguns in high-crime urban areas, and is thus a permissible legislative response to a serious, indeed life-threatening, problem. The right protected by the Second Amendment, even assuming it is an individual right to possess and carry weapons for self-defense purposes in keeping with the majority's position, is not absolute and is subject to government regulation. Any attempt in theory to apply strict scrutiny to gun regulations will in practice turn into an interest-balancing inquiry, with the interests protected by the Second Amendment on one side and the governmental public-safety concerns on the other, the only question being whether the regulation at issue impermissibly burdens the former in the course of advancing the latter. Statistics show that for every intruder stopped by a homeowner with a firearm, there are four gun-related accidents within the home. While Heller (P) argues that the handgun ban will not reduce these types of accidents, and that crime and homicide rates are higher since the ban went into effect, the question is whether it was reasonable for the District's (D) legislative body to reject such empirically based arguments. Here, the District's (D) decision represents the kind of empirically based judgment that legislatures, not courts, are best suited to make, and the interests that the District (D) properly seeks to further are "compelling." The handgun ban is a proportionate response to very high rates of crime in urban areas. There is no less restrictive alternative, because the objective is to eliminate handguns, with some exceptions. Moreover, the popularity of a particular weapon, such as the handgun, should not be dispositive of whether its use and possession is protected, since it feasible that very dangerous weapons could be invented that would become the preferred choice of American citizens for self-defense. In essence, the majority determines what regulations are permissible by looking to see what existing regulations permit. There is

Continued on next page.

no basis for believing that the Framers intended such circular reasoning.

▶ *ANALYSIS*

Some commentators have argued that the District's (D) ban on one class of weapons (handguns) does not violate the Second Amendment even under an individual rights view, since individuals are not barred from possessing or using all weapons for self-defense. Others would take a property approach to the regulation of guns, whereby such regulations are analyzed in the same way as other regulation of property under modern constitutional law and are permitted as long as they are rationally related to achieving a legitimate government purpose—essentially the approach taken by Justice Breyer in his dissent. Judge Posner, of the Seventh Circuit, believes that the majority opinion created new constitutional rights that did not previously exist. He has said, "The text of the amendment, whether viewed alone or in light of the concerns that actuated its adoption, creates no right to the private possession of guns for hunting or other sport, or for the defense of person or property. It is doubtful that the amendment could even be thought to require that members of state militias be allowed to keep weapons in their homes, since that would reduce the militias' effectiveness." Finally, others have criticized the opinion as circumventing the legislative process and being a form of judicial legislation.

■≡■

Quicknotes

SELF-DEFENSE The right to protect an individual's person, family or property against attempted injury by another.

■≡■

McDonald v. City of Chicago

Citizens (P) v. State (D)

___ U.S. ___, 130 S. Ct. 3020, 177 L.Ed.2d 894 (2010).

NATURE OF CASE: Appeal to Supreme Court from federal appeals court.

FACT SUMMARY: [Several plaintiffs (P) challenged a ban on handguns in Chicago.]

RULE OF LAW
The Second Amendment applies to the states by incorporation through the Due Process Clause.

FACTS: [The cities of Chicago and Oak Park in Illinois had gun bans. Several lawsuits were filed against the cities challenging those bans after the Supreme Court decided *District of Columbia v. Heller,* 554 U.S. 570 (2008), where the Court held that a District of Columbia handgun ban violated the Second Amendment because the D.C. law was enacted under the authority of the federal government and, therefore, the Second Amendment was applicable. The plaintiffs (P) in this case argued that the Second Amendment also applies to the states, and because it does, the Chicago handgun bans were unconstitutional. The district court dismissed the suits and on appeal, the U.S. Court of Appeals for the Seventh Circuit affirmed.]

ISSUE: Does the Second Amendment apply to the states by incorporation through the Due Process Clause?

HOLDING AND DECISION: (Alito, J.) Yes. The Second Amendment applies to the states by incorporation through the Due Process Clause. In *Heller,* it was decided that the right to self-defense is a right that is "fundamental to the Nation's scheme of ordered liberty" and "deeply rooted in this Nation's history and tradition." The question is not whether a civilized society can exist without recognizing this particular right; it's whether our civilized society must recognize the right. The Due Process Clause of the Fourteenth Amendment incorporates the Second Amendment right recognized in *Heller,* a fundamental, deeply rooted right. Reversed and remanded.

CONCURRENCE: (Thomas, J.) The judgment is correct, and the Fourteenth Amendment incorporates the Second Amendment against the states, but the Due Process Clause is not the appropriate mechanism for incorporation. Instead, the Privileges or Immunities Clause is the more appropriate avenue for incorporation. The framers of the Privileges or Immunities Clause and the ratifying-era public understood that the right to keep and bear arms was essential to the preservation of liberty. A constitutional provision that guarantees only "process" before a person is deprived of life, liberty, or property cannot define the substance of rights not mentioned in the Constitution.

DISSENT: (Breyer, J.) There are many reasons why applying the Second Amendment to state and local governments is unwise. Nothing in our history shows a consensus that the right to private-armed defense is deeply rooted in history or tradition, or is otherwise fundamental. To incorporate the right in *Heller* may change the law in many of the states. In addition, incorporation will not necessarily further any other constitutional objective. It does not comprise a necessary part of the democratic process, and does not significantly protect individuals who might otherwise suffer unfair or inhumane treatment at the hands of a majority. The state legislature is in a much better position to assess any particular gun law.

DISSENT: (Stevens, J.) The Fourteenth Amendment incorporates the Second Amendment against the states. But owning a personal firearm was not a "liberty" interest protected by the Due Process Clause. Recognizing a new liberty right is a huge step and is not warranted here. Firearms have an ambivalent relationship to liberty, because they can help criminals murder innocent victims. Owning a handgun is not critical to leading a life of autonomy, dignity, or political equality. And while Americans' interest in firearms may be deeply rooted, it is also true that the states have a long history of regulating firearms. Finally, the strength of any liberty claim has to be evaluated in connection with its status in the democratic process, and gun control opponents have considerable political power. History is also a factor, but it should not be the determinative factor, and the net result of Justice Scalia's approach is to give federal judges unprecedented lawmaking powers in an area in which they have no special qualifications, and where the political process has handled the issue for decades.

CONCURRENCE: (Scalia, J.) Justice Stevens's dissent is wrong. His assertion that firearms have an ambivalent relationship to liberty because they sometimes are used to cause harm to others is wrong, because the criteria—harm to others—is inapposite. The Clause does not cover only those rights that have zero harmful effects on anyone, or even the First Amendment is out. His argument that owning a handgun is not a fundamental right because it is not critical to their way of life or security, but deciding what is essential to a life is an inherently political, moral judgment. Finally, his argument that we ought not to find the right to keep and bear arms is incorporated because it is prudent, even if we had the authority to do so based on history. But historically focused methods may be

Continued on next page.

the best means available to determine constitutional questions, even if the method is not a perfect method.

▶ ANALYSIS

Most scholars agree that when the Bill of Rights was adopted, it was intended to limit the federal, not state, government. After the adoption of the Fourteenth Amendment in 1868, the Supreme Court held that rights from the Bill of Rights may be selectively applied, or "incorporated," through the Due Process Clause. In *McDonald*, the Court stated that provisions of the Bill of Rights may be incorporated only if they are "fundamental to *our* scheme of ordered liberty," or "deeply rooted in this Nation's history and tradition." The case therefore represents a restriction on the application of the Due Process Clause.

■══■

Quicknotes

DUE PROCESS CLAUSE Clauses found in the Fifth and Fourteenth Amendments to the United States Constitution providing that no person shall be deprived of "life, liberty, or property, without due process of law."

FOURTEENTH AMENDMENT Declares that no state shall make or enforce any law that shall abridge the privileges and immunities of citizens of the United States. No state shall deny to any person within its jurisdiction the equal protection of the laws.

PRIVILEGES AND IMMUNITIES CLAUSE Refers to the guarantee set forth in the Fourteenth Amendment to the United States Constitution recognizing that any individual born in any of the United States is entitled to both state and national citizenship and guaranteeing such citizens the privileges and immunities thereof.

■══■

McCleskey v. Kemp

Convicted black man (P) v. State (D)

481 U.S. 279 (1987).

NATURE OF CASE: Appeal from denial of federal habeas corpus relief.

FACT SUMMARY: In McCleskey's (P) action against Kemp (D) for federal habeas corpus relief, McCleskey (P) contended that the Georgia capital sentencing process was administered in a racially discriminatory manner in violation of the Eighth Amendment and the Equal Protection Clause of the Fourteenth Amendment.

RULE OF LAW
The Constitution does not require that a state eliminate any demonstrable disparity that correlates with a potentially irrelevant factor, such as race, in order to operate a criminal justice system that includes capital punishment.

FACTS: McCleskey (P), a black man, was convicted in a Georgia trial court of armed robbery and the murder of a white police officer in the course of the robbery and was sentenced to death. McCleskey (P) sought federal habeas corpus relief, contending that the Georgia capital sentencing process was administered in a racially discriminatory manner in violation of the Eighth Amendment and the Equal Protection Clause of the Fourteenth Amendment. In support of his claim, McCleskey (P) offered a statistical study, "Baldus, Pulaski and Woodworth, Comparative Review of Death Sentences: An Empirical Study of the Georgia Experience," 74 J. Crim. L. & C. 661 (1983) (The Baldus Study). This study examined over 2,000 murder cases occurring in Georgia in the 1970's and concluded that black defendants, such as McCleskey (P), who kill whites have the greatest likelihood of being sentenced to death. The federal district court ruled that the Baldus Study did not contribute anything of value to McCleskey's (P) claim and denied relief. The court of appeals affirmed. McCleskey (P) appealed.

ISSUE: Does the Constitution require that a state eliminate any demonstrable disparity that correlates with a potentially irrelevant factor, such as race, in order to operate a criminal justice system that includes capital punishment?

HOLDING AND DECISION: (Powell, J.) No. The Constitution does not require that a state eliminate any demonstrable disparity that correlates with a potentially irrelevant factor, such as race, in order to operate a criminal justice system that includes capital punishment. It is the ultimate duty of courts to determine on a case-by-case basis whether state laws are applied consistently with the Constitution. Despite McCleskey's (P) arguments that

basically challenge the validity of capital punishment in our multi-race society, the only question here was if the law of Georgia was properly applied. McCleskey's (P) sentence was imposed under Georgia sentencing procedures that focus discretion on the particularized nature of the crime and the particularized characteristics of the individual defendant. The sentence was not wantonly or freakishly imposed and thus not disproportionate with any recognized meaning under the Eighth Amendment. Statistics at most may show only a likelihood that a particular factor entered into some decisions. Here, the Baldus Study is insufficient as the constitutional measure of an unacceptable risk of racial prejudice influencing a capital decision. Affirmed.

DISSENT: (Brennan, J.) The majority misreads the Court's Eighth Amendment jurisprudence in concluding that McCleskey (P) has not demonstrated a degree of risk sufficient to raise constitutional concern. The determination of the significance of this evidence is at its core an exercise in human moral judgment, not a mechanical statistical analysis. This Court has determined a uniquely high degree of rationality in imposing the death penalty. A capital sentencing system in which race more likely than not plays a role does not meet this standard.

ANALYSIS

In another dissent in the *McCleskey* case, Justice Stevens stated that the studies supporting McCleskey's (P) claim demonstrated a strong probability that the sentencing jury was influenced by the fact that McCleskey (P) was black and his victim was white. The jury's sense that a defendant had lost his moral entitlement to live would most likely not have been generated if he had killed a member of his own race. Justice Stevens concluded that this sort of disparity is constitutionally intolerable.

Quicknotes

EIGHTH AMENDMENT The eighth amendment to the federal constitution prohibiting the imposition of excessive bail, fines and cruel and unusual punishment.

EQUAL PROTECTION CLAUSE A constitutional guarantee that no person should be denied the same protection of the laws enjoyed by other persons in like circumstances.

Continued on next page.

HABEAS CORPUS A proceeding in which a defendant brings a writ to compel a judicial determination of whether he is lawfully being held in custody.

THE BALDUS STUDY A report of statistical research conducted in 1983 which indicated that, in Georgia, persons who murder whites receive the death penalty more often than persons who murder blacks, and that black murderers of whites receive the death penalty more often than white murderers of whites.

■=■

Freedom of Expression and Association

Quick Reference Rules of Law

Abrams v. United States

[Parties not identified in casebook excerpt.]

250 U.S. 616 (1919).

NATURE OF CASE: Appeal from conviction for conspiracy to violate the Espionage Act amendments of 1918.

FACT SUMMARY: Abrams (D) and others distributed thousands of leaflets in New York City in opposition to what Abrams (D) believed to be an American attempt "to crush the Russian Revolution."

 RULE OF LAW
[Rule of Law not stated in casebook excerpt.]

FACTS: In the summer of 1918, the government sent a small contingent of Marines to Siberia, an action which Abrams (D) and others viewed as an attempt "to crush the Russian Revolution" with which they sympathized. In response, several thousand leaflets were printed and distributed in New York City. The Supreme Court upheld convictions for conspiracy to violate the provisions of the 1918 amendments to the Espionage Act (the Act), one prohibiting language intended "to incite, provoke or encourage resistance to the United States" (count 3); the other prohibiting the urging of curtailment of war production "with intent to cripple or hinder the United States in the prosecution of the war" (count 4). The United States had declared war on Germany, but not on Russia.

ISSUE: [Issue not stated in casebook excerpt.]

HOLDING AND DECISION: [Holding and Decision not stated in casebook excerpt.]

DISSENT: (Holmes, J.) The Act requires intent, which did not appear to exist. "When words are used exactly, a deed is not done with intent to produce a consequence unless that consequence is the aim of the deed." One "does not do the act with intent to produce it unless the aim to produce it is the proximate motive of the specific act although there may be some deeper motive behind it." The government may punish speech that is intended to produce a clear and imminent danger which will bring about evils the government may constitutionally prevent, and that power is greater in time of war when there are dangers that at other times do not exist. Here, the publishing of a "silly leaflet by an unknown man" did not present such an immediate danger. The first leaflet claimed that the President's silence about German intervention in Russia showed that the government was just as much against workers as the Russians and Germans. The second leaflet warned munitions workers that the bullets they made were being used against their fellow workers. Neither leaflet was intended to impede the United States in its declared war against Germany. "I wholly disagree with the argument of the government that the First Amendment left the common law as to seditious libel in force."

ANALYSIS

Reaction to this case has been vigorous and mixed. Professor Chafee thought it ridiculous to give a twenty-year sentence to each of "five obscure and isolated young aliens, misguided by their loyalty to their endangered country and ideals." Wigmore has argued the opposite. He feared that if the five here could be allowed to urge a general munitions workers strike, then anyone could do the same, "and a thousand disaffected undesirables, aliens and natives alike, were ready and waiting to do so."

Quicknotes

ESPIONAGE ACT Federal law prohibiting espionage.

Whitney v. California

Political organizer (D) v. State (P)

274 U.S. 357 (1927).

NATURE OF CASE: Appeal from conviction for violation of Criminal Syndicalism Act.

FACT SUMMARY: Miss Whitney (D), organizer and member of the Communist Labor Party of California, was convicted of aiding in that organization's violation of the Criminal Syndicalism Act.

RULE OF LAW

A state may, in the exercise of its police power, punish abuses of freedom of speech where such utterances are inimical to the public welfare as tending to incite crime, disturb the peace, or endanger organized government through threats of violent overthrow.

FACTS: In 1919, Miss Whitney (D) attended a convention of the Socialist Party. When the convention split into factions, Miss Whitney (D) went with the radicals and helped form the Communist Labor Party (CLP). Later that year, Miss Whitney (D) attended another convention to organize a new California unit of CLP. There, Miss Whitney (D) supported a resolution that endorsed political action and urged workers to vote for CLP member-candidates at all elections. This resolution was defeated and a more extreme program of action was adopted, over Miss Whitney's (D) protests. At trial, upon indictment for violation of the California Criminal Syndicalism Act, which held it unlawful to organize a group that advocated unlawful acts of violence as a means of effecting change in industrial ownership and in political change, Miss Whitney (D) contended that she never intended the CLP to become a terrorist organization. Miss Whitney (D) further contended that since she had no intent to aid the CLP in a policy of violent political reform, her mere presence at the convention was not a crime. Miss Whitney (D) contends that the Act thus deprived her of her liberty and freedom of speech, assembly, and association without due process.

ISSUE: May a state, in the exercise of its police power, punish abuses of freedom of speech where such utterances are inimical to the public welfare as tending to incite crime, disturb the peace, or endanger organized government through threats of violent overthrow?

HOLDING AND DECISION: (Sanford, J.) Yes. A state may, in the exercise of its police power, punish abuses of freedom of speech where such utterances are inimical to the public welfare as tending to incite crime, disturb the peace, or endanger organized government through threats of violent overthrow. Freedom of speech, secured by the Constitution, does not confer an absolute right to speak, without responsibility. A state may in the exercise of its police power, punish abuses of freedom of speech where such utterances are inimical to the public welfare as tending to incite crime, disturb the peace, or endanger organized government through violent overthrow. Here, the Syndicalism Act of California declared that to become a knowing member of or assist in an organization that advocates crimes involving danger to the public peace and security of the state was punishable in the exercise of the state's police powers. The essence of the offense was the combining with others to accomplish desired ends through advocacy and use of criminal means. This is in the nature of criminal conspiracy and involves an even greater danger to public security than individual acts. Miss Whitney's (D) contentions that the California Criminal Syndicalism Act as applied to her in this case is unconstitutional is foreclosed to the court, since it is an effort to review a trial verdict. Affirmed.

CONCURRENCE: (Brandeis, J.) Miss Whitney (D) is here punished for a step in the preparation of incitement which threatens the public only remotely. The Syndicalism Act of California aims at punishing those who propose to preach, not put into action, criminal syndicalism. The right of freedom of speech, assembly, and association, protected the Due Process Clause of the Fourteenth Amendment and binding on the states, are restricted if they threaten political, moral, or economic injury to the state. However, such restriction does not exist unless speech would produce a clear and imminent danger of some substantive evil to the state. The Court has not yet fixed standards in determining when a danger shall be clear. But no danger flowing from speech can be deemed clear and present unless the threatened evil is so imminent that it may strike before opportunity for discussion on it. There must be, however, probability of serious injury to the state. As to review by this Court of an allegation of unconstitutionality of a criminal syndicalism act, whenever fundamental rights of free speech and assembly are alleged to have been invaded, the defendant must be allowed to present the issue of whether a clear and present danger was imminent by his actions. Here, mere advocacy of revolution by mass action at some future date was within the Fourteenth Amendment protection. But our power of review was lacking since there was evidence of a criminal conspiracy, and such precludes review by this Court of errors at a criminal trial absent a showing that constitutional rights were deprived.

Continued on next page.

▶ *ANALYSIS*

The *Whitney* case is important for having added to the *Schenck* test of "clear and present danger" the further requirement that the danger must be "imminent." See *Schenck v. United States*, 249 U.S. 47 (1919). The Brandeis opinion in the *Whitney* case should be viewed as a dissenting opinion. His addition of "imminent" flies directly in the face of the majority opinion that punished "mere advocacy" of threatened action against the state. The "mere advocacy" test has not survived. Modernly, through the Smith Act that continues to punish criminal syndicalism, "mere advocacy" is not punishable. The urging of action for forcible overthrow is necessary before punishment will be imposed. Thus, the "urging of action" is the modern test of "clear and present imminent danger" espoused by Brandeis in *Whitney*.

■══■

Quicknotes

CRIMINAL SYNDICALISM The advocating of unlawful conduct to effect a change in ownership or control.

DUE PROCESS The constitutional mandate requiring the courts to protect and enforce individuals' rights and liberties consistent with prevailing principles of fairness and justice and prohibiting the federal and state governments from such activities that deprive its citizens of life, liberty, or property interest.

DUE PROCESS CLAUSE Clause found in the Fifth and Fourteenth Amendments to the United States Constitution providing that no person shall be deprived of "life, liberty, or property, without due process of law."

SMITH ACT Federal law prohibiting the violent overthrow of government.

■══■

Dennis v. United States

Political organizer (D) v. Federal government (P)

341 U.S. 494 (1951).

NATURE OF CASE: Appeal from conviction of violating the Smith Act.

FACT SUMMARY: Ringleaders (D) of the American Communist Party were convicted, under the Smith Act, of knowingly advocating the overthrow of government by violent means, and conspiracy.

🏛 RULE OF LAW
In reviewing legislation that restricts freedom of speech, the court, in determining whether a "clear and present danger" exists, must ask whether the gravity of the evil, discounted by its improbability, justifies such invasion of free speech as is necessary to avoid the evil.

FACTS: The Smith Act (the Act), passed by Congress in 1940, made it a crime for anyone to knowingly advocate the overthrow of government by force or violence or by the assassination of any officer. The Act also prohibited an attempt or conspiracy to accomplish the same. Dennis (D) and other ringleaders (D) of the American Communist Party had been conducting seminars, making speeches, and writing articles advocating the overthrow of the United States government. They were charged with conspiracy in violation of the Smith Act. At their trial, the judge instructed the jury that their only duty was to determine whether a violation of the Act had occurred, and if so, as a matter of law, he had determined that there is sufficient danger of a substantive evil that Congress had a right to prevent that justified the Act's application under the First Amendment. Dennis (D) and the other ringleaders (D) were convicted, and they appealed.

ISSUE: Is the Smith Act, as applied against the leaders of the American Communist Party, constitutional?

HOLDING AND DECISION: (Vinson, C.J.) Yes. [The Court initially held that Congress has the power to pass the Smith Act since government has a right to protect itself against armed rebellion.] Congress, by passing the Act, intended not to prohibit the free discussion of political theories, but only advocacy of a dangerous nature. The words of the standard test, "clear and present danger," cannot mean that before the government may act it must wait until the rebellion is about to be executed, the plans have been laid, and the signal is awaited. The fact that those plotting the rebellion are small and weak, while the government is strong, is irrelevant; success or probability of success is not the criterion. In determining whether a "clear and present danger exists," the court must determine the gravity of the evil as discounted by the improbability of its

occurrence. In the present case, the trial court concluded that the Communist Party, composed of rigidly disciplined members subject to call at the will of the leaders, posed a sufficient danger to justify an intrusion on First Amendment rights. Furthermore, the doctrine that there must be a clear and present danger of a substantive evil that Congress has a right to prevent is a judicial rule to be applied as a matter of law by the courts. The convictions are affirmed.

CONCURRENCE: (Frankfurter, J.) The independence of the judiciary would be jeopardized were courts to become embroiled in the passions of the day and assume primary responsibility in choosing between competing political, economic, and social pressures. How best to reconcile competing interests is the business of legislatures and should not be second-guessed by the judiciary if there is any reasonable basis to sustain it.

CONCURRENCE: (Jackson, J.) The "clear and present danger" test should be applied only in those cases where the issue is criminality of a hot-headed speech on a street corner or circulation of a few pamphlets, etc. It should not be applied in cases like the instant one where the court must appraise imponderables, including international and national phenomena which baffle the best informed foreign offices and our most experienced politicians.

DISSENT: (Black, J.) The First Amendment as construed in the light of "reasonableness" is not likely to protect any but those safe or orthodox views which rarely need its protection.

DISSENT: (Douglas, J.) The defendants here were indicted for organizing people to teach and themselves teach certain books. These books, by Marx and Lenin, may lawfully remain on library shelves. Thus, the Smith Act punishes not what is said but on the intent with which it is said. Furthermore, pure speech, without seditious conduct, is prohibited. The "clear and present danger" test requires that before speech can be curtailed, conditions must be so critical that there will be no time to avoid the evil which is threatened. That is not the situation here; while the force of Communism may be prevalent in the world, its strength in this country is minimal.

▌ ANALYSIS

After *Dennis*, the Court retreated from its apparent carte blanche approval of congressional attempts to fight domestic Communism. In *Yates v. United States*, 354 U.S. 298

Continued on next page.

(1957), the Court held that in order for a defendant to be convicted under the Smith Act, the trial judge must instruct the jury to acquit unless it found that there had been some advocacy of action and not merely an argument for the desirability of the action.

■━━■

Quicknotes

FIRST AMENDMENT   Prohibits Congress from enacting any law respecting an establishment of religion, prohibiting the free exercise of religion, abridging freedom of speech or the press, the right of peaceful assembly and the right to petition for a redress of grievances.

SMITH ACT   Federal law prohibiting the violent overthrow of government.

■━━■

Brandenburg v. Ohio

Ku Klux Klan leader (D) v. State (P)

395 U.S. 444 (1969).

NATURE OF CASE: Appeal from conviction for violation of the Ohio criminal syndicalism statute.

FACT SUMMARY: Brandenburg (D) was convicted under a state statute which proscribes advocacy of the duty, necessity, or propriety of crime, sabotage, violence, or unlawful methods of terrorism as a means of accomplishing reform.

🏛 RULE OF LAW
The constitutional guarantees of freedom of speech and freedom of press do not permit a state to forbid or proscribe advocacy of the use of force or of law violation except where such advocacy is directed to inciting or producing imminent lawless action and is likely to produce or incite such action.

FACTS: Brandenburg (D), a Ku Klux Klan leader, was convicted under Ohio's criminal syndicalism statute. The statute prohibits advocacy of the duty, necessity, or propriety of crime, sabotage, violence, or unlawful methods of terrorism as a means of accomplishing reform, and the assembling with any group formed to teach or advocate the doctrine of criminal syndicalism. The case against Brandenburg (D) rested on some films. One film showed 12 hooded figures, some carrying firearms, gathered around a wooden cross which they burned. Scattered words could be heard that were derogatory to Jews and Blacks. Brandenburg (D) made a speech and stated, "We are not a revengent group, but if our President, our Congress, and our Supreme Court, continues to suppress the White, Caucasian race, it's possible that there might have to be some revengence taken."

ISSUE: Do the constitutional guarantees of free speech and free press permit a state to forbid or proscribe advocacy of the use of force or law violation except where such advocacy is directed to inciting or producing imminent lawless action and is likely to incite or produce such action?

HOLDING AND DECISION: (Per curiam) No. The constitutional guarantees of free speech and free press do not permit a state to forbid or proscribe advocacy of the use of force or of law violation except where such advocacy is directed to inciting or producing imminent lawless action and is likely to incite or produce such action. The mere abstract teaching of the moral propriety, or even moral necessity for a resort to force and violence, is not the same as preparing a group for violent action and steering it to such action. A statute which fails to draw this distinction impermissibly intrudes upon the freedoms guaranteed by the First and Fourteenth Amendments. It sweeps within its condemnation speech which the Consti-

tution has immunized from governmental control. The Ohio statute purports to punish mere advocacy and to forbid assembly with others merely to advocate the described type of action. Hence, it cannot be sustained. Brandenburg's (D) conviction is reversed.

CONCURRENCE: (Black, J.) The "clear and present danger" doctrine should not be used in interpreting the First Amendment. The Court's opinion is correct in citing *Dennis v. United States*, 341 U.S. 494 (1951), but not in indicating agreement with the "clear and present danger" doctrine on which *Dennis* purportedly relied.

CONCURRENCE: (Douglas, J.) It is doubtful that the "clear and present danger" is congenial with the First Amendment. "The line between what is permissible and not subject to control and what may be made impermissible and subject to regulation is the line between ideas and overt acts." Apart from where "speech is brigaded with action," speech should be immune from prosecution.

▶ ANALYSIS

This case demonstrates that the imminence of danger is an essential requirement to the validity of any statute curbing freedom of speech. This requirement was reiterated in *Bond v. Floyd*, 385 U.S. 116 (1966), in which the Court reversed a state legislature's resolution excluding Bond from membership. The exclusion was based on the ground that Bond could not take the oath to support the state and federal Constitutions after his endorsement of a statement by the Student Nonviolent Coordinating Committee (a civil rights organization of which Bond was then the Communications Director) and his remarks criticizing the draft and the Vietnam war. The Court found no incitement to violation of law in Bond's remarks.

■═■

Quicknotes

CLEAR AND PRESENT DANGER A threat that is proximate and impending.

FIRST AMENDMENT Prohibits Congress from enacting any law respecting an establishment of religion, prohibiting the free exercise of religion, abridging freedom of speech or the press, the right of peaceful assembly and the right to petition for a redress of grievances.

SYNDICALISM The advocating of unlawful conduct to effect a change in ownership or control.

■═■

New York Times Co. v. Sullivan

Newspaper (D) v. City commissioner (D)

376 U.S. 254 (1964).

NATURE OF CASE: Appeal of defamation judgment.

FACT SUMMARY: New York Times Co. (D) published an editorial advertisement in which false statements were made which concerned Sullivan (P).

🏛 RULE OF LAW
The First Amendment requires that a public official may not recover damages for defamatory falsehoods relating to his official conduct unless he proves that the statement involved was made with "actual malice—that is, with knowledge that it was false or with reckless disregard of whether it was false or not."

FACTS: Sullivan (P) was a commissioner in the city of Montgomery, Alabama, charged with supervision of the Police Department. During a series of civil rights demonstrations in that city in 1960, the New York Times Co. (D) published an editorial advertisement entitled, "Heed Their Rising Voices," in which several charges of terrorism were leveled at the Police Department. The falsity of some of these statements is uncontroverted. The advertisement charged that nine students at a local college had been expelled for leading a march on the state capitol when, in fact, the reason had been an illegal lunch counter sit-in. The advertisement charged that the police had padlocked the dining hall of the college to starve the demonstrators into submission when, in fact, no padlocking had occurred. Other false statements also were made. Sullivan (P) brought a defamation action against New York Times (D) for these statements and recovered $500,000. Under Alabama law, a publication is libel per se (no special damages need be proved—general damages are presumed), whenever a defamatory falsehood is shown to have injured its subject in his public office or impute misconduct to him in his office. New York Times (D) appealed the Alabama judgment, challenging this rule.

ISSUE: May a public official recover damages under a First Amendment claim for defamatory falsehoods relating to his official conduct without proving that the statement involved was made with "actual malice—that is, with knowledge that it was false or with reckless disregard of whether it was false or not"?

HOLDING AND DECISION: (Brennan, J.) No. The First Amendment requires that a public official may not recover damages for defamatory falsehoods relating to his official conduct unless he proves that the statement involved was made with "actual malice—that is, with

knowledge that it was false or with reckless disregard of whether it was false or not." First Amendment protections do not turn upon the truth, popularity, or social utility of ideas and beliefs which are involved. Rather, they are based upon the theory that erroneous statements are inevitable in free debate and must be protected if such freedom is to survive. Only where malice is involved do such protections cease. Here, the Alabama rule falls short of this standard, and the evidence at trial was insufficient to determine its existence. The decision must, therefore, be reversed.

CONCURRENCE: (Black, J.) Justice Black would go further and hold that all statements about public officials should be constitutionally protected, even malicious ones.

▶ ANALYSIS

New York Times is the landmark case in constitutional defamation law. The subsequent cases have expanded this concept even further. In *Rosenblatt v. Baer*, 383 U.S. 75 (1966), the Court defined "public official" as anyone having substantial responsibility for conduct of government affairs. In *Curtis Publishing v. Butts*, 388 U.S. 130 (1967), *New York Times* was extended to "public figures" as well as officials. In *Gertz v. Robert Welch, Inc.*, 418 U.S. 323 (1974), however, the Court retreated a bit by stating that, "As long as they do not impose liability without fault, the states may define for themselves the appropriate standard of liability for publisher . . . of defamatory falsehood injurious to a private individual." Note that the Court has also taken steps to toughen the *New York Times'* recklessness standard. In *St. Amant v. Thompson*, 390 U.S. 727 (1968), the Court ruled that recklessness was not to be measured by the reasonable man standard but rather by the subjective standard of whether or not the defendant in the case subjectively entertained serious doubts about the truth of his statements.

━■━

Quicknotes

DEFAMATION An intentional false publication, communicated publicly in either oral or written form, subjecting a person to scorn, hatred or ridicule, or injuring him or her in relation to his or her occupation or business.

FREEDOM OF THE PRESS The right to publish and publicly disseminate one's views.

FREEDOM OF SPEECH The right to express oneself without governmental restrictions on the content of that expression.

Continued on next page.

LIBEL PER SE A false or malicious publication that subjects a person to scorn, hatred or ridicule, or that injures him in relation to his occupation or business of such an extreme nature that the law will presume that the person has suffered such injury.

■▬■

Gertz v. Robert Welch, Inc.

Attorney (P) v. Publisher (D)

418 U.S. 323 (1974).

NATURE OF CASE: Action for defamation.

FACT SUMMARY: Gertz (P) sued Robert Welch, Inc. (D), a publisher of a John Birch Society newsletter, when Welch (D) published an article calling Gertz (P) a long-time communist who helped frame a Chicago policeman's conviction for murder, all of which was untrue.

🏛 RULE OF LAW
In an action for defamation, a private individual must show the publisher to be at fault and may recover no more than actual damages when liability is not based on a showing of knowledge of falsity or reckless disregard for the truth.

FACTS: Robert Welch, Inc. (D) published "American Opinion," a monthly newsletter of the John Birch Society. An article appeared in that publication purporting to illustrate that Gertz (P) framed a policeman for the murder of a child of Gertz's (P) clients. The article also alleged Gertz (P) was a member of communist organizations. At trial, the evidence showed that managing editor of "American Opinion" knew nothing of the defamatory content but had relied on the reputation and accuracy of the author. The jury found the matter libelous per se and not privileged and awarded a $50,000 judgment, but the judge applied the *New York Times* standard as pertaining to any discussion of a public issue without regard to the status of the person defamed. Judgment n.o.v. was entered for Welch (D). The court of appeals affirmed, and Gertz (P) appealed.

ISSUE: In an action for defamation, must a private individual show the publisher to be at fault and recover no more than actual damages when liability is not based on a showing of knowledge of falsity or reckless disregard for the truth?

HOLDING AND DECISION: (Powell, J.) Yes. In an action for defamation, a private individual must show the publisher to be at fault and may recover no more than actual damages when liability is not based on a showing of knowledge of falsity or reckless disregard for the truth. The *New York Times* standard applies to public figures and public officials, but the state interest in compensating injury to reputation of private individuals requires that a different rule should apply to them. A public figure or official has greater access to the media to counteract false statements than private individuals normally enjoy. Being more vulnerable to injury, the private individual deserves greater protection and recovery. As long as the states do not impose liability without fault, the states themselves may define the appropriate standard of liability for a publisher of defamatory matter injurious to a private person. And the states may not permit the recovery of presumed or punitive damages, at least when liability is not based on a showing of knowledge of falsity or reckless disregard for the truth. Juries' largely uncontrolled discretion to award damages beyond the suffered loss inhibits the exercise of free speech. Also, the doctrine of presumed damages invites juries to punish unpopular opinion rather than compensate an injured party. The states have no interest in compensating petitioners with awards far in excess of actual injury. Here, Gertz (P) was not publicly involved. The public figure question should look to the nature and extent of an individual's participation in the controversy giving rise to the action. Reversed and remanded for new trial, as the jury was allowed to impose liability without fault and presume damages without proof of damages.

DISSENT: (Brennan, J.) "We strike the proper accommodation between avoidance of media self-censorship and protection of individual reputations only when we require states to apply the *New York Times'* knowing-or-reckless falsity standard in civil libel actions concerning media reports of the involvement of private individuals in events of public or general interest."

DISSENT: (White, J.) Federalizing major aspects of libel law is a radical change and a severe invasion of the prerogatives of the states not shown to be necessitated by present circumstances or required by the First Amendment. Neither *New York Times* nor the First Amendment should deprive this private citizen of his historic recourse to redress damaging falsehoods. The risk of falsehood is here shifted to the victim. While a statement may be wholly false, wrong, and unjustified, a defamation case will be dismissed if the victim cannot prove negligence or other fault.

▌ ANALYSIS

The majority advances the view that it is necessary to restrict victims of defamation who do not prove knowledge of falsity or reckless disregard for the truth to compensation for actual injury only. Actual injury is not limited to out-of-pocket loss. Actual harm includes impairment of reputation and standing in the community, personal humiliation, and mental anguish and suffering. While the Court discusses that juries in the past were tempted to award excess damages, there was no proof that trial judges have failed to keep judgments within reasonable bounds. This

Continued on next page.

decision has not yet established a clear trend as to its application.

■════■

Quicknotes

DEFAMATION An intentional false publication, communicated publicly in either oral or written form, subjecting a person to scorn, hatred or ridicule, or injuring him or her in relation to his or her occupation or business.

JUDGMENT N.O.V. A judgment entered by the trial judge reversing a jury verdict if the jury's determination has no basis in law or fact.

LIBEL PER SE A false or malicious publication that subjects a person to scorn, hatred or ridicule, or that injures him in relation to his occupation or business of such an extreme nature that the law will presume that the person has suffered such injury.

■════■

Florida Star v. B.J.F.

Newspaper (D) v. Rope victim (P)

491 U.S. 524 (1989).

NATURE OF CASE: Appeal of award of damages for invasion of privacy.

FACT SUMMARY: The Florida Star (D) published the name of rape victim B.J.F. (P), which it had lawfully obtained.

RULE OF LAW
A state may not prohibit a newspaper from publishing the name of a crime victim when it obtains the information lawfully.

FACTS: Florida enacted a statute prohibiting the publication of the names of rape victims. The Florida Star (D), having obtained the name of rape victim B.J.F. (P) from a police report, published her name. B.J.F. (P) brought an action alleging invasion of privacy. A jury awarded $100,000. The Supreme Court granted review.

ISSUE: May a state prohibit a newspaper from publishing the name of a crime victim when it obtains the information lawfully?

HOLDING AND DECISION: (Marshall, J.) No. A state may not prohibit a newspaper from publishing the name of a rape victim when it obtains the information lawfully. When a newspaper lawfully obtains information, a state may not prohibit publication thereof absent a need to further a state interest of the highest order. The interests cited here are safety of the victim, privacy of the victim, and the goal of encouraging victims to report. As to the privacy argument, considering that the information was obtained from a public record, little merit can be found in that. As to the victim's safety, the law is underinclusive, as it does not prohibit dissemination of such information in ways other than the mass media. The rebuttal against the reporting argument is basically the same. Since the law does not properly advance a public interest of the highest order, the law is contrary to the First Amendment. Reversed.

CONCURRENCE: (Scalia, J.) The underinclusiveness of the law alone makes it invalid.

DISSENT: (White, J.) The bases of the Court's decision are wrong. A major difference exists between a release of information by a government agency and mass media dissemination. Also, it is proper for a legislature to decide that mass media dissemination of harmful information has a unique capacity to do damage. This invalidates the underinclusiveness argument.

ANALYSIS

The Court took pains to point out the scope of its holding. It stated that it did not hold that truthful information will always be constitutionally protected, or that there is no unprotectable zone of privacy. However, the Court offered no dicta to indicate where the boundaries might lie.

Quicknotes

INVASION OF PRIVACY The violation of an individual's right to be protected against unwarranted interference in his personal affairs, falling into one of four categories: (1) appropriating the individual's likeness or name for commercial benefit; (2) intrusion into the individual's seclusion; (3) public disclosure of private facts regarding the individual; and (4) disclosure of facts placing the individual in a false light.

Paris Adult Theatre I v. Slaton

Film theatre (D) v. State (P)

413 U.S. 49 (1973).

NATURE OF CASE: Civil proceeding to enjoin continued showing of two adult films.

FACT SUMMARY: Two adult films were shown at theatres (D) which advertised the nature of the films and required proof that all patrons were over 21.

🏛 RULE OF LAW
A state can forbid the dissemination of obscene material to consenting adults to preserve the quality of the community and to prevent the possibility of resulting antisocial behavior.

FACTS: Two movie theatres (D) in Atlanta showed "adult" films exclusively. The State of Georgia (P) sought to enjoin the showing of sexually explicit movies in these theatres (D) under an obscenity statute. It was determined that the exterior advertising was not obscene or offensive, but that there were signs at the entrance stating that patrons must be 21 years of age and able to prove it. There was a further warning that those who would be offended by nudity should not enter. However, the films in question included, in addition to nudity, various simulated sex acts.

ISSUE: Can a state forbid the dissemination of obscene material to consenting adults to preserve the quality of the community and to prevent the possibility of resulting antisocial behavior?

HOLDING AND DECISION: (Burger, C.J.) Yes. A state can forbid the dissemination of obscene material to consenting adults to preserve the quality of the community and to prevent the possibility of resulting antisocial behavior. Even if exposure to juveniles and unwilling observers is prevented, the state has a further interest in preserving the quality of life, the community environment, and possible threats to public safety, which will allow the regulation of obscenity. Here, even though only consenting adults are involved, the state can make a judgment that public exhibition of obscenity has a tendency to injure the community and can, therefore, enjoin the distribution of obscenity.

DISSENT: (Brennan, J.) Prior obscenity standards have proved unworkable because they fail to give adequate notice of the definition of obscenity, producing a chilling effect on constitutionally protected speech. Because of the vague nature of these standards, every case is marginal, producing a vast number of constitutional questions which creates institutional stress in the judicial system. States do have a valid interest in protecting children and unconsenting adults from exposure to allegedly obscene material, but other possible state interests, as discussed in the majority opinion, are vague, speculative, and cannot be proven. Therefore, in the absence of threat of exposure to juveniles or unconsenting adults, material cannot be suppressed, but the state can regulate the manner of distribution.

DISSENT: (Douglas, J.) Art and literature reflect tastes; and tastes, like musical appreciation, are not reducible to precise definitions; hence, "obscenity" should not be deemed an exception to the First Amendment. Matters of taste, like matters of belief, turn on the idiosyncrasies of individuals.

▶ ANALYSIS

Interestingly, Justice Douglas in his dissent notes that he never reads nor sees the materials coming to the Court under charges of obscenity on the theory that "I have thought the First Amendment made it unconstitutional for me to act as a censor."

━■━

Quicknotes

ENJOIN The ordering of a party to cease the conduct of a specific activity.

FIRST AMENDMENT Prohibits Congress from enacting any law respecting an establishment of religion, prohibiting the free exercise of religion, abridging freedom of speech or the press, the right of peaceful assembly and the right to petition for a redress of grievances.

━■━

Miller v. California

Advertiser (D) v. State (P)

413 U.S. 15 (1973).

NATURE OF CASE: Criminal prosecution for knowingly distributing obscene matter.

FACT SUMMARY: Miller (D) sent out advertising brochures for adult books to unwilling recipients.

RULE OF LAW

Material is obscene and not protected by the First Amendment if: (1) the average person, applying contemporary community standards, would find that the work, taken as a whole, appeals to the prurient interest; (2) the work depicts in a patently offensive way sexual conduct specifically defined by the applicable state law; and (3) the work, taken as a whole, lacks serious literary, artistic, political, or scientific value.

FACTS: Miller (D) conducted a mass mailing campaign to advertise the sale of adult books. The advertising brochures were themselves found obscene. These brochures were sent to unwilling recipients who had not requested the material. Miller (D) was convicted of violating a statute which forbade knowingly distributing obscene matter.

ISSUE: Is the *Memoirs* requirement that material must be "utterly without redeeming social value" to be considered obscene a proper constitutional standard?

HOLDING AND DECISION: (Burger, C.J.) No. The proper standard for judging obscenity is (1) whether the average person, applying contemporary community standards, would find that the work, taken as a whole, appeals to the prurient interest; (2) whether the work depicts in a patently offensive way sexual conduct specifically defined by the applicable state law; and (3) whether the work, taken as a whole, lacks serious literary, artistic, political, or scientific value. If material meets this definition of obscenity, then the state can prohibit its distribution if the mode of distribution entails the risk of offending unwilling recipients or exposing the material to juveniles. The burden of proof of the *Memoirs* test [*Memoirs v. Massachusetts*, 383 U.S. 413 (1966)] that the material be utterly without redeeming value, is virtually impossible for the prosecution to meet and must be abandoned. There is no fixed national standard of "prurient interest" or "patently offensive" and these first two parts of the test are questions of fact to be resolved by the jury by applying contemporary community standards.

DISSENT: (Douglas, J.) Until a civil proceeding has placed a tract beyond the pale, no criminal prosecution should be sustained. Certainly, men should not be sent to prison or fined when they had no "fair warning" that what they did was criminal conduct. Only after a specific book, play, paper or movie has been adjudged obscene, should it be possible to criminally charge someone with publishing, showing, or displaying that particular work.

DISSENT: (Brennan, J.) The obscenity statute at issue is overly broad and unconstitutional. Courts historically have been unable to provide rules to discern between protected sexually explicit speech and obscene speech. It is likely impossible to balance community interests with free speech interests and still have a bright-line rule. Obscenity is typically defined within the parameters of the defining person's experience, tastes, and objectives. The Court must set forth a standard so that the lower courts do not continue developing multiple, vague tests. The existing vague statutes also create a problem for those attempting to abide by the law without a true sense of what violates it. A bright-line rule would undoubtedly protect government action and intrude upon First Amendment protections. Today's decision provides that works must have "serious" value, which will render some works obscene although admittedly retaining some social value. This does not provide fairer notice to the public of what constitutes obscenity. The Court is left with only a case-by-case analysis. Allowing the lower courts significant deference in the obscenity determination does not solve the problem because those cases would lead to mixed results with no clear rule to follow. Suppressing all sexual materials is not the answer because of the violation of the First and Fourteenth Amendments. States must have the option to regulate materials but cannot suppress them altogether.

ANALYSIS

The *Miller* test of obscenity is the most current test. If the three requirements are met, then the material in question is considered obscene and outside the protection of the First Amendment. *Miller* is a turnaround from *Memoirs* for many reasons: the *Memoirs* standard was too difficult to prove and the lower courts had no clear cut guidelines because *Memoirs* was a plurality opinion. The Court decided to use local community standards to allow greater jury power, and the Court was beginning to feel institutional pressures, since every obscenity question was a constitutional question. Therefore, *Miller* was an attempt by the Court to decentralize decisionmaking.

Continued on next page.

Quicknotes

FIRST AMENDMENT Prohibits Congress from enacting any law respecting an establishment of religion, prohibiting the free exercise of religion, abridging freedom of speech or the press, the right of peaceful assembly and the right to petition for a redress of grievances.

OBSCENITY Conduct tending to corrupt the public morals by its indecency or lewdness.

Cohen v. California

Citizen (D) v. State (P)

403 U.S. 15 (1971).

NATURE OF CASE: Criminal prosecution for violation of disturbing the peace statute.

FACT SUMMARY: Cohen (D) wore a jacket with the words "Fuck the Draft" on it in a courthouse corridor and was arrested and convicted under a disturbing the peace statute.

> 🏛 **RULE OF LAW**
> A state cannot bar the use of offensive words either because such words are inherently likely to cause a violent reaction or because the state wishes to eliminate such words to protect the public morality.

FACTS: Cohen (D) was arrested in a courthouse because he was wearing a jacket bearing the words, "Fuck the Draft." Cohen (D) did not engage in any act of violence or any other unlawful act. There was also no evidence that anyone who saw the jacket became violently aroused or even protested the jacket. Cohen (D) testified that he wore the jacket to inform people of his feelings against the Vietnam war and the draft. He was convicted under a statute prohibiting "maliciously and willfully disturbing the peace or quiet ... by offensive conduct." The state court held that "offensive conduct" meant conduct which had a tendency to provoke others to disturb the peace.

ISSUE: Can a state constitutionally prevent the use of certain words on the ground that the use of such words is offensive conduct?

HOLDING AND DECISION: (Harlan, J.) No. A state cannot constitutionally prohibit the use of offensive words. Here, Cohen (D) could not be punished for criticizing the draft, so the statute could be upheld, if at all, only as a regulation of the manner, not the substantive content, of his speech. Cohen's (D) speech does not come within any of the exceptions to the general rule that the form and content of speech cannot be regulated: (1) this is not a prohibition designed to protect courthouse decorum because the statute is not so limited; (2) this is not an obscenity case because Cohen's (D) words were not erotic; (3) this is not a case of fighting words which are punishable as inherently likely to provoke a violent reaction because here the words were not directed as a personal insult to any person; and (4) this is not a captive audience problem since a viewer could merely avert his eyes, there is no evidence of objection by those who saw the jacket, and the statute is not so limited. The state tries to justify the conviction because the words are inherently likely to cause a violent reaction, but this argument cannot be upheld because these are not fighting words and there is no evidence that words that are merely offensive would cause such a response. Next the state justifies the conviction on the ground that the state is guardian of the public morality. This argument is unacceptable because "offensive" is an unlimited concept and forbidding the use of such words would also cause the risk of suppressing the accompanying ideas. Therefore, there are no valid state interests which support the regulation of offensive words in public. Reversed.

DISSENT: (Blackmun, J.) Cohen's (D) conviction can be upheld both because his speech was fighting words and also because his act was conduct and not speech. Additionally, the state court subsequently restricted the statute in question to the fighting words context, so the case should be remanded and reconsidered under this construction.

▶ ANALYSIS

This case reasserts the *Chaplinsky* holding that fighting words are not protected by the First Amendment. See *Chaplinsky v. New Hampshire*, 315 U.S. 568 (1942). Fighting words, then, are only those words which are likely to cause an immediate breach of the peace by another person and are not just offensive words. More importantly, this case holds that a state has no valid interest in preventing the use of offensive words when there is no competing privacy interest. Here, the public in general has no right to protection from hearing either offensive words or offensive ideas.

■━■

Quicknotes

FIGHTING WORDS Unprotected speech that inflicts injury by its very utterance and provokes violence from the audience.

FIRST AMENDMENT Prohibits Congress from enacting any law respecting an establishment of religion, prohibiting the free exercise of religion, abridging freedom of speech or the press, the right of peaceful assembly and the right to petition for a redress of grievances.

■━■

United States v. O'Brien

Federal government (P) v. Draft card burner (D)

391 U.S. 367 (1968).

NATURE OF CASE: Appeal from conviction for draft card burning.

FACT SUMMARY: O'Brien (D) was convicted of a violation of a federal statute after he publicly burned his draft card during a demonstration against the compulsory draft and the war in Vietnam.

🏛 RULE OF LAW
When both speech and non-speech elements are combined in the same conduct, a sufficiently important governmental interest in regulating the non-speech element can justify incidental limitations of First Amendment freedoms.

FACTS: During a public demonstration directed against the compulsory draft and the war in Vietnam, O'Brien (D) and several others burned their Selective Service Registration Certificates. His act was witnessed by several Federal Bureau of Investigation (FBI) agents who arrested him. The arrest was for violating a federal statute prohibiting the knowing destruction or knowing mutilation of a Selective Service Certificate. The act also prohibited any changes, alterations, or forgeries of the Certificates. O'Brien (D) was convicted and now appeals, contending a violation of his First Amendment right to free speech.

ISSUE: When both speech and non-speech elements are combined in the same conduct, can a sufficiently important governmental interest in regulating the non-speech element justify incidental limitations of First Amendment freedoms?

HOLDING AND DECISION: (Warren, C.J.) Yes. When both speech and non-speech elements are combined in the same conduct, a sufficiently important governmental interest in regulating the non-speech element can justify incidental limitations of First Amendment freedoms. The Court considered two aspects of O'Brien's (D) appeal. First, that the statute was unconstitutional in its application to him, and secondly, that the statute was unconstitutional as enacted. Where conduct is composed of speech and non-speech elements, the speaker can invoke his freedom of speech rights to defend against unwarranted governmental interference. What must be determined is whether the attempted regulation of the nonspeech element also impermissibly inhibits the speech aspect. An incidental restriction on speech can be justified where the government can show a substantial interest in furthering a constitutional power which is not directed at the suppression of speech. In order to facilitate the implementation of its power to

raise and support armies, Congress has enacted a system for classifying individuals as to eligibility for military service. The Selective Service cards provide an efficient and reasonable method for identifying those persons previously deemed fit for military service should a national emergency arise. The Court found the requirement that the card be in the possession of the holder to be a valid requirement. The Court also found an independent justification for both the possession requirement and the prohibition against mutilation or destruction. While admitting some overlap, the possession requirement was intended for a smooth functioning of the draft system while the prohibition against mutilation was a sabotage prevention measure. A person could destroy another's card while retaining his own intact. The statute was intended as a necessary and proper method to carry out a vital governmental interest. No reasonable alternative is apparent and the narrow construction of the statute indicates it was not intended to suppress communication. As to the contention the statute was unconstitutional on its face, the Court found congressional intent to be the smooth functioning of the draft system, not the suppression of anti-war sentiment. Reversed.

CONCURRENCE: (Harlan, J.) This statute did not prohibit all means of expressing the ideas O'Brien (D) sought to advance. He was free to communicate his concepts in a variety of ways that did not conflict with other governmental interests.

DISSENT: (Douglas, J.) Both the litigants and this Court have failed to address the basic issue of whether the government can enforce conscription for all undeclared war and the case should be remanded for a trial on that point.

▶ ANALYSIS

Many articles written about this decision have been critical of the Court's superficial analysis of the interests involved on both sides of this case. The commentators felt that O'Brien's (D) contention that the draft card was not a vital document was dismissed out of hand. They also felt there should have been a more probing analysis of the operation of the Selective Service System and an examination of the actual, not supposed, importance of the draft card in that system. The strongest criticism of this case has been that the Court justified the suppression of expression, not on the basis of a compelling interest, but on a bureaucratic system designed for convenience. There was no analysis of alternative systems. Finally, some observers

Continued on next page.

saw in this decision a desire to counterbalance the long string of cases decided by the Warren Court upholding individual rights in the face of much stronger governmental interests.

■══■

Quicknotes

FIRST AMENDMENT Prohibits Congress from enacting any law respecting an establishment of religion, prohibiting the free exercise of religion, abridging freedom of speech or the press, the right of peaceful assembly and the right to petition for a redress of grievances.

FREEDOM OF SPEECH The right to express oneself without governmental restrictions on the content of that expression.

■══■

Texas v. Johnson

State (P) v. Flag burner (D)

491 U.S. 397 (1989).

NATURE OF CASE: Appeal of conviction for flag desecration.

FACT SUMMARY: Johnson (D) was convicted under a Texas (P) statute criminalizing desecration of the American flag.

🏛 RULE OF LAW
A government may not criminalize desecration of the American flag as an act of protest.

FACTS: As part of a protest, Johnson (D) burned an American flag. Johnson (D) was prosecuted under a Texas (P) law criminalizing desecration of the American flag. The court of appeals found the statute in violation of the First Amendment. The Supreme Court granted certiorari.

ISSUE: May a government criminalize desecration of the American flag as an act of protest?

HOLDING AND DECISION: (Brennan, J.) No. A government may not criminalize desecration of the American flag as an act of protest. One doing this is engaging in an act of expression, an act protected under the First Amendment. Any restriction on such expression requires an interest unrelated to stifling such expression. One proffered interest is the avoidance of breaches of the peace. However, the Court is not satisfied that breaches of the peace necessarily follow from the conduct here proscribed. In fact, in this case there was none. The second proffered interest is the necessity of respecting the flag as a symbol of national unity. As this interest necessarily involves stifling protected expression, the most rigorous scrutiny must be applied. Under this analysis, the law cannot pass muster. It is underinclusive, as there are other items, such as the Presidential Seal and the Constitution, that are similar symbols. More importantly, one does not advance respect for the flag by limiting the freedom it represents. Persuasion, not sanction, is the proper manner for this. For these reasons, the law violates the First Amendment. Reversed.

CONCURRENCE: (Kennedy, J.) The perspective of the dissenters is understandable, and the decision here made is not an agreeable one. Nonetheless, the First Amendment requires it to be made, and this Court must make it.

DISSENT: (Rehnquist, C.J.) The flag is not simply an idea competing in the marketplace of ideas. It is a unique national symbol deserving special protection. Furthermore, it is fallacious to suggest that burning the flag does not run a serious risk of leading to breaches of the peace.

DISSENT: (Stevens, J.) One wishing to denounce the United States has many options that are absolutely protected under the First Amendment. The burden of proscribing this one manner is trivial and is outweighed by the damage done to this unique symbol.

▶ ANALYSIS

Johnson (D) made a facial challenge to the statute. The Court chose instead to rule on the law as it was applied to him. A state could prohibit desecration of the flag when not done as an act of expression, said the Court. Cited as an example was a tired man dragging a flag rather than carrying it.

■=■

Quicknotes

CERTIORARI A discretionary writ issued by a superior court to an inferior court in order to review the lower court's decisions; the Supreme Court's writ ordering such review.

FIRST AMENDMENT Prohibits Congress from enacting any law respecting an establishment of religion, prohibiting the free exercise of religion, abridging freedom of speech or the press, the right of peaceful assembly and the right to petition for a redress of grievances.

■=■

Virginia State Board of Pharmacy v. Virginia Citizens Consumer Council

State agency (D) v. Consumer group (P)

425 U.S. 748 (1976).

NATURE OF CASE: Action for declaratory judgment.

FACT SUMMARY: The Virginia State Board of Pharmacy (D) is charged with enforcing a state law which makes it illegal for a pharmacist to advertise the prices of his prescription drugs.

RULE OF LAW
The First Amendment guarantee of freedom of speech extends to the recipients as well as the sources of the speech; and, as such, the consumer's interest in the free flow of advertising information brings such "commercial speech" within the protection of the First Amendment.

FACTS: Virginia law provides that licensed pharmacists are guilty of "unprofessional conduct" if they advertise "in any manner whatsoever, any amount, price, fee, premium, discount, rebate or credit terms . . . for any drugs which may be dispensed only by prescription." Virginia Citizens Consumer Council (P) is comprised of Virginia residents who require prescription drugs. Citing statistics which show that drugs vary in price strikingly from outlet to outlet (e.g., from $2.59 to $6 for one drug), they filed this action to have the advertising ban declared an unconstitutional infringement on their First Amendment right to free speech. From a judgment for the Consumer Council (P), the Virginia State Board of Pharmacy (D) appealed contending that "commercial speech" such as this is not protected by the First Amendment.

ISSUE: Does the First Amendment guarantee of freedom of speech extend to the recipients as well as the sources of the speech; and, as such, does the consumer's interest in the free flow of advertising information bring such "commercial speech" within the protection of the First Amendment?

HOLDING AND DECISION: (Blackmun, J.) Yes. The First Amendment guarantee of freedom of speech extends to the recipients as well as the sources of the speech; and, as such, the consumer's interest in the free flow of advertising information brings such "commercial speech" within the protection of the First Amendment. The traditional rule that "commercial speech" is not protected has been gradually eroded by the Court and, today, it is set to rest. Advertising, however tasteless, is information nevertheless, and entitled to constitutional deference thereby. To be sure, the holding today does not prevent reasonable regulation as to "time, place and manner" or prevent illegal or misleading speech. It only recognizes the legitimacy of commercial speech for First Amendment purposes.

CONCURRENCE: (Stewart, J.) Today's ruling in no way narrows the government power to promulgate broad regulations for the protection of the public from false or deceptive advertising.

DISSENT: (Rehnquist, J.) The Court today improperly overrules a legislative determination that advertising by pharmacists is not in the public interest.

ANALYSIS

Justice Burger's concurrence to the contrary notwithstanding, this case has brought many observers to the conclusion that advertising bans on professionals are no longer constitutional. Indeed, the American Bar Association and several state bar associations have begun to promulgate standards for advertising by attorneys which will protect the public from the perceived evils of a competitive bar. *Consumer Council* claims to overrule the 1951 case of *Breard v. Alexandria*, 341 U.S. 622 (1951). Note, however, that the ban on door-to-door sales upheld therein would appear to be precisely the kind of "time, place, and manner restriction" which the Court in *Consumer Council* expressly sanctioned.

■==■

Quicknotes

COMMERCIAL SPEECH Any speech that proposes a commercial transaction, or promotes products or services.

FIRST AMENDMENT Prohibits Congress from enacting any law respecting an establishment of religion, prohibiting the free exercise of religion, abridging freedom of speech or the press, the right of peaceful assembly and the right to petition for a redress of grievances.

■==■

Lorillard Tobacco Co. v. Reilly

Tobacco manufacturers (P) v. Attorney General of Massachusetts (D)

533 U.S. 525 (2001).

NATURE OF CASE: Appeal from upholding the constitutionality of Massachusetts's regulations governing outdoor advertising of the sale of tobacco.

FACT SUMMARY: Tobacco manufacturers argued that Massachusetts's regulations governing outdoor advertising of the sale of tobacco was so overinclusive as to violate the First Amendment.

🏛 **RULE OF LAW**
State regulations that prohibit smokeless tobacco or cigar advertising within a 1,000-foot radius of a school or playground violate the First Amendment.

FACTS: In 1999, the Attorney General of Massachusetts (D) promulgated comprehensive regulations governing the advertising and sale of cigarettes, smokeless tobacco, and cigars. A section of these rules consisted of outdoor advertising regulations prohibiting smokeless tobacco or cigar advertising within a 1,000-foot radius of a school or playground. Lorillard Tobacco Co. (P) and other tobacco manufacturers sued the Attorney General (D) in federal district court claiming that the outdoor advertising regulations, inter alia, violated the First Amendment by the state's overinclusiveness in its effort to prevent tobacco sales to minors. The district court held the regulations to be valid and enforceable. The federal court of appeals affirmed on this issue, and Lorillard Tobacco Co. (P) appealed.

ISSUE: Do state regulations that prohibit smokeless tobacco or cigar advertising within a 1,000-foot radius of a school or playground violate the First Amendment?

HOLDING AND DECISION: (O'Connor, J.) Yes. State regulations that prohibit smokeless tobacco or cigar advertising within a 1,000-foot radius of a school or playground violate the First Amendment. Whatever the strength of the Massachusetts Attorney General's (D) evidence to justify the outdoor advertising regulations as to tobacco, this Court concludes that the regulations do not satisfy the critical inquiry in this case, which requires a reasonable fit between the means and ends of the regulatory scheme. The broad sweep of the regulations indicates that the Attorney General (D) did not carefully calculate the costs and benefits associated with the burden on speech imposed by the regulations. The 1,000-foot radius of a school or playground prohibition comprises prohibition of such advertising "in a substantial portion" of the major metropolitan areas of Massachusetts. The substantial geographical reach of these regulations is compounded by other factors. The ban includes not only advertising outside

an establishment, but also advertising inside a store if visible from outside the store. In some geographical areas, these regulations would constitute nearly a complete ban on the communication of truthful information about smokeless tobacco and cigars to adult consumers. Furthermore, there is here a lack of tailoring; to the extent that studies have identified particular advertising and promotion practices that appeal to youth, tailoring would involve targeting those practices while permitting others. As crafted, the regulations make no distinction among practices on this basis. The state's interest in preventing underage tobacco use is substantial, and even compelling, but it is no less true that the sale and use of tobacco products by adults is a legal activity. Tobacco retailers and manufacturers have an interest in conveying truthful information about their products to adults, and adults have a corresponding interest in receiving truthful information about tobacco products. As the state protects children from tobacco advertisements, tobacco manufacturers and retailers and their adult consumers still have a protected interest in communication. The Attorney General (D) has failed to show that the outdoor advertising regulations for smokeless tobacco and cigars are not more extensive than necessary to advance the state's substantial interest in preventing underage tobacco use. Reversed.

CONCURRENCE: (Kennedy, J.) The obvious overbreadth of the outdoor advertising restrictions suffice to invalidate them.

CONCURRENCE: (Thomas, J.) An asserted government interest in keeping people ignorant by suppressing expression is per se illegitimate and can no more justify regulation of commercial speech than it can justify regulation of noncommercial speech. A prohibited zone defined solely by circles drawn around schools and playgrounds is necessarily overinclusive, regardless of the radii of the circles.

CONCURRENCE AND DISSENT: (Souter, J.) The case should be remanded for a review of the constitutionality of the distance limitation of 1,000 feet.

CONCURRENCE AND DISSENT: (Stevens, J.) Because the present record does not enable the Court to adjudicate the merits of the parties' claims on summary judgment, the Court should vacate the lower court's decision and remand for trial on the constitutionality of the outdoor advertising regulations.

Continued on next page.

▶ *ANALYSIS*

In *Lorillard*, the Supreme Court noted that a careful calculation of the costs of a speech regulation does not mean that a state must demonstrate that there is no incursion on legitimate speech interests, but a speech regulation cannot unduly impinge on the speaker's ability to propose a commercial transaction and the adult listener's opportunity to obtain information about products.

■■■■

Quicknotes

FIRST AMENDMENT Prohibits Congress from enacting any law respecting an establishment of religion, prohibiting the free exercise of religion, abridging freedom of speech or the press, the right of peaceful assembly and the right to petition for a redress of grievances.

INTER ALIA Among other things.

■■■■

R.A.V. v. St. Paul

Cross burner (D) v. City (P)

505 U.S. 377 (1992).

NATURE OF CASE: Appeal of reversal of dismissal of disorderly conduct.

FACT SUMMARY: R.A.V. (D) burned a cross and was charged with violating St. Paul, Minnesota's (P) hate crime ordinance.

🏛 RULE OF LAW
The government may not proscribe some fighting words and permit others, where the distinction is based on content or viewpoint.

FACTS: A St. Paul, Minnesota (P) ordinance provided: "Whoever places on public or private property a [symbol], including, but not limited to, a burning cross or Nazi swastika, which one knows or has reasonable grounds to know arouses anger, alarm or resentment in others on the basis of race, color, creed, religion or gender commits disorderly conduct and shall be guilty of a misdemeanor." R.A.V. (D) allegedly burned a cross in the yard of a black family and was charged under the ordinance. R.A.V. (D) challenged the ordinance on First Amendment grounds. The Minnesota Supreme Court upheld the ordinance, limiting the reach of the ordinance to "fighting words." *Chaplinsky v. New Hampshire*, 315 U.S. 568 (1942). R.A.V. (D) appealed.

ISSUE: May the government proscribe some fighting words and permit others, where the distinction is based on content or viewpoint?

HOLDING AND DECISION: (Scalia, J.) No. The government may not proscribe some fighting words and permit others where the distinction is based on content or viewpoint. The government may proscribe fighting words, but proscribable categories of speech are not beyond the First Amendment. Speech may be proscribable for one reason, but not for another. For example, a city may ban obscenity, but not just obscenity which criticizes city government. Here, St. Paul (P) may prohibit the conduct that is fighting words, but may not, as it has, ban fighting words only if they go to the topics of "race, color, creed, religion or gender." This ordinance goes beyond content to viewpoint discrimination, prohibiting, for example, fighting words aimed at religion, while permitting fighting words aimed at religious opponents. Content discrimination may permissibly single out speech presenting a heightened version of the harm that is the basis for the category of proscribable speech (e.g., an obscenity law prohibiting only the most lascivious displays of sexual activity). Or it may single out speech with secondary effects (e.g., a law only prohibiting live obscene performances by minors, the

secondary effect being harm to minors). These bases for distinction ensure the restriction is not based on opposition to the speaker's message. Here, however, St. Paul (P) certainly attempted to suppress particular ideas. Reversed.

CONCURRENCE: (White, J.) The majority strikes down the ordinance for the wrong reason. The categorical approach is firmly entrenched in First Amendment law. Certain categories of speech are not protected by the First Amendment. Fighting words are not a means of expressing views; they are directed against individuals to provoke violence or inflict injury. It is inconsistent to hold that fighting words may be completely proscribed, but that the government may not treat some fighting words differently than others. The irrationally discriminatory laws which the majority is concerned about would be prohibited by the Equal Protection Clause. The majority's exceptions, while designed to cover obvious flaws in its rule, also swallow the rule.

CONCURRENCE: (Blackmun, J.) The majority seems to abandon the categorical approach, which will lead to a relaxation of the level of scrutiny applicable to content-based laws. No First Amendment values are compromised by prohibiting acts designed to drive minorities from their homes by cross burning, but there is great harm in preventing St. Paul (P) from specifically punishing race-based fighting words which prejudice the community. Nevertheless, the ordinance is overbroad and invalid.

CONCURRENCE: (Stevens, J.) Under First Amendment decisions core political speech is most protected, commercial speech and nonobscene, sexually explicit speech is more protected, and obscenity and fighting words are least protected. Even if the last category is not unprotected, it should not receive, as the majority gives it, as much protection as core political speech and more protection than commercial speech. The absolutist approaches of the majority and of Justice White are unsound. Courts must consider the content and context of the regulated speech and the scope of the restrictions.

▶ ANALYSIS

The majority also held that the ordinance failed to survive strict-scrutiny review. St. Paul (P) had a compelling interest in protecting the rights of certain group members to live where they wish in peace, but the ordinance was held not necessary to achieve this interest. The majority ruled a content-neutral ordinance could have achieved the same

Continued on next page.

results. Justice White disagreed, stating that the Court, as recently as *Burson v. Freeman*, 504 U.S. 191 (1992), has always rejected the view that a narrowly drawn, content-based ordinance is unconstitutional if the object of legislation could be achieved by banning a wider category of speech.

■≡■

Quicknotes

FIGHTING WORDS Unprotected speech that inflicts injury by their very utterance and proves violence from the audience.

■≡■

Near v. Minnesota

Publisher (D) v. State (P)

283 U.S. 697 (1931).

NATURE OF CASE: Action to abate publication of newspaper as a public nuisance.

FACT SUMMARY: Minnesota (P) sought to have an injunction issued against the Saturday Press (D), which was publishing articles charging public officials with dereliction and complicity in dealing with gangsters.

🏛 RULE OF LAW
A state statute which authorizes previous restraints on publication violates the liberty of the press guaranteed by the Fourteenth Amendment if such publication relates to the malfeasance of public officials.

FACTS: A Minnesota statute authorized abatement as a public nuisance of a "malicious, scandalous and defamatory" newspaper. The law permitted the defense of good motives and justifiable ends. The Saturday Press (the Press) (D) had published a series of articles which charged that gangsters were in control of gambling, bootlegging, and racketeering in Minneapolis, and that public officials were either derelict in their duties or had illicit relations with the gangsters. Minnesota (P) sought to abate further publication of the Press (D) which is "malicious, scandalous, or defamatory." The trial court issued a permanent injunction, and the Press (D) appealed.

ISSUE: Is a state statute which authorizes abatement of a newspaper publication dealing with the corruption of public officials unconstitutional?

HOLDING AND DECISION: (Hughes, C.J.) Yes. It is the chief purpose of the constitutional guaranty of freedom of press to prevent previous restraint on publication. Placing previous restraints on the press endangers the very nature of a free state. Only in exceptional circumstances may previous restraints be imposed. These would include where a government seeks to prevent actual obstruction to its recruiting service or the publication of the sailing dates of transports or the number and location of troops. Similarly, obscene publications, and incitements to acts of violence or the overthrow by force of orderly government, may be enjoined. However, previous restraint on a publication which seeks to expose the malfeasance of public officials is prohibited by the Fourteenth Amendment. Public officials have recourse against false accusations under the libel law. Finally, requiring newspapers to present proof of their good intentions is merely an additional step to a complete system of censorship. So far as the

Minnesota statute authorized the abatement proceedings against the Press (D), it is unconstitutional. Reversed.

DISSENT: (Butler, J.) The Minnesota statute does not operate as a "previous restraint on publication within the proper meaning of that phrase." It does not authorize administrative control in advance such as was formerly exercised by the licensers and censors but prescribes a remedy to be enforced by a suit in equity. Existing libel laws are ineffective to suppress the evils occasioned by false and malicious publications.

▶ ANALYSIS

"The issue is not whether the government may impose a particular restriction of substance in an area of public expression, such as forbidding obscenity in newspapers, but whether it may do so by a particular method, such as advance screening of newspaper copy. In other words, restrictions which could be validly imposed when enforced by subsequent punishment are, nevertheless, forbidden if attempted by prior restraint." Emerson, "The Doctrine of Prior Restraint," 20 L. & Contemp. Prob. 648 (1956). Traditionally, the judicial concern in prior restraint cases is on the broad discretion over free expression vested in administrative officers.

■═■

Quicknotes

FOURTEENTH AMENDMENT 42 U.S.C. § 1983 Defamation by state officials in connection with a discharge implies a violation of a liberty interest protected by the due process requirements of the United States Constitution.

FREEDOM OF THE PRESS The right to publish and publicly disseminate one's views.

PRIOR RESTRAINT A restriction imposed on speech imposed prior to its communication.

■═■

Times Film Corp. v. Chicago

Film corporation (P) v. City (D)

365 U.S. 43 (1961).

NATURE OF CASE: Appeal from denial of film permit.

FACT SUMMARY: Times Film Corp. (P) contended Chicago's (D) ordinance requiring films to be submitted for governmental approval before exhibition was an unconstitutional prior restraint on freedom of speech.

🏛 RULE OF LAW
Local governments may validly protect their citizens from exhibition of obscene material.

FACTS: Times Film Corp. (P) refused to submit its film "Don Juan" to the City of Chicago (D) for review prior to the issuance of a permit allowing its exhibition. The permit was refused, and Times (P) sued, challenging the ordinance requiring such submission on the basis it was an unconstitutional prior restraint on free speech. The trial and appellate courts upheld the ordinance, and the Supreme Court granted certiorari.

ISSUE: May local governments validly protect their citizens from exhibition of obscene material?

HOLDING AND DECISION: (Clark, J.) Yes. Local governments may validly protect their citizens from exhibitions of obscene material. It has long been recognized that obscenity is not protected speech. Thus there is no basis for holding invalid an ordinance imposing prior restraint on the publication of obscenity. Thus the ordinance was valid. Affirmed.

DISSENT: (Warren, C.J.) This holding invites invidious censorship not only in motion pictures but in all forms of communication.

▶ ANALYSIS

The obvious question presented by this case is: "What is obscene?" The second question is: "Who determines what is obscene?" Logically, these questions must be resolved before the holding in this case can be supported. Each piece of material must be judged according to the prevailing community standards and the existence of any redeeming social value inherent in the material.

Quicknotes

OBSCENITY Conduct tending to corrupt the public morals by its indecency or lewdness.

PRIOR RESTRAINT A restriction imposed on speech imposed prior to its communication.

RIGHT OF FREE SPEECH Right guaranteed by the first amendment to the United States Constitution prohibiting Congress from enacting any law abridging freedom of speech or the press.

New York Times Co. v. United States (The Pentagon Papers Case)

Newspaper (D) v. Federal government (P)

403 U.S. 713 (1971).

NATURE OF CASE: Action by federal government to restrain newspaper publication.

FACT SUMMARY: Government (P) sought to enjoin, in the interests of "national security," the New York Times (D) and the Post (D) from further publishing of portions of the "Pentagon Papers," a classified, "top secret" study.

🏛 RULE OF LAW
Any system of prior restraints on the freedom of the press bears a heavy presumption against its constitutional validity.

FACTS: During the Vietnam War, the New York Times (the Times) (D) and the Washington Post (the Post) (D) published portions of a study that the Government (P) had classified as "Top Secret." The classified study was entitled "History of U.S. Decision-Making Process on Viet Nam Policy," and was popularly known as the "Pentagon Papers." The Government (P), maintaining that "national security" interests were threatened by further publication, sought prior restraints against the Times (D) and the Post (D).

ISSUE: Must any system of prior restraints on the freedom of the press bear a heavy presumption against its constitutional validity?

HOLDING AND DECISION: (Per curiam) Yes. Any system of prior restraints of expression comes to the court bearing a heavy presumption against its constitutional validity. The Government (P) thus carries a heavy burden of showing justification for the enforcement of such a restraint. No restraining order or injunction will issue. Vacated.

CONCURRENCE: (Black, J.) The guarding of military and diplomatic secrets at the expense of informed representative government provides no real security for the Republic and would wipe out the First Amendment.

CONCURRENCE: (Douglas, J.) There is no congressional enactment barring the kind of publication in this case. Secrecy in government is fundamentally antidemocratic, perpetuating bureaucratic errors.

CONCURRENCE: (Brennan, J.) The First Amendment tolerates absolutely no prior restraints of the press predicated upon surmise or conjecture that untoward consequences may result. The country is not at war, and the Government (P) has failed to show that continued publication here would cause war, a nuclear holocaust, or would directly and immediately imperil our troops. The Government (P) must clearly define the basis for enlisting judicial aid in suppression of the press.

CONCURRENCE: (Stewart, J.) I cannot say that disclosure of any of the "Pentagon Papers" will surely result in direct, immediate, and irreparable damage to our nation or its people.

CONCURRENCE: (White, J.) The President, who is charged with conducting foreign policy and protecting the Nation's security, is entitled to an injunction when he can convince a court that the information to be revealed threatens "grave and irreparable" injury to the public interest. The injunction should issue whether or not the material to be published is classified, whether or not publication would be lawful under relevant criminal statutes enacted by Congress, and regardless of the circumstances by which the newspaper came into possession of the information. That burden, however, has not been met in the present case.

DISSENT: (Harlan, J.) The judiciary must satisfy itself that the subject matter of the dispute does lie within the proper compass of the President's foreign relations power. It may also properly insist that the determination that disclosure of the subject matter would irreparably impair the national security be made by the head of the Executive Department concerned (i.e., State or Defense) after actual personal consideration by that officer. However, since the very nature of executive decisions as to foreign policy is political, the judiciary should not go beyond these two inquiries to redetermine for itself the probable impact of disclosure on the national security. Even if some additional review is permitted, some deference must be given to the decision of the Executive Branch, a coequal partner in government.

DISSENT: (Blackmun, J.) First Amendment absolutism has never commanded a majority of this Court. What is needed here is a weighing, upon properly developed standards, of the broad right of the press to print and of the very narrow right of the Government to prevent. The question is one of proximity and degree.

▶ ANALYSIS

In *Pittsburgh Press Co. v. Pittsburgh Commission on Human Relations*, 413 U.S. 376 (1973), the Court upheld an administrative order which forbade a newspaper from carrying sex-designated "help wanted" ads, except for exempt jobs. Justice Powell, in writing for the majority, commented, "The

Continued on next page.

present order does not endanger arguably protected speech. Because the order is based on a continuing course of repetitive conduct, this is not a case in which the Court is asked to speculate as to the effect of publication. [Cf. *New York Times v. United States.*] Moreover, the order is clear and sweeps no more broadly than necessary. And because no interim relief was granted, the order will not have gone into effect until it was finally determined that the actions of Pittsburgh Press were unprotected."

■▬■

Quicknotes

INJUNCTION A court order requiring a person to do, or prohibiting that person from doing, a specific act.

■▬■

Branzburg v. Hayes

Reporters (D) v. Grand jury (P)

408 U.S. 665 (1972).

NATURE OF CASE: Appeal from contempt citations for failure to testify before state and federal grand juries.

FACT SUMMARY: Newsmen refused to testify before state and federal grand juries, claiming that their news sources were confidential.

🏛 RULE OF LAW
The First Amendment's freedom of press does not exempt a reporter from disclosing to a grand jury information that he has received in confidence.

FACTS: Branzburg (D), who had written articles for a newspaper about drug activities he had observed, refused to testify before a state grand jury regarding his information. Pappas (D), a television newsman, even though he wrote no story, refused to testify before a state grand jury on his experiences inside Black Panther headquarters. Caldwell (D), a reporter who had interviewed several Black Panther leaders, and written stories about the articles, refused to testify before a federal grand jury which was investigating violations of criminal statutes dealing with threats against the President and traveling interstate to incite a riot. Branzburg (D) and Pappas (D) were held in contempt.

ISSUE: Does the First Amendment protect a newsman from revealing his sources before a grand jury which has subpoenaed him to testify, even if the information is confidential?

HOLDING AND DECISION: (White, J.) No. The First Amendment does not invalidate every incidental burdening of the press that may result from the enforcement of civil or criminal statutes of general applicability. Newsmen cannot invoke a testimonial privilege not enjoyed by other citizens. The Constitution should not shield criminals who wish to remain anonymous from prosecution through disclosure. Forcing newsmen to testify will not impede the flow of news. The newsman may never be called. Many political groups will still turn to the reporter because they are dependent on the media for exposure. Grand jury proceedings are secret and the police are experienced in protecting informants. More importantly, the public's interest in news flow does not override the public's interest in deterring crime. Here, the grand juries were not probing at will without relation to existing need; the information sought was necessary to the respective investigations. A grand jury is not restricted to seeking information from non-newsmen—it may choose the best method for its task. The contempt citations are affirmed.

CONCURRENCE: (Powell, J.) The newsman always has resort to the courts to quash subpoenas where his testimony bears only a remote and tenuous relationship to the subject of the investigation.

DISSENT: (Douglas, J.) A newsman has an absolute right not to appear before a grand jury so as to have absolute privacy in uncovering information in the course of testing his hunches. Effective government depends upon a free flow of opinion and reporting.

DISSENT: (Stewart, J.) The press should not be treated as an investigating tool of the government. Fear of an unbridled subpoena power deters sources. The Court requests concrete, empirical studies but those are never required such studies to support a First Amendment right. The government should be compelled to prove that the desired information from the press is clearly relevant to the issue at hand, cannot be obtained through less intrusive means, and the government's interest in the information is compelling and overriding. Such a rule would protect the press and the public's right to a free flow of information while balancing judicial interests.

▶ ANALYSIS

Guidelines promulgated by the Attorney General for federal officials to follow when subpoenaing members of the press to testify before grand juries or at criminal trials included the following test for information: whether there is "sufficient reason to believe that the information sought is essential to a successful investigation" and cannot be obtained from non-press sources. However, in "emergencies and other unusual situations," "subpoenas which do not conform to the guidelines may be issued."

■=■

Quicknotes

CONTEMPT An act of omission that interferes with a court's proper administration of justice.

FIRST AMENDMENT Prohibits Congress from enacting any law respecting an establishment of religion, prohibiting the free exercise of religion, abridging freedom of speech or the press, the right of peaceful assembly and the right to petition for a redress of grievances.

FREEDOM OF THE PRESS The right to publish and publicly disseminate one's views.

■=■

Richmond Newspapers, Inc. v. Virginia

Newspaper (P) v. State (D)

448 U.S. 555 (1980).

NATURE OF CASE: Action to overturn a closure order.

FACT SUMMARY: At the behest of the criminal defendant and without objection by the prosecutor, a trial judge closed a criminal trial to the public and press, including Richmond Newspapers, Inc. (P).

🏛 RULE OF LAW
Absent an overriding interest articulated in findings, the trial of a criminal case must be open to the public, including the press.

FACTS: A criminal defendant facing his fourth trial on a murder charge moved to close his trial to the public and press to prevent information from "being shuffled back and forth" during recesses among witnesses and/or "contamination" of the jurors. The prosecutor did not object, so the judge granted the notice without specifically finding such was necessary to preserve the fairness of the trial and without considering less drastic measures to ensure a fair trial. Reporters from Richmond Newspapers, Inc. (P) were compelled to leave the courtroom. They appeared at a hearing later that same day on their motion to vacate the closure order. The judge denied their motion, and Richmond Newspapers (P) sought to overturn that ruling.

ISSUE: Must the trial of a criminal case be open to public and press unless there is an overriding interest articulated in findings?

HOLDING AND DECISION: (Burger, C.J.) Yes. A criminal trial must be open to the public and press unless there is an overriding interest articulated in findings, e.g., that closure is required to protect the defendant's superior right to a fair trial. The right of the public, and the press as its representative, to attend criminal trials is implicit in the guarantees of the First Amendment and cannot be disregarded. Reversed.

CONCURRENCE: (Brennan, J.) Public access to trials, in addition to being part of this country's tradition, serves to maintain public confidence in the administration of justice and acts as a type of check and balance on the judicial system. Absent compelling countervailing interests sufficient to reverse the presumption of openness that thus arises, closure of trials is constitutionally impermissible.

CONCURRENCE: (Stewart, J.) The First and Fourteenth Amendments clearly give the press and the public a right of access to trials themselves, civil as well as criminal, but it is not an absolute right. A judge may impose reasonable limitations upon the unrestricted occupation of a

courtroom by representatives of the press and members of the public, much like the legislature may impose reasonable time, place, and manner restrictions on the exercise of First Amendment freedoms. In this case, the judge did not even consider the right of the press and public.

CONCURRENCE: (White, J.) Had the Court been willing to accept the proposition advanced by four of us in *Gannett Co. v. DePasquale*, 443 U.S. 368 (1979), to construe the Sixth Amendment as forbidding exclusion of the public from criminal proceedings except in narrowly defined circumstances, this case would have been unnecessary. However, inasmuch as the First Amendment issue must be addressed in this case, I concur in the opinion of the Chief Justice.

CONCURRENCE: (Blackmun, J.) I continue to believe the right to a public trial is to be found where the Constitution explicitly placed it, in the Sixth Amendment, and that *Gannett* was in error insofar as it failed to recognize this principle. Setting the Sixth Amendment aside, however, I adopt the secondary position that the First Amendment must provide some measure of protection for public access to the trial.

CONCURRENCE: (Stevens, J.) This watershed case marks the first time the Court unequivocally holds that an arbitrary interference with access to important information about the operation of the government is an abridgement of the freedom of speech and of the press protected by the First Amendment. While I agree, I find it ironic that the Court should find more reason to recognize a right of access today than it did in prior cases whose facts seemed even more compelling.

DISSENT: (Rehnquist, J.) Constitutional review is not appropriate when a state denies public access to a trial after prosecution and defense agree to a closure order. The Constitution cannot be read to prohibit such a closure order and the issue is not a balancing of the press's rights with the defendant's rights.

▶ ANALYSIS

In the case of *Gannett Co. v. DePasquale*, 443 U.S. 368 (1979), the Court had faced the question of the right of public/press access to hearings on pretrial motions as opposed to trials. It refused to decide whether such a right existed under the Sixth Amendment, although broadly hinting that that amendment conferred a right only upon the defendant. Even if a public access right did exist, the

Continued on next page.

Court said, the circumstances of the case showed that the defendant's right to a fair trial required closure in that particular case. The decision left legal commentators and journalists confused as to the posture of the Court in this whole area of public access to criminal proceedings.

■═■

Quicknotes

FIRST AMENDMENT Prohibits Congress from enacting any law respecting an establishment of religion, prohibiting the free exercise of religion, abridging freedom of speech or the press, the right of peaceful assembly and the right to petition for a redress of grievances.

FOURTEENTH AMENDMENT Declares that no state shall make or enforce any law that shall abridge the privileges and immunities of citizens of the United States. No state shall deny to any person within its jurisdiction the equal protection of the laws.

■═■

International Society for Krishna Consciousness, Inc. v. Lee

Religious group (P) v. State authority (D)

505 U.S. 672 (1992).

NATURE OF CASE: Appeal of ruling upholding solicitation ban.

FACT SUMMARY: The Krishna (P) sought to overturn a regulation of the Port Authority of New York and New Jersey (D) prohibiting solicitation and leafleting in airport terminals.

> **RULE OF LAW**
> A ban on solicitation in airport terminals, which are not public forums, is reasonable and does not violate the First Amendment.

FACTS: The Krishna (P) perform a religious ritual that consists of going into public places to disseminate religious literature and solicit funds. The Port Authority (D) issued a regulation prohibiting sale of merchandise, sale or distribution of written material, and solicitation and receipt of funds inside the terminals at the three main New York City airports. These activities were allowed on the sidewalks outside the terminals. The Krishna (P) sued the Port Authority (D), including police superintendent Lee (D), claiming the regulation violated the First Amendment. The court of appeals upheld the ban as to solicitation, but not as to leafleting. The Krishna (P) appealed the solicitation ruling [while the Port Authority (D) appealed the leafleting decision in a companion case, *Lee v. International Society for Krishna Consciousness, Inc.*, 505 U.S. 830 (1992)].

ISSUE: Does a ban on solicitation in airport terminals violate the First Amendment?

HOLDING AND DECISION: (Rehnquist, C.J.) No. A solicitation ban in airport terminals is reasonable and does not violate the First Amendment. Airport terminals are not public forums. Airports are recent developments, with an even more recent history of use for religious and speech activities, so they are not traditional areas of public speech. Bus and train stations might be public forums, but airports have heightened security needs and are less compatible with certain expressive activity. Airports are commercial enterprises dedicated to the facilitation of air travel and do not have a primary purpose of "promoting the free exchange of ideas." As a speech restriction in a nonpublic forum, the regulation only must be reasonable. Solicitation disrupts airport traffic. Airport users are often in a hurry, and a missed flight creates major inconvenience. Face-to-face solicitation also presents risks of duress and fraud, and airport travelers on tight schedules are unlikely to report such activity. The sidewalk outside the terminal is a completely satisfactory alternative channel for solicitors.

Affirmed. [In a per curiam decision, the Court denied the Port Authority's (D) appeal, upholding the lower court opinion which overturned the leafleting ban.]

CONCURRENCE: (O'Connor, J.) Airports are not public forums. Speech restrictions in nonpublic forums must be reasonable in light of the forum's purpose. New York airports are open to travelers and nontravelers, and house restaurants, commercial and government offices, shops, and even a branch of Bloomingdale's. The Port Authority (D) is operating a shopping mall as well as an airport. Thus, while the Court accurately finds the solicitation ban reasonable, a ban on leafleting is not. A leaflet may be taken and read later; people need not stop. There is no disruption of traffic. The Port Authority (D) may issue only reasonable time, place, and manner restrictions on leafleting.

CONCURRENCE: (Kennedy, J.) Airports are public forums. Streets and sidewalks, quintessential public forums, have a primary purpose of transportation, just like airports. Airport terminals share with streets and sidewalks many characteristics that make them suitable as public forums. An airport is one of the few government-owned places where many people have extensive contact with other members of the public, so it is critical to preserve the area for protected speech. Such characteristics, not a tradition of speech activities, should determine whether a forum is public. The record indicates that when adequate time, place, and manner restrictions are in place, expressive activity is compatible with the uses of major airports.

CONCURRENCE AND DISSENT: (Souter, J.) Airports are public forums, thus both the leafleting and solicitation bans are unconstitutional. Government may not ban solicitation just because it could be coercive or fraudulent. A regulation aimed at coercion and fraud can be more narrowly tailored by making such conduct a crime, instead of banning solicitation altogether.

> **ANALYSIS**

The result of this case and its companion was to uphold solicitation restrictions but strike down the leafleting ban. The majority to uphold solicitation restrictions was six justices (Rehnquist; White, Scalia, and Thomas, who joined Rehnquist's opinion; O'Connor; and Kennedy). The majority joining the per curiam opinion to strike down the leafleting ban was five justices (O'Connor; Kennedy; and Souter,

Continued on next page.

Blackmun, and Stevens, who joined Kennedy's concurrence in the solicitation case as to the leafleting issue but dissented as to the solicitation issue).

■▬■

Quicknotes

FIRST AMENDMENT   Prohibits Congress from enacting any law respecting an establishment of religion, prohibiting the free exercise of religion, abridging freedom of speech or the press, the right of peaceful assembly and the right to petition for a redress of grievances.

■▬■

Lee v. International Society for Krishna Consciousness, Inc.

State authority (D) v. Religious group (P)

505 U.S. 830 (1992).

NATURE OF CASE: Appeal of order striking down leafleting ban.

FACT SUMMARY: The Krishna (P) sought to overturn a regulation of the Port Authority of New York and New Jersey (D) prohibiting solicitation and leafleting in airport terminals.

RULE OF LAW
A total ban on leafleting in airport terminals violates the First Amendment.

FACTS: The Krishna (P) perform a religious ritual which consists of going into public places to disseminate religious literature and solicit funds. The Port Authority (D) issued a regulation prohibiting sale of merchandise, sale or distribution of written material, and solicitation and receipt of funds inside the terminals at the three main New York City airports. These activities were allowed on the sidewalks outside the terminals. The Krishna (P) sued the Port Authority (D), including police superintendent Lee (D), claiming the regulation violated the First Amendment. The court of appeals upheld the ban as to solicitation, but not as to leafleting. The Port Authority (D) appealed the leafleting ruling [while the Krishna (P) appealed the solicitation decision in a companion case, *International Society for Krishna Consciousness, Inc. v. Lee*, 505 U.S. 672 (1992)].

ISSUE: Does a total ban on leafleting in airport terminals violate the First Amendment?

HOLDING AND DECISION: (Per curiam) Yes. A total ban on leafleting in airport terminals violates the First Amendment. Support for this rule is found in the concurrences to *International Society for Krishna Consciousness, Inc., v. Lee*. Affirmed.

DISSENT: (Rehnquist, C.J.) Leafleting presents risks of congestion similar to solicitation. Instead of simply taking a leaflet from the leafleter's hand, a person may choose to debate. Additionally, leaflets may be dropped, creating an eyesore, a safety hazard, and additional cleanup for airport staff. By striking down the ban on leafleting, the Court may have rendered meaningless its upholding of the solicitation ban. Monitoring leafleting to make sure that no solicitation occurs may prove as burdensome to the Port Authority (D) as the monitoring that would be required if soliciting were allowed.

terminals, as per its regulation, but instead limited them to a relatively uncongested part of the terminals. Justice O'Connor suggested that such a time, place, and manner restriction on leafleting would be constitutional. Chief Justice Rehnquist suggested that a total ban on leafleting might prove constitutional in the future if the Port Authority (D) develops evidence that a rule banning solicitation, but permitting leafleting is too burdensome to enforce.

Quicknotes

FIRST AMENDMENT Prohibits Congress from enacting any law respecting an establishment of religion, prohibiting the free exercise of religion, abridging freedom of speech or the press, the right of peaceful assembly and the right to petition for a redress of grievances.

⏵ ANALYSIS

During the pendency of this litigation, the Port Authority (D) did not ban Krishna (P) adherents completely from

Hill v. Colorado

Counselors (P) v. State (D)

530 U.S. 703 (2000).

NATURE OF CASE: Suit challenging constitutionality of a state statute.

FACT SUMMARY: Petitioners challenged the constitutionality of a Colorado statute regulating speech-conduct within 100 feet of the entrance to any health care facility.

> ## 🏛 RULE OF LAW
> A statute may be upheld as a valid time, place and manner regulation where it serves governmental interests that are significant and legitimate, the restrictions are content neutral and the statute is narrowly tailored to serve such interests, leaving open ample alternative channels for communication.

FACTS: Colorado (D) enacted a statute prohibiting a person within 100 feet of an entrance of a health care facility from "knowingly" coming with eight feet of another person entering that facility if the approach is to provide literature, display a sign, or attempt to protest or counsel the entering person. The statute does not prohibit the content of any speech or other forms of communication inside or outside the facility. Hill (P) claimed that the legislation was specifically enacted to affect abortion clinics, but the actual statute applies to all health care facilities throughout Colorado (D). Hill (P) also contends that the prohibited communications are protected by the First Amendment and that the affected public sidewalks, streets, and ways are traditionally public speech forums.

ISSUE: May a statute be upheld as a valid time, place and manner regulation where it serves governmental interests that are significant and legitimate, the restrictions are content neutral and the statute is narrowly tailored to serve such interests, leaving open ample alternative channels for communication?

HOLDING AND DECISION: (Stevens, J.) Yes. A statute may be upheld as a valid time, place and manner regulation where it serves governmental interests that are significant and legitimate, the restrictions are content neutral, and the statute is narrowly tailored to serve such interests, leaving open ample alternative channels for communication. While the petitioners enjoy First Amendment interests in communicating freely in areas which are "public forums," the state's interest may justify a special focus on unimpeded access to health care facilities and the avoidance of potential trauma to patients associated with confrontational protests. When balancing these competing interests it is important to recognize the significant difference between state restrictions on a speaker's right to

address a willing audience and those intended to protect listeners from unwanted communications. The right to free speech includes the right to attempt to persuade others to change their views, and may not be restricted simply because the speaker's message may be offensive to his audience. However, offensive speech is not always protected when it is so intrusive that the unwilling audience cannot avoid it. All of the lower court opinions upheld the statute as a valid content-neutral time, place and manner regulation. This is true for three reasons: (1) it does not regulate speech but rather some of the places where speech may occur; (2) it was not adopted because of disagreement with the message it conveys; and (3) the state's interests in protecting access and privacy and providing the police with clear guidelines are unrelated to the content of the demonstrators' speech. The petitioners argued that the statute is not content neutral because it applies to some oral communication. The Court rejects this argument since the statute here places no restrictions on and does not prohibit either a particular viewpoint or any subject matter that may be discussed by a speaker. Furthermore, it is narrowly tailored to serve the state's interest and leaves open ample alternative channels for communication.

CONCURRENCE: (Souter, J.) A restriction is content-based only if it is imposed because of the content of speech and not because of any distinctive, offensive behavior of the speaker that is associated with the delivery of the speech. Thus, not every regulation of such distinctive offensive behavior is content-based. The question is simply whether the ostensible reason for the regulation is really about the ideas expressed in the speech. Here, the evidence shows that the ostensible reason for the regulation is the true reason—to prevent an encounter when the person addressed does not want to get close; to regulate the protesters' behavior, not their anti-abortion message. This regulation is significantly different from the injunction that was struck down in *Schenck*, 249 U.S. 47 (1919), where the floating bubble was larger and involved near-absolute prohibitions on speech. However, the issue of the inherent difficulty in administering floating bubble zones is not before the Court and should not be considered on a facial challenge.

DISSENT: (Scalia, J.) The Court concludes that a regulation requiring speakers on the public streets bordering medical facilities to speak from a distance of eight feet is not a regulation of speech but a regulation of the places where some speech may occur, and that regulation of

Continued on next page.

certain categories of speech (protect, education and counseling) is not content-based. This decision represents a blatant distortion of First Amendment principles that the Court seems to invoke when abortion is involved.

DISSENT: (Kennedy, J.) The Court's holding contradicts well-established First Amendment principles, approving a law which bars a private citizen from peacefully communicating a message to a fellow citizen on a public sidewalk. The statute here imposes content-based restrictions and limits speech with respect to certain topics. Not only is the statute not content neutral but it is not viewpoint neutral and prohibits only those persons who speak "against" certain medical procedures.

▌ANALYSIS

The Court also rejects the petitioners' argument that the statute is overbroad because it protects too many people in too many places, rather than simply patients at medical facilities where confrontational speech has occurred. The Court rejects this argument on the basis that it fails to identify a constitutional defect and that it misinterprets the overbreadth doctrine. The Court maintains that the statute does not "ban" any message but merely regulates the places at which such communications can take place.

■■■■

Quicknotes

FIRST AMENDMENT   Prohibits Congress from enacting any law respecting an establishment of religion, prohibiting the free exercise of religion, abridging freedom of speech or the press, the right of peaceful assembly and the right to petition for a redress of grievances.

PUBLIC FORUM   Public area so associated with freedom of speech so that restriction of access to it for that purpose is unconstitutional (e.g., sidewalks, streets, parks, etc.).

■■■■

Rust v. Sullivan

[Parties not identified in casebok excerpt.]

500 U.S. 173 (1991).

NATURE OF CASE: Review of order dismissing constitutional challenge to regulations promulgated under the Public Health Service Act.

FACT SUMMARY: The Department of Health and Human Services (HHS) promulgated regulations prohibiting clinics receiving funding under the Public Health Service Act (PHSA) from providing abortion counseling or referrals.

🏛 RULE OF LAW
Clinics receiving funding under the PHSA may be prohibited from providing abortion counseling or referrals.

FACTS: In 1970, Congress enacted Title X to the Public Health Service Act (PHSA). This provision authorized the use of federal funds for clinics providing family planning services. In 1988, the Department of Health and Human Services (HHS) promulgated regulations under Title X, prohibiting clinics receiving funding under the Act from either providing services relating to abortion or providing counseling with respect to abortion services. Rather, those seeking family planning services after conception would be referred to facilities not providing abortion as an option. Further, grantees could not engage in activities promoting or encouraging abortions. A constitutional challenge under the Fourteenth Amendment was made to the regulations. The court of appeals upheld the regulations, and the Supreme Court granted review.

ISSUE: May clinics receiving funding under the PHSA be prohibited from providing abortion counseling or referrals?

HOLDING AND DECISION: (Rehnquist, C.J.) Yes. Clinics receiving funding under the PHSA may be prohibited from providing abortion counseling or referrals. It has long been accepted that, as a matter of constitutional law, Congress may discourage by use of its spending power that which it cannot directly prohibit. While Congress can neither legislate against the right to an abortion or the right of physicians to discuss matters pertaining thereto, it can legitimately withhold funding from persons or entities who engage in such activities. Simply put, Congress may legitimately decide one set of values is superior to another, and choose to fund in such a manner as to promote that set. Here, Congress has not prohibited any protected activity, it has merely chosen not to fund such activities. This was well within its powers. Affirmed.

DISSENT: (Blackmun, J.) The Court today has upheld viewpoint-based suppression of speech simply because that suppression was a condition upon acceptance of public funds. This is a dangerous precedent.

▶ ANALYSIS

The carrot-and-stick approach to regulation, as opposed to direct regulation, has been used by Congress in many areas. In recent times, however, abortion has been the most controversial arena of its application. The most well-known case dealing with this subject prior to *Rust* was *Maher v. Roe*, 432 U.S. 464, decided in 1977. This decision permitted Congress to prohibit the use of Medicare funds for abortions.

Quicknotes

FOURTEENTH AMENDMENT Declares that no state shall make or enforce any law which shall abridge the privileges and immunities of citizens of the United States.

SPENDING POWER The power delegated to Congress by the Constitution to spend money in providing for the nation's welfare.

Tinker v. Des Moines School District

Students (P) v. School district (D)

393 U.S. 503 (1969).

NATURE OF CASE: Appeal from denial of an injunction.

FACT SUMMARY: The Tinkers (P), brother and sister, were high school students who sought to enjoin school officials from disciplining them for wearing black arm bands in class in protest of the Vietnam conflict.

🏛 RULE OF LAW
The prohibition of a particular opinion without evidence that it is necessary to avoid material and substantial interference with school work or discipline is not constitutionally permissible.

FACTS: The Tinkers (P), brother and sister, were high school students who sought to enjoin school officials from disciplining them. They wore black arm bands to school as a symbolic protest of their opposition to the continuing American participation in the Vietnam conflict. They refused to remove the arm bands when asked to do so. In accordance with a ban on arm bands adopted by the district's (D) principals two days before the anticipated protest, the Tinkers (P) were suspended from school until they returned to school without the arm bands. The lower federal courts uphold the district's (D) action on grounds that it was reasonable in order to prevent a disturbance which might result.

ISSUE: Is the prohibition of a particular opinion without evidence that it is necessary to avoid material and substantial interference with school work or discipline constitutionally permissible?

HOLDING AND DECISION: (Fortas, J.) No. The prohibition of a particular opinion without evidence that it is necessary to avoid material and substantial interference with school work or discipline is not constitutionally permissible. Under the circumstances here, the wearing of arm bands "was entirely divorced from actually or potentially disruptive conduct by those participating in it." The symbolic action was closely akin to pure speech which receives great First Amendment protection. Students and teachers do not lose the right to free expression at the schoolhouse gate. There was no evidence of interference with the school's work or with the rights of other students. "Undifferentiated fear or apprehension of disturbance is not enough to overcome the right of freedom of expression." The state must show more than a mere desire to avoid the unpleasantness that accompanies an unpopular viewpoint. Reversed and remanded.

CONCURRENCE: (Stewart, J.) Children and adults do not share the same First Amendment rights because children may not have full individual choice in certain situations, such as captive audiences in school.

DISSENT: (Black, J.) The evidence demonstrates that the armbands did in fact disrupt school and distract other students. The students intended to draw attention so that they could draw attention to the Vietnam conflict.

DISSENT: (Harlan, J.) The school must balance its respect for freedom of expression with its authority to maintain discipline. Nothing in the record indicates the school acted on the basis of anything other than a sincere intention to prevent disruption to the learning process.

▶ ANALYSIS

The Second Circuit held that school officials violated a teacher's rights by firing him for wearing a black arm band in class as a symbolic protest to American involvement in Vietnam. The court noted that the teacher's action did not disrupt the classroom, *James v. Board of Educ.*, 461 F.2d 566 (1972). The Supreme Court denied certiorari to a Tenth Circuit case that upheld the indefinite suspension of male Pawnee Indian students who wore their hair in long braids in violation of the school dress code which forbade hair from touching the ears or collar, *Rider v. Board of Education*, 414 U.S. 1088 (1974), Justices Douglas and Marshall dissenting.

◼▬◼

Quicknotes

FIRST AMENDMENT Prohibits Congress from enacting any law respecting an establishment of religion, prohibiting the free exercise of religion, abridging freedom of speech or the press, the right of peaceful assembly and the right to petition for a redress of grievances.

INJUNCTION A court order requiring a person to do or prohibiting that person from doing a specific act.

SYMBOLIC ACTION Conduct that is expressive of a person's thoughts or opinions.

◼▬◼

Hazelwood School District v. Kuhlmeier

School district (D) v. Students (P)

484 U.S. 260 (1988).

NATURE OF CASE: Appeal from finding of unconstitutional censorship.

FACT SUMMARY: The Hazelwood School District (D) appealed from a decision finding its decision to delete two newspaper articles from the school newspaper, *Spectrum*, because of the nature of the articles, was violative of the students' (P) First Amendment rights of expression.

🏛 RULE OF LAW
Educators do not violate the First Amendment by exercising editorial control over the style and content of a school-sponsored student newspaper so long as the actions are reasonably related to legitimate pedagogical concerns.

FACTS: Hazelwood East High School published a school newspaper, *Spectrum*, as part of its journalism class. The paper was published several times over the course of the year, and it was the practice of the journalism teacher to present proofs of each issue prior to publication to the principal, Reynolds (D). The students (P) sought to publish two articles dealing with student pregnancy and the effect of divorce on students. The proofs were presented to Reynolds (D) prior to publication of the May 13th issue. Reynolds (D) found that the article on teenage pregnancy was inappropriate for some of the younger students, and that the divorce article should have allowed some of the parents mentioned to respond to comments. He determined that the paper could not be effectively edited without canceling the issue, so he published the issue, deleting the two pages containing the articles. The students (P) brought suit, contending the editorial deletion violated their First Amendment rights of freedom of expression. From the court of appeals decision finding that the deletion of the articles violated the First Amendment rights of the students (P), the Hazelwood School District (the District) (D) appealed.

ISSUE: Do educators violate the First Amendment by exercising editorial control over the style and content of a school-sponsored newspaper so long as their actions are reasonably related to legitimate pedagogical concerns?

HOLDING AND DECISION: (White, J.) No. Educators do not violate the First Amendment by exercising editorial control over the style and content of a school-sponsored newspaper so long as their actions are reasonably related to legitimate pedagogical concerns. While students retain their constitutional rights even at school,

these rights are not coextensive with the rights of individuals in other public settings. Student speech is considered in light of the special characteristics of the school environment, and the determination of what manner of speech in the classroom or school assembly is appropriate properly rests with the District (D). There is no evidence in the present case that the District (D) intended to create a public forum, and therefore the District's (D) officials were entitled to regulate the content of *Spectrum* in any reasonable manner. When judged by this standard, the District's (D) decision to regulate on the grounds that the articles were unsuitable for less mature audiences must be upheld. Reversed.

DISSENT: (Brennan, J.) The publication of a school newspaper, to the extent it is a noncurricular activity, is less likely to disrupt any legitimately pedagogical purpose. The "sensitive topic" standard used to censor in the present case invites discretionary manipulation to achieve ends that can have a chilling effect on student speech.

▶ ANALYSIS

The Court in the present case distinguished the *Tinker* case, 393 U.S. 503 (1969), as being a case involving student discipline, as the present case involved only content regulation of a school newspaper. The *Tinker* standard is much stricter and allows the restriction of student expression only when such expression substantially interferes with the work of the school or impinges on the rights of other students.

■=■

Quicknotes

FIRST AMENDMENT Prohibits Congress from enacting any law respecting an establishment of religion, prohibiting the free exercise of religion, abridging freedom of speech or the press, the right of peaceful assembly and the right to petition for a redress of grievances.

FREEDOM OF EXPRESSION The guarantee of the First Amendment to the United States Constitution prohibiting Congress from enacting any law respecting an establishment of religion, prohibiting the free exercise of religion, abridging freedom of speech or the press, the right of peaceful assembly and the right to petition for a redress of grievances.

■=■

FCC v. Pacifica Foundation

Government commission (D) v. Radio station (P)

438 U.S. 726 (1978).

NATURE OF CASE: Challenge to a ruling by the Federal Communications Commission.

FACT SUMMARY: A monologue by George Carlin was broadcast on a radio station owned by the Pacifica Foundation (P).

🏛 RULE OF LAW
The Federal Communications Commission may regulate or apply sanctions for the use of "indecent" language broadcast over the airways.

FACTS: A monologue by George Carlin entitled "Dirty Words" was broadcast on a radio station owned by Pacifica Foundation (P). The monologue involved a satire of swearing and censorship. It was broadcast as a part of a program about contemporary society's attitude toward language and was preceded by a warning that the monologue might contain material which would be sensitive to some listeners. The Federal Communications Commission (FCC) (D), in response to a listener's complaint, found that the language contained indecent, but not obscene language. The FCC (D) found that it had the power to regulate or prohibit the broadcasting of such language under 18 U.S.C. § 1464, which prohibits the broadcasting of any obscene, indecent, or profane language. No disciplinary action was taken against Pacifica (P), but the finding was to be included in its file and could be considered if such conduct was repeated in determining whether disciplinary action was warranted at that time. The FCC (D) subsequently stated that not all such language was prohibited, but its use when children were obviously in the audience should not be permitted. Pacifica (P) appealed, alleging that the language was not obscene and that its broadcasting freedom was protected under the First Amendment.

ISSUE: May the FCC regulate or apply sanctions for the use of "indecent" language broadcast over the airways?

HOLDING AND DECISION: (Stevens, J.) Yes. The FCC may regulate or apply sanctions for the use of "indecent" language broadcast over the airways. Section 1464 prohibits the broadcasting of obscene, indecent, or profane language. "Indecent" language is the use of words not accepted under contemporary standards of morality. They need not be obscene to be subjected to FCC (D) regulation. The fact that they were used in a specific context will not foreclose FCC (D) regulation of patently offensive words. The FCC (D) order was limited to words involving patently offensive references to excretory and sexual organs and will involve a minimum of self-censorship. Thus narrowed, the issue becomes whether the FCC

(D) may be consistent with the First Amendment and still restrict the use of indecent language on the public airways under any circumstances. The mere fact that society may find various language offensive is not grounds for censorship. However, patently offensive words themselves are accorded little protection by the First Amendment, since they have no real intrinsic value. Within the context of the broadcast media, we find that the use of patently offensive sexual and excretory language is improper and is not protected under the First Amendment. Because of the pervasiveness of such broadcasts and the possibility that warnings may not be heard, the public cannot adequately protect itself from exposure to such language. Broadcasting is also uniquely accessible to children. The FCC (D) could find that such language constituted a nuisance which is afforded no constitutional protection. The FCC's (D) order was proper. Reversed.

CONCURRENCE: (Powell, J.) The FCC (D) order sought to channel this type of programming to more suitable hours to protect children. Radio programs come directly into the house and listeners have a right not to be assaulted by indecent language. The FCC (D) order merely states that such language is not appropriate in the manner and at the time it was broadcasted. Our decision turns solely on the unique position of radio and television.

DISSENT: (Brennan, J.) The word "indecent" in § 1464 must be defined as meaning only "obscene." The majority has created yet another exception to First Amendment protections. While the right to privacy is entitled to protection, offensive language may be turned off. Radio shows are voluntarily "admitted" into the listener's home. Any intrusion is minor based on this fact. Indecent language which is not obscene will have little or no impact on children. Thus, neither rationale supports the curtailment of otherwise protectable speech. The FCC (D) order will create an unacceptable air of self-censorship, and certain "dirty words" may be appropriate in certain contexts.

▌ ANALYSIS

Pacifica is limited in scope to radio and television transmissions. The meaning of "indecent" is limited to sexual and excretory references by the FCC, otherwise it would not have withstood a vagueness challenge. The FCC also limited its ruling to hours when children could be expected in the audience, thereby limiting self-censorship. Indecent

Continued on next page.

language is not deemed so important as to require First Amendment protection in this context.

■══■

Quicknotes

OBSCENITY   Conduct tending to corrupt the public morals by its indecency or lewdness.

■══■

Buckley v. Valeo

Senator (D) v. Government (P)

424 U.S. 1 (1976).

NATURE OF CASE: Action for declaration of unconstitutionality.

FACT SUMMARY: Senator Buckley (P) and others challenged the Federal Election Campaign Act's contribution and expenditures limitations.

🏛 RULE OF LAW

The strong governmental interest in preventing election corruption does not justify imposition of substantial restrictions on the effective ability of any individual to express his political beliefs and engage in political association.

FACTS: In order to curtail political corruption, Congress in the Federal Election Campaign Act of 1971, as amended in 1974, developed an intricate statutory scheme for the regulation of federal political campaigns. Inter alia, Congress imposed a $1000 limitation on individual contributions "to a single candidate" in § 608(b)(1), a $5000 limitation on "contributions" to a single candidate by political committees in § 608(b)(2), a $25,000 limitation on total "contributions" by any individual in one year to political candidates in § 608(b)(3), a $1000 ceiling in "expenditures" relative to a known candidate in § 608(e)(1), and similar ceilings on "expenditures" by the candidate and his family and on overall campaign "expenditures" in § 608(a) and (c). Senator Buckley (D) and others pursuant to a special section in the Act of 1971, brought this action to have all the above-mentioned sections declared an unconstitutional violation of their First Amendment rights of freedom of expression and association. This appeal followed.

ISSUE: Does the strong governmental interest in preventing election corruption justify imposition of substantial restrictions on the effective ability of any individual to express his political beliefs and engage in political association?

HOLDING AND DECISION: (Per curiam) No. The strong governmental interest in preventing election corruption does not justify imposition of substantial restrictions on the effective ability of any individual to express his political beliefs and engage in political association. Although "the First Amendment protects political association as well as political expression . . . a limitation upon the amount that any one person or group may contribute to [and associate with] a candidate or a political committee entails only a marginal restriction on the contributor's ability to engage in free communication [and association];" but "a restriction on the amount of money a person or group can spend on political communication [as a whole] during a campaign [excessively] reduces the quantity of expression by restricting the number of issues discussed, the depth of their exploration, and the size of the audience reached." As such, the so-called "contribution" (i.e., to candidates) limitations here (§ 608(b)(1-3)) may be upheld as valid means for limiting political corruption by "fat cats." The so-called "expenditure" (on political expression) limitations (§ 608(a, c, e)), however, places too broad a restriction on the individuals ability to speak out and must therefore be avoided as constitutionally invalid.

CONCURRENCE AND DISSENT: (Burger, C.J.) The Court is correct in holding that the First Amendment intrusions involved here may only be justified by the "strongest of state interests;" but it is difficult to see why the interests which invalidate the expenditure limitations should not do the same to the contribution limitations. Limiting contributions, as a practical matter, will limit expenditures as well. Both sets of limitations should be struck down.

CONCURRENCE AND DISSENT: (White, J.) Since the contribution and expenditure limitations involved here are all neutral as to the content of speech and are not motivated by fear of the consequences of speech by any candidate, the strong government interest in avoiding the evils of unlimited political campaign spending should suffice to uphold both. The argument that money is speech (or "money talks") simply proves too much in a First Amendment context.

▶ ANALYSIS

In this case, the Court has identified one of the few "compelling governmental interests" which may be employed to justify congressional regulation of an area subject to strict judicial scrutiny. That interest is the interest in maintaining the integrity of the political process. Note, however, that even though the interest is held compelling, the Court does not automatically affirm its imposition. Note that the Court's decision left the Federal Election Campaign Act rife with loopholes. Perhaps the most exploited was that which permitted individuals to "expend" (i.e., separately from any candidate or his organization) large sums to endorse a vote for a particular candidate.

Continued on next page.

Quicknotes

FIRST AMENDMENT Prohibits Congress from enacting any law respecting an establishment of religion, prohibiting the free exercise of religion, abridging freedom of speech or the press, the right of peaceful assembly and the right to petition for a redress of grievances.

FREEDOM OF ASSOCIATION The right to peaceably assemble.

FREEDOM OF EXPRESSION The guarantee of the First Amendment to the United States Constitution prohibiting Congress from enacting any law respecting an establishment of religion, prohibiting the free exercise of religion, abridging freedom of speech or the press, the right of peaceful assembly and the right to petition for a redress of grievances.

■■■

Citizens United v. FEC

Non-profit organization (D) v. Government commission (P)

___ U.S. ___, 130 S.Ct. 876, 175 L.Ed.2d 753 (2010).

NATURE OF CASE: Supreme Court review of a lower court decision denying Citizens United's motion for a preliminary injunction to stop the Federal Election Commission from enforcing provisions of the Bipartisan Campaign Reform Act of 2002, which would prevent the airing of a film criticizing a presidential candidate.

FACT SUMMARY: During the presidential campaign for the 2008 election, Citizens United, a conservative, non-profit organization, sought to advertise and then air a movie that was critical of then-Senator Hillary Clinton.

RULE OF LAW

The government may not suppress political speech on the basis of the speaker's corporate identity.

FACTS: In January 2008, Citizens United (D), a non-profit organization, released a 90-minute documentary highly critical of then-Senator Hillary Clinton. The movie mentioned Clinton by name and featured interviews with commentators who were highly critical of the candidate. The movie was released in theatres, and Citizens United (D) attempted to increase distribution by making it available through video-on-demand. To do this, Citizens United (D) created advertisements containing short, pejorative statements about Clinton. It then wanted to promote the video-on-demand offering by running ads on broadcast and cable television. The Federal Election Commission (FEC) (P), using provisions of the Bipartisan Campaign Reform Act of 2002 (BCRA), stopped Citizens United (D) from running the film within 30 days of the 2008 Democratic primaries. Citizens United (D) tried unsuccessfully in district court to get a restraining order against the FEC's (P) action. The Supreme Court heard the appeal.

ISSUE: May the government suppress political speech on the basis of the speaker's corporate identity?

HOLDING AND DECISION: (Kennedy, J.) No. The government may not suppress political speech on the basis of the speaker's corporate identity. There is no basis for the proposition that the government may impose restrictions on certain disfavored speakers, and this First Amendment protection extends to corporations as well. In *Austin v. Michigan Chamber of Commerce*, 494 U.S. 652 (1990), the Court identified a new governmental interest in preventing the "corrosive distorting effects of immense aggregations of wealth that are accumulated with the help of the corporate form and that have little or no correlation to the public's support for the corporation's political ideas." The Court's anti-distortion rationale thus states

that the corporate form of an entity is the problem to be feared, yet media corporations, which can aggregate huge wealth as well, are exempt from the ban on corporate expenditures. Thus the anti-distortion rationale of *Austin* seems to be undercut by this exemption. Next, the Government (P) says that corporate political speech can be banned in order to prevent "corruption or its appearance." The anticorruption interest, however, is not sufficient to displace the speech in question. Furthermore, the government says that corporate expenditures can be limited because if its interest in protecting dissenting shareholders from being compelled to fund corporate political speech. The First Amendment does not allow that power, and additionally, nothing prevents shareholders from exercising their powers, which includes the possibility of removing board members, through the corporate process. *Austin* is not well reasoned, and for this reason, it must be overruled.

CONCURRENCE AND DISSENT: (Stevens, J.) In the context of election to public office, the distinction between corporate and human speakers is significant. Corporations are not truly members of our society, despite the significant contributions that they make to it. The financial resources and legal structure of the corporate entity raise complicated questions about its proper role in the election process. Since they are not natural persons, it does not make sense to treat corporations as such when one considers the role they can play when making expenditures to support or attack a political candidate. Today's decision marks a troubling departure from this Court's previous rulings.

ANALYSIS

This five-to-four decision stands as one of the most important First Amendment cases in years. Section 441b of the BCRA (commonly known as the McCain-Feingold Act) made it a felony for corporations to expressly advocate the election or defeat of a political candidate or to broadcast electioneering communications within 30 days of an election. There was an exemption for political action committees created by a corporation, and the dissent noted this fact to rebut the argument that it was opposed to all forms of corporate speech. The dissent was troubled by the fact that a corporation, due to its structure, can marshal huge amounts of wealth and resources and thus distort the nature of the election discourse in ways that are not available to the individual advocate. The majority seemed less troubled by this fact and claimed it was simply

Continued on next page.

ridding this issue of contradictions inherent in previous rulings.

■ ■ ■

Quicknotes

FIRST AMENDMENT Prohibits Congress from enacting any law respecting an establishment of religion, prohibiting the free exercise of religion, abridging freedom of speech or the press, the right of peaceful assembly and the right to petition for a redress of grievances.

■ ■ ■

Freedom of Religion

Quick Reference Rules of Law

Zelman v. Simmons-Harris

School superintendent (D) v. Taxpayers (P)

536 U.S. 639 (2002).

NATURE OF CASE: Appeal from affirmance of injunction against a school voucher program that can be used for parochial school education.

FACT SUMMARY: To address the dismal performance of the Cleveland public school system, Ohio enacted a school voucher program that enabled parents to choose to send their children to participating private schools. An overwhelming number of the private schools participating in the program had a religious affiliation, and Ohio taxpayers (P) challenged the voucher program as a violation of the Establishment Clause.

🏛 RULE OF LAW
A school voucher program that gives parents the choice to send their children to a private school does not violate the Establishment Clause where the overwhelming number of participating private schools is comprised of religiously-affiliated parochial schools.

FACTS: Ohio's Pilot Project Scholarship Program gave educational choices to families in any Ohio school district that was under state control pursuant to a federal-court order. The program provided tuition aid for certain students in the Cleveland City School District, the only covered district because of its dismal performance as compared to most other districts in the nation, to attend participating public or private schools of their parents' choosing and tutorial aid for students who chose to remain enrolled in public school. Both religious and nonreligious schools in the district could participate, as could public schools in adjacent school districts. Tuition aid was distributed to parents according to financial need, and where the aid was spent depended solely upon where parents chose to enroll their children. The number of tutorial assistance grants provided to students remaining in public school had to equal the number of tuition aid scholarships. In the 1999–2000 school year, 82% of the participating private schools had a religious affiliation, none of the adjacent public schools participated, and 96% of the students participating in the scholarship program were enrolled in religiously affiliated schools. Sixty percent of the students were from families at or below the poverty line. Cleveland schoolchildren also had the option of enrolling in community schools, which were funded under state law but run by their own school boards and received twice the per-student funding as participating private schools, or magnet schools (public schools emphasizing a particular subject area, teaching method, or service). Ohio taxpayers (P) sought to enjoin the program on the ground that it violated the Establishment Clause. The district court granted them

summary judgment, and the court of appeals affirmed. The Supreme Court granted review.

ISSUE: Does a school voucher program that gives parents the choice to send their children to a private school violate the Establishment Clause where the overwhelming number of participating private schools is comprised of religiously-affiliated parochial schools?

HOLDING AND DECISION: (Rehnquist, C.J.) No. A school voucher program that gives parents the choice to send their children to a private school does not violate the Establishment Clause where the overwhelming number of participating private schools is comprised of religiously-affiliated parochial schools. Because the program here was undisputedly enacted for the valid secular purpose of providing educational assistance to poor children in a demonstrably failing public school system, the question is whether the program nonetheless has the forbidden effect of advancing or inhibiting religion. The Court's jurisprudence [see, e.g, *Mueller v. Allen*, 463 U.S. 388 (1983), and its progeny] makes clear that a government aid program is not readily subject to challenge under the Establishment Clause if it is neutral with respect to religion and provides assistance directly to a broad class of citizens who, in turn, direct government aid to religious schools wholly as a result of their own genuine and independent private choice. The instant program is one of true private choice, and is thus constitutional. It is neutral in all respects toward religion, and is part of Ohio's general and multifaceted undertaking to provide educational opportunities to children in a failed school district. It confers educational assistance directly to a broad class of individuals defined without reference to religion and permits participation of all district schools—religious or nonreligious—and adjacent public schools. The only preference in the program is for low-income families, who receive greater assistance and have priority for admission. Rather than creating financial incentives that skew it toward religious schools, the program creates financial disincentives: Private schools receive only half the government assistance given to community schools and one-third that given to magnet schools, and adjacent public schools would receive two to three times that given to private schools. Families, too, have a financial disincentive, for they have to copay a portion of private school tuition, but pay nothing at a community, magnet, or traditional public school. Thus, no reasonable observer would think that such a neutral private choice program carries with it the imprimatur of

Continued on next page.

government endorsement. Nor is there evidence that the program fails to provide genuine opportunities for Cleveland parents to select secular educational options: Their children may remain in public school as before, remain in public school with funded tutoring aid, obtain a scholarship and choose to attend a religious school, obtain a scholarship and choose to attend a nonreligious private school, enroll in a community school, or enroll in a magnet school. The Establishment Clause question whether Ohio is coercing parents into sending their children to religious schools must be answered by evaluating all options Ohio provides Cleveland schoolchildren, only one of which is to obtain a scholarship and then choose a religious school. The taxpayers' (P) additional argument that constitutional significance should be attached to the fact that 96% of the scholarship recipients have enrolled in religious schools was flatly rejected in *Mueller*. The constitutionality of a neutral educational aid program simply does not turn on whether and why, in a particular area, at a particular time, most private schools are religious, or most recipients choose to use the aid at a religious school. In sum, the Ohio program is entirely neutral with respect to religion. It provides benefits directly to a wide spectrum of individuals, defined only by financial need and residence in a particular school district. It permits such individuals to exercise genuine choice among options public and private, secular and religious. The program is therefore a program of true private choice. Reversed.

CONCURRENCE: (O'Connor, J.) Here, it is clear that the voucher program is neutral as between religious and nonreligious schools. Nonreligious schools provide parents reasonable alternatives to religious schools in the voucher program, competing effectively with the parochial schools. Many parents sent their children to nonreligious private, magnet, and community schools. The parents have a genuine choice when all the choices available are considered, and, therefore, the voucher program is consistent with the Establishment Clause.

DISSENT: (Souter, J.) Under the voucher program, public tax money will be used to pay not only for instruction in secular subjects but also for religious indoctrination. The Court's unrepudiated precedent in *Everson v. Board of Ed.*, 330 U.S. 1 (1947), makes it clear that no tax may be used to support religious activities or institutions. However, in Cleveland, the overwhelming proportion of large appropriations for voucher money must be spent on religious schools if it is to be spent at all, and will be spent in amounts that cover almost all of tuition. The money will thus pay for eligible students' instruction not only in secular subjects but in religion as well, in schools that can fairly be characterized as founded to teach religious doctrine. Thus, tax money will pay for teaching religion. The Court cannot leave *Everson* on the books and approve the vouchers unless it ignores *Everson* and ignores the meaning of neutrality and private choice. From a historical perspective, the majority is creating a new phase of Establishment

Clause jurisprudence in which the substantial character of government aid is held to have no constitutional significance, and the espoused criteria of neutrality in offering aid, and private choice in directing it, are shown to be nothing but examples of verbal formalism. Thus, even though *Everson*'s rule is still the touchstone of sound law, the reality is that with regard to educational aid, given the majority opinion, the Establishment Clause has largely been read away.

DISSENT: (Breyer, J.) Voucher programs direct financing to a core function of the Church: the teaching of religious truths to young children. Parental choice cannot help the taxpayer who does not want to finance the religious education of children.

▶ ***ANALYSIS***

The Court has traditionally been satisfied that a law has a neutral primary effect if the religious impact of the law is remote, indirect, and incidental. Here, the dissent seems to argue that the voucher program's impact was not remote or incidental, because by its very design, given the demographic realities of the school district, it encouraged enrollment in religious schools. The case leaves several constitutional questions unanswered, including whether provisions in voucher programs that prohibit discrimination by recipient schools are now constitutionally mandated, and whether state laws that expressly prohibit the use of aid for religious schools are themselves unconstitutional.

■■■

Quicknotes

ESTABLISHMENT CLAUSE The constitutional provision prohibiting the government from favoring any one religion over others, or engaging in religious activities or advocacy.

FOURTEENTH AMENDMENT Declares that no state shall make or enforce any law that shall abridge the privileges and immunities of citizens of the United States. No state shall deny to any person within its jurisdiction the equal protection of the laws.

INJUNCTION A court order requiring a person to do, or prohibiting that person from doing, a specific act.

SUMMARY JUDGMENT Judgment rendered by a court in response to a motion made by one of the parties, claiming that the lack of a question of material fact in respect to an issue warrants disposition of the issue without consideration by the jury.

■■■

Wallace v. Jaffree

State (D) v. Parent (P)

472 U.S. 38 (1985).

NATURE OF CASE: Appeal from dismissal of challenge to state period-of-silence laws.

FACT SUMMARY: Alabama's (D) law authorizing a one-minute period of silence in all public schools "for meditation" was replaced by a similar law which provided the silent period "for meditation or voluntary prayer."

 RULE OF LAW
State statutes enacted for the purpose of endorsing or disapproving religion violate the Establishment Clause of the First Amendment.

FACTS: In 1978, Alabama (D) enacted a statute which authorized a one-minute period of silence in all public schools "for meditation." In 1981, it replaced the 1978 law with a similar statute which also authorized a silent period, but "for meditation or voluntary prayer." The sponsor of the 1981 legislation entered into the legislative record a statement that the legislation was an "effort to return voluntary prayer" to the public schools. Jaffree (P), who had three children enrolled in Alabama public schools, filed a challenge to the 1981 law on the grounds that it violated the Establishment Clause of the First Amendment. The district court dismissed Jaffree's (P) challenge based on its interpretation of the history underlying the Establishment Clause. The court of appeals reversed, and the state of Alabama (D) appealed.

ISSUE: Do state statutes which are enacted for the purpose of endorsing or disapproving religion violate the Establishment Clause of the First Amendment?

HOLDING AND DECISION: (Stevens, J.) Yes. State statutes which are enacted for the purpose of endorsing or disapproving religion violate the Establishment Clause of the First Amendment. The individual freedom of conscience protected by the First Amendment embraces the right to select any religious faith or none at all. A statute which does not have a secular legislative purpose, or which is entirely motivated by a purpose to advance religion, violates the "purpose" test of *Lemon v. Kurtzman*, 403 U.S. 602 (1971), and the Establishment Clause. Here, Alabama (D), in the hearings below, introduced no evidence at all of secular purpose in adopting the 1981 law requiring the silent period "for meditation or voluntary prayer." In fact, the legislative record surrounding adoption of the 1981 law shows that the legislation was explicitly intended "to return voluntary prayer" to public schools in Alabama and to characterize prayer as a favored practice. This is a markedly different purpose than merely protecting

every student's right to engage in voluntary prayer during an appropriate moment of silence during the school day, which the 1978 law already protected. Such an endorsement of religion is not consistent with the established principle that the government must pursue a course of complete neutrality toward religion. Affirmed.

CONCURRENCE: (O'Connor, J.) The *Lemon v. Kurtzman* test should be replaced. Instead, religious liberty protected by the Establishment Clause should be deemed infringed when the government makes adherence to religion relevant to a person's standing in the political community. Government action which conveys the message that religion or a particular religion is favored or preferred leaves the nonadherent with the distasteful choice of participating in or accepting the religious message, thereby compromising the nonadherent's belief, or withdrawing, thereby calling attention to his nonconformity. Here, then, the crucial question is whether Alabama (D) conveyed the message that children should use the moment of silence for prayer. If an objective observer, acquainted with the text, legislative history, and implementation of the Alabama (D) statute would perceive it as a state endorsement of prayer in public schools, then it should be held to violate the Establishment Clause.

DISSENT: (Burger, C.J.) Hostility to religion is as much forbidden by the Constitution as an official establishment of religion. The Establishment Clause allows states such as Alabama (D) to accommodate, in a wholly neutral and noncoercive manner, the religious observances of others. Here, Alabama's (D) 1981 statute does only that: it creates an opportunity to pray without pressuring those who do not wish to pray, much in the same way Congress provides chaplains and chapels to its members.

DISSENT: (Rehnquist, J.) Madison and the founders did not view the Establishment Clause as requiring neutrality on the part of the government between religion and nonreligion. Rather, the Establishment Clause was aimed only at preventing the establishment of a national church and perhaps the preference of one religious sect over another; it was definitely not concerned about whether the government might aid all religions evenhandedly.

▶ *ANALYSIS*

In cases involving students who are temporarily released from ordinary class time in order to participate in religious services or observances, the Supreme Court has reached

Continued on next page.

conflicting results. In *McCollum v. Board of Educ.*, 333 U.S. 203 (1948), privately employed religion teachers held classes once a week on school premises for children whose parents had granted permission to attend. Even though non-attending students attended academic studies in other parts of the same building, the Court per Justice Black held that the use of "the state's compulsory public school machinery" as well as "tax-supported public school buildings" invalidated the practice. In *Zorach v. Clauson*, 343 U.S. 306 (1952), however, the Court per Justice Douglas upheld a New York City program which released students for participation in religious classes in private, off-premises religious buildings.

■═■

Quicknotes

ESTABLISHMENT CLAUSE The constitutional provision prohibiting the government from favoring any one religion over others, or engaging in religious activities or advocacy.

■═■

Allegheny County v. ACLU

County (D) v. Civil liberties group (P)

492 U.S. 573 (1989).

NATURE OF CASE: Appeal from ruling that holiday displays violate the Establishment Clause of the First Amendment.

FACT SUMMARY: Every year Allegheny County (D) erected two holiday displays: a creche on the grand staircase of the county courthouse and a Chanukah menorah next to a Christmas tree and sign saluting liberty outside another public building.

🏛 RULE OF LAW

The government's use of religious symbols or displays violates the Establishment Clause if, given the context of their use, it is sufficiently likely that the public will understand them as endorsing or disapproving of its individual religious choices.

FACTS: Every year during the holiday season, Allegheny County (D) erected two displays in Pittsburgh. The first was a creche perched on the steps of the county courthouse, featuring a nativity scene with an angel and banner proclaiming "Gloria in excelsis Deo!" The second was a Chanukah menorah placed just outside another county building and next to a Christmas tree. Next to the menorah and tree was a sign from the mayor of Pittsburgh, stating that the city "salutes liberty during the holiday season." Certain Pittsburgh citizens, represented by the American Civil Liberties Union (ACLU) (P), challenged the constitutionality of the holiday displays as violative of the Establishment Clause on the grounds that each has the impermissible effect of endorsing either Christianity or Judaism or both. The third circuit court of appeals agreed and held for the ACLU (P), but Allegheny County (D), in which Pittsburgh is situated, appealed.

ISSUE: Does the government's use of religious symbols or displays violate the Establishment Clause if, given the context of their use, it is sufficiently likely that the public will understand them as endorsing or disapproving of its individual religious choices?

HOLDING AND DECISION: (Blackmun, J.) Yes. The government's use of religious symbols or displays violates the Establishment Clause if, given the context of their use, it is sufficiently likely that the public will understand them as endorsing or disapproving of its individual religious choices. Any such perceived endorsement of religion by the government is invalid because it sends a message to nonadherents that they are outsiders, not full members of the political community. The effect on minority religious groups is to convey the message that their views are not similarly worthy of public recognition nor

entitled to public support. Here, the creche itself communicates a religious message; it sits on the grand staircase, which is the "main" and "most beautiful" part of the building which is the seat of Allegheny County (D) government. No viewer could reasonably think that it occupies this location without the support and approval of the government. Because the creche suggests a "denominational preference" for a particular religion, i.e., Christianity, it is subject to strict scrutiny. On the other hand, the Chanukah menorah next to the Christmas tree (which in itself is not a religious symbol) simply recognizes that both Christmas and Chanukah are part of the same winter-holiday season. Further, the mayor's sign linking the symbols to liberty and freedom assures that the purpose and message are secular and merely celebratory of the winter season. In contrast to the creche, it is not sufficiently likely that residents of Pittsburgh will perceive the combined display of the tree, sign, and menorah as an endorsement or disapproval of their individual religious choices. Affirmed as to the creche; reversed as to the menorah/tree/liberty sign display.

CONCURRENCE AND DISSENT: (Kennedy, J.) Church-state contacts have existed throughout our history, and governments may recognize and accommodate the central role religion plays in our society. Whether government use of religious symbols or displays survives Establishment Clause scrutiny should not depend on the reaction of the reasonable observer, as held by the majority, but on whether the use represents an effort to proselytize or actually establish a state religion. Here, neither the creche nor the menorah/tree/liberty sign display was impermissible because they did not coerce nonadherents to participate in religious ceremonies or activities; in fact, just as when confronted with offensive speech, observers who disagreed with Allegheny County's (D) holiday message were free to turn their backs on the displays. Allegheny County (D) was entitled to celebrate the religious as well as secular aspects of the holiday season, and the displays here were merely further examples of "ceremonial deism" such as the long-accepted practices of the President's Thanksgiving Proclamations or the Pledge of Allegiance. Both displays were constitutionally acceptable.

CONCURRENCE: (O'Connor, J.) The Establishment Clause also takes into account subtle displays of governmental favoritism toward a particular religion. Demonstration of coercion is not a requirement to prove a violation of the Establishment Clause. The endorsement test must take the particular facts of each case into account.

Continued on next page.

Justice Kennedy's fear that traditional practices will become prohibited under the endorsement test is not a justification to allow the traditional practices to continue if they have always violated the Establishment Clause. The holiday display at issue here does not constitute an endorsement of religion, so today's opinion is appropriate. The rule that a religious symbol in place of a secular one creates an inference of endorsement is too rigid, however.

CONCURRENCE AND DISSENT: (Brennan, J.) The display of an object with a religious meaning, such as a Chanukah menorah, is incompatible with the separation of church and state. The Establishment Clause requires neutrality between religion and nonreligion and does not accept government promotion of religion so long as one religion is not favored. Both displays were constitutionally impermissible.

CONCURRENCE AND DISSENT: (Stevens, J.) The Establishment Clause should be construed to create a strong presumption against the display of religious symbols on public property because there is always a risk that such symbols will offend nonmembers of the faith being advertised as well as adherents who find the particular advertisement disrespectful. Both displays were constitutionally impermissible.

▶ *ANALYSIS*

Justice Brennan's dissent in the case relied upon for the majority's holding and rule of law, here, *Lynch v. Donnelly*, 465 U.S. 668 (1984), which suggests three categories of government activity with differing degrees of acceptability under the Establishment Clause. First, if governments recognize public holidays, they legitimately accommodate citizens who will be otherwise occupied on that day. Second, if governments actually participate in secular celebrations of religious holidays which also have seasonal aspects (as in a Christmas party), they still engage in acceptable behavior though they are "closer to the limits of their constitutional power." However, if governments participate in or appear to endorse the distinctively religious elements of otherwise secular events, they encroach upon First Amendment freedoms.

■≡■

Quicknotes

ESTABLISHMENT CLAUSE The constitutional provision prohibiting the government from favoring any one religion over others, or engaging in religious activities or advocacy.

FIRST AMENDMENT Prohibits Congress from enacting any law respecting an establishment of religion, prohibiting the free exercise of religion, abridging freedom of speech or the press, the right of peaceful assembly and the right to petition for a redress of grievances.

STRICT SCRUTINY Method by which courts determine the constitutionality of a law, when a law affects a fundamental right. Under the test, the legislature must have a compelling interest to enact the law and measures prescribed by the law must be the least restrictive means possible to accomplish its goal.

■≡■

Hobbie v. Unemployment Appeals Commission

Unemployed (P) v. Commission (D)

480 U.S. 136 (1987).

NATURE OF CASE: Appeal from denial of unemployment compensation benefits.

FACT SUMMARY: The Florida Unemployment Appeals Commission (D) denied Hobbie (P) unemployment compensation benefits after she was fired for refusing to work on Saturdays because of sincerely held religious convictions.

RULE OF LAW
Where a state conditions receipt of an important benefit on conduct proscribed by a religious faith, it must be justified by a compelling interest to survive strict scrutiny under the Free Exercise Clause of the First Amendment.

FACTS: Hobbie (P) was discharged from her job when she refused to work on Saturdays because to do so would violate the precepts of her newly adopted religion. The Florida Unemployment Appeals Commission (D) disqualified Hobbie (P) from receiving unemployment compensation benefits, and Hobbie (P) sued the Appeals Commission (D) on the grounds that its disqualification of her for benefits burdened her religion in violation of the Free Exercise Clause of the First Amendment.

ISSUE: Where a state conditions receipt of an important benefit on conduct proscribed by a religious faith, must it be justified by a compelling interest to survive strict scrutiny under the Free Exercise Clause of the First Amendment?

HOLDING AND DECISION: (Brennan, J.) Yes. Where a state conditions receipt of an important benefit upon conduct proscribed by a religious faith, or where it denies such a benefit because of conduct mandated by religious belief, thereby putting substantial pressure on an adherent to modify his behavior and to violate his beliefs, a burden upon religion in violation of the Free Exercise Clause of the First Amendment exists. Such infringements will be subjected to strict scrutiny and will be justified only by proof by the state of a compelling interest. Here, Hobbie's (P) faith precluded her from working on Saturdays, and the Unemployment Appeals Commission (D) denied her unemployment compensation benefits because of this conduct mandated by her religion. It has shown no state interest in doing so; therefore, its disqualification of Hobbie (P) was constitutionally impermissible under the Free Exercise Clause. Nor does it matter that Hobbie (P) adopted her beliefs subsequent to beginning employment, unlike earlier cases in which the adherent's beliefs preceded employment, because the religious convert is entitled to no

less favorable treatment than the longstanding, stalwart follower. Reversed.

DISSENT: (Rehnquist, C.J.) The Unemployment Appeals Commission (D) here did not prohibit Hobbie's (P) religious practices, it merely made them more expensive by requiring her to forego certain jobs or unemployment benefits. Such behavior, which imposes only an indirect burden on the exercise of religion but does not make unlawful the religious practice itself, is not constitutionally impermissible.

ANALYSIS

The majority here rejected a more lenient standard urged on it by the Unemployment Appeals Commission (D), and which had been advocated by former Chief Justice Burger in *Bowen v. Roy*, 476 U.S. 693 (1986), in a concurring opinion. Justice Burger would have allowed the government in such cases to meet its burden "when it demonstrates that a challenged requirement for governmental benefits, neutral and uniform in its application, is a reasonable means of promoting a legitimate public interest." This less strict rule met with immediate disapproval even from some of the Court's more conservative members. For example, in Justice O'Connor's concurrence in the same case, she noted: "Such a test has no basis in precedent and relegates a serious First Amendment value to the barest level of minimal scrutiny that the Equal Protection Clause already provides."

Quicknotes

EQUAL PROTECTION CLAUSE A constitutional guarantee that no person should be denied the same protection of the laws enjoyed by other persons in like circumstances.

FREE EXERCISE CLAUSE The guarantee of the First Amendment to the United States Constitution prohibiting Congress from enacting laws regarding the establishment of religion or prohibiting the free exercise thereof.

STRICT SCRUTINY Method by which courts determine the constitutionality of a law, when a law affects a fundamental right. Under the test, the legislature must have a compelling interest to enact the law and measures prescribed by the law must be the least restrictive means possible to accomplish its goal.

Employment Div., Oregon Dept. of Human Resources v. Smith

Government agency (D) v. Native American (P)

494 U.S. 872 (1990).

NATURE OF CASE: Review of denial of unemployment compensation.

FACT SUMMARY: Smith (P) was terminated for ingesting peyote in contravention to state law, although his ingestion thereof was purportedly for religious reasons.

🏛 RULE OF LAW
The fact that drug consumption is pursuant to religious belief will not exempt such ingestion from a general prohibition thereof.

FACTS: Smith (P), an American Indian, ingested peyote during a religious ceremony. State law extended a blanket prohibition on such ingestion. Smith (P) was consequently terminated from his employment. He sought state unemployment compensation but was denied same because his termination had been for misconduct. Smith (P) appealed, contending that the law under which he was terminated violated his rights under the Free Exercise Clause of the First Amendment. The Oregon Supreme Court agreed and reversed. The United States Supreme Court granted certiorari.

ISSUE: Will the fact that drug consumption is pursuant to religious belief exempt such ingestion from a general prohibition thereon?

HOLDING AND DECISION: (Scalia, J.) No. The fact that drug consumption is pursuant to religious belief will not exempt such ingestion from a general prohibition thereon. The government may not mandate religious belief, nor may it pass laws that single out religion for preferential or burdensome treatments. However, with respect to conduct, the situation is different. A law of general application which does not single out religion in its intent or execution may not be disobeyed on the grounds that doing so violates a religious belief. To hold otherwise in a country characterized by religious diversity would be to invite anarchy. Here, the law against peyote consumption is religion-neutral on its face and as applied. Consequently, Smith (P) may not involve a religious justification for disobedience thereto. Reversed.

CONCURRENCE: (O'Connor, J.) A law that prohibits conduct that happens to be an act of worship for someone does interfere with that person's free exercise of religion. To so prohibit such conduct should require a compelling governmental interest, which has been shown here.

DISSENT: (Blackmun, J.) The state must show a compelling interest to prohibit religious conduct as part of a law of general application, which it has not done here.

▶ ANALYSIS

Prior to this decision, precedents existed for the contention Smith (P) made in this case. In *Pierce v. Society of Sisters*, 268 U.S. 510 (1925), for instance, the Court struck down a state law requiring children to attend public schools, on the basis that this violated the Free Exercise Clause. The Court here distinguished *Pierce* by noting that not only was freedom of religion implicated there, but also the right of parents to control their children.

Quicknotes

CERTIORARI A discretionary writ issued by a superior court to an inferior court in order to review the lower court's decisions; the Supreme Court's writ ordering such review.

COMPELLING GOVERNMENT INTEREST Defense to an alleged Equal Protection Clause violation that a state action was necessary in order to protect an interest that the government is under a duty to protect.

FIRST AMENDMENT Prohibits Congress from enacting any law respecting an establishment of religion, prohibiting the free exercise of religion, abridging freedom of speech or the press, the right of peaceful assembly and the right to petition for a redress of grievances.

FREE EXERCISE CLAUSE The guarantee of the First Amendment to the United States Constitution prohibiting Congress from enacting laws regarding the establishment of religion or prohibiting the free exercise thereof.

Corporation of the Presiding Bishop of the Church of Jesus Christ of Latter-Day Saints v. Amos

Mormon Church (D) v. Employee (P)

483 U.S. 327 (1987).

NATURE OF CASE: Appeal from judgment that a § 702 exemption of the Civil Rights Act of 1964 violates the Establishment Clause of the First Amendment.

FACT SUMMARY: In Amos's (P) action on behalf of Mayson against the Latter Day Saints (Mormon) Church (D) for Mayson's discharge as a Church (D) employee because Mayson was not a Church (D) member, Amos (P) contended that if construed to allow religious employers to discriminate on religious grounds in hiring for nonreligious jobs, § 702 of the Civil Rights Act of 1964 violates the Establishment Clause of the First Amendment.

RULE OF LAW
Section 702 of the Civil Rights Act of 1964 is rationally related to the legitimate purpose of alleviating significant governmental interference with the ability of religious organizations to define and carry out their religious missions.

FACTS: Mayson worked for 16 years as a building engineer at the Deseret Gymnasium, a nonprofit facility, open to the public and run by the Latter Day Saints (Mormon) Church (D). Mayson was discharged because he failed to qualify for a temple recommend, or certificate, that he was a member of the Church (D) and eligible to attend its temples. Amos (P), on Mayson's behalf, sued the Church (D) for discriminating on religious grounds in hiring for nonreligious jobs. The Church (D) argued that § 702 of the Civil Rights Act of 1964 exempts religious organizations from Title VII's prohibition against discrimination in employment on the basis of religion. Amos (P), at trial, contended that if construed to allow religious employers to discriminate on religious grounds in hiring for nonreligious jobs, § 702 violated the Establishment Clause of the First Amendment. The district court held that § 702 did violate the Establishment Clause and ruled in Amos's (P) favor. The Church (D) appealed.

ISSUE: Is § 702 of the Civil Rights Act rationally related to the legitimate purpose of alleviating significant governmental interference with the ability of religious organizations to define and carry out their religious missions?

HOLDING AND DECISION: (White, J.) Yes. Section 702 is rationally related to the legitimate purpose of alleviating significant governmental interference with the ability of religious organizations to define and carry out their religious missions. To be constitutional, a law must serve a secular legislative purpose. Congress's purpose, in enacting § 702, was to minimize governmental interference with the decisionmaking process in religions. This purpose does not violate the Establishment Clause of the First Amendment. Constitutionality of a law under the Establishment Clause also depends on the principal or primary effect of that law neither advancing nor inhibiting religion. For a law to be forbidden, it must be fair to say that the government itself has advanced religion through its own activities and influence. Section 702, does not single out religious entities for a benefit. Rather § 702 is neutral on its face and motivated by a permissible purpose of limiting governmental interference with the exercise of religion and, therefore, is not violative of the Establishment Clause. Reversed.

CONCURRENCE: (Brennan, J.) Ideally, religious organizations should be able to discriminate on the basis of religion only with respect to religious activities, so that a determination should be made in each case whether an activity is religious or secular.

CONCURRENCE: (O'Connor, J.) In cases such as this, the inquiry should always be whether the government's purpose is to endorse religion and whether the statute actually conveys a message of endorsement.

ANALYSIS

The Establishment Clause applies to both the federal and local governments. It is a prohibition of sponsorship of religion which requires that government neither aid nor formally establish a religion. At its inception, the clause might not have been intended to prohibit governmental aid to all religion, but today the accepted view is that it also prohibits a preference for religion over nonreligion.

■══■

Quicknotes

ESTABLISHMENT CLAUSE The constitutional provision prohibiting the government from favoring any one religion over others, or engaging in religious activities or advocacy.

FIRST AMENDMENT Prohibits Congress from enacting any law respecting an establishment of religion, prohibiting the free exercise of religion, abridging freedom of speech or the press, the right of peaceful assembly and the right to petition for a redress of grievances.

■══■

Equal Protection

Quick Reference Rules of Law

Railway Express Agency v. New York

Freight transport company (D) v. City (P)

336 U.S. 106 (1949).

NATURE OF CASE: Appeal from conviction for violation of a state advertising statute.

FACT SUMMARY: New York has a regulation that prohibits advertising on business vehicles unless the vehicles are engaged in their owner's usual work and are not used mainly for advertising.

RULE OF LAW
The Equal Protection Clause does not require that a statute eradicate all evils of the same type or none at all.

FACTS: A New York City regulation prohibits advertising vehicles. The statute does not prohibit, however, advertising on business vehicles so long as the vehicles are engaged in their owner's usual work and are not used merely or mainly for advertising. Railway Express Agency (D) is engaged in a nationwide express business. It operates 1900 trucks in New York City (P). It sells space on the exterior of its trucks for advertising. Such advertising is generally unconnected with its business.

ISSUE: Does the Equal Protection Clause require that a statute eradicate all evils of the same type or none at all?

HOLDING AND DECISION: (Douglas, J.) No. The Equal Protection Clause does not require that a statute eradicate all evils of the same type or none at all. The court of special sessions concluded that advertising on vehicles using the streets of New York City (P) constituted a distraction to vehicle drivers and pedestrians, therefore affecting the public's safety in the use of the streets. The local authorities may well have concluded that those who advertise their own products on their trucks do not present the same traffic problem in view of the nature and extent of their advertising. The Court cannot say that such a judgment is now an allowable one. The classification has relation to the purpose for which it is made and does not contain the kind of discrimination against which the Equal Protection Clause protects. The fact that New York City (P) does not eliminate all distractions from its streets is immaterial. It is not a requirement of equal protection that all evils of the same genus be eradicated or none at all. Conviction affirmed.

CONCURRENCE: (Rutledge, J.) The opinion and judgment are appropriate but the equal protection of the laws analysis is doubtful.

CONCURRENCE: (Jackson, J.) Laws must not discriminate between people except upon some reasonable differentiation fairly related to the object of regulation.

There is a real difference between doing in self-interest and doing for hire so that it is one thing to tolerate an action done in self-interest and another thing to permit the same action to be done for hire.

ANALYSIS

Traditionally, the Equal Protection Clause supported only minimal judicial intervention. During the late sixties, however, it became the favorite and most far-reaching tool for judicial protection of fundamental rights not specified in the Constitution. For many years, the impact of the Equal Protection Clause was a very limited one. During the decades of extensive Court intervention with state economic legislation, substantive due process, not equal protection, provided the cutting edge to determine a statute's constitutionality. Also, as the concurring opinion points out, equal protection demanded only a "reasonable differentiation fairly related to the object of regulation." As demonstrated by this case, the rational classification requirement could be satisfied fairly easily, as the courts were deferential to legislative judgment and were extremely easily convinced that the means used might relate rationally to a plausible end.

Quicknotes

ESTABLISHMENT CLAUSE The constitutional provision prohibiting the government from favoring any one religion over others, or engaging in religious activities or advocacy.

FUNDAMENTAL RIGHT A liberty that is either expressly or impliedly provided for in the United States Constitution, the deprivation or burdening of which is subject to a heightened standard of review.

New Orleans v. Dukes

Municipality (D) v. Pushcart vendor (P)

427 U.S. 297 (1976).

NATURE OF CASE: Challenge to constitutionality of a local ordinance.

FACT SUMMARY: A pushcart operator (P) attacked a New Orleans (D) ordinance banning all pushcart food vendors from the French Quarter who had not operated there for at least eight years.

🏛 RULE OF LAW

Unless a classification trammels fundamental personal rights or is drawn upon inherently suspect distinctions such as race, religion or alienage, the constitutionality of the statutory discriminations is presumed and all that is required is that the challenged classification be rationally related to a legitimate state interest.

FACTS: A New Orleans (D) ordinance banned all pushcart food vendors from operating in the French Quarter except those who had continuously operated there for eight or more years. Plaintiff, who had operated a pushcart for only two years, challenged the ordinance.

ISSUE: Unless a classification trammels fundamental personal rights or is drawn upon inherently suspect distinctions such as race, religion or alienage, is the constitutionality of the statutory discriminations presumed and is all that is required that the challenged classification be rationally related to a legitimate state interest?

HOLDING AND DECISION: (Per curiam) Yes. Unless a classification trammels fundamental personal rights or is drawn upon inherently suspect distinctions such as race, religion or alienage, the constitutionality of the statutory discriminations is presumed and all that is required is that the challenged classification be rationally related to a legitimate state interest. When local economic regulation is challenged as solely violating the Equal Protection Clause, this Court consistently defers to the legislature's determinations as to the desirability of particular statutory discriminations. States are accorded wide latitude in the regulation of their local economies under their police powers. Here the classification rationally furthers the purpose identified by New Orleans (D) as its objective in enacting the provision as a means of preserving the appearance and custom valued by the Quarter's residents and attractive to tourists. Such objective is legitimate. Reversed.

▶ ANALYSIS

This case represents an equal protection challenge to an economic regulation. The Court typically deferred to the legislatures in such challenges so long as the classifications were not arbitrary. The Court here rejected the argument that the grandfather provision was arbitrary, since the city could rationally decide that newer businesses were less likely to have established substantial reliance interests in continued operation.

Quicknotes

EQUAL PROTECTION CLAUSE A constitutional guarantee that no person should be denied the same protection of the laws enjoyed by other persons in like circumstances.

POLICE POWERS The power of a state or local government to regulate private conduct for the health, safety and welfare of the general public.

RATIONAL BASIS TEST A test employed by the court to determine the validity of a statute in equal protection actions, whereby the court determines whether the challenged statute is rationally related to the achievement of a legitimate state interest.

United States R.R. Retirement Board v. Fritz

Railroad retirement system (D) v. Employees (P)

449 U.S. 166 (1980).

NATURE OF CASE: Appeal of order invalidating statutory changes in railroad retirement system.

FACT SUMMARY: Congress made certain changes in the railroad retirement system that included the taking away of vested benefits.

🏛 RULE OF LAW
Congress may enact a statute stripping vested benefits from selected portions of eligible railroad employees.

FACTS: Prior to 1974, railroad retirees received benefits from the Social Security and railroad retirement systems. In 1974, Congress passed an act mandating that railroad workers with less than 10 years' seniority as of January 1, 1975, would not qualify for dual benefits. Workers with more than 10 years who were still connected to the industry would receive dual benefits, as would current retirees. Fritz (P) and other employees who did not qualify for dual benefits under the new law challenged it as a violation of equal protection. The lower courts overturned the law.

ISSUE: May Congress enact a statute stripping vested benefits from selected portions of eligible railroad employees?

HOLDING AND DECISION: (Rehnquist, J.) Yes. Congress may enact a statute stripping vested benefits from selected portions of eligible railroad employees. Congress could have eliminated these windfall benefits for all employees, but rather chose to do this to only some. The only remaining question is whether the classification was arbitrary or capricious. This was not so here. Congress could have assumed that those having a current connection with the industry in 1974 were most likely to remain in the railroad industry and were thus more worthy of benefits. Where plausible reasons for congressional action exist, inquiry into the actual reasons, if any, is improper. Reversed.

DISSENT: (Brennan, J.) The purpose of the legislation was to preserve vested benefits for employees. The legislation not only does not rationally further this goal, but is inimical to it. A challenged classification may be sustained only if it is related to the achievement of an actual governmental purpose.

▶ ANALYSIS

Brennan's dissent would have the Court look to the actual purpose of challenged legislation. The majority approach, which validates an act of Congress if any valid purpose can be articulated, represents the mainstream thought on this issue. The approach promoted by Justice Brennan saw its high point of acceptance during the *Lochner* era.

Quicknotes

EQUAL PROTECTION CLAUSE A constitutional guarantee that no person should be denied the same protection of the laws enjoyed by other persons in like circumstances.

Plessy v. Ferguson

Passenger (D) v. State (P)

163 U.S. 537 (1896).

NATURE OF CASE: Appeal from criminal prosecution for violating a state railway accommodation segregation law.

FACT SUMMARY: Plessy (D) was arrested for trying to sit in a railroad car that was designated "for whites only."

🏛 RULE OF LAW
Segregation of the races is reasonable if based upon the established custom, usage and traditions of the people in the state.

FACTS: Plessy (D), who was seven-eighths white and whose skin color was white, was denied a seat in an all-white railroad car. When he (D) resisted, he was arrested for violating a state law that provided for segregated "separate but equal" railroad accommodations. Plessy (D) appealed the conviction on the basis that separation of the races stigmatized blacks and stamped them with the badge of inferiority. He (D) claimed that segregation violated the Thirteenth and Fourteenth Amendments. The trial court found Plessy (D) guilty on the basis that the law was a reasonable exercise of the state's police powers based upon custom, usage and tradition in the state.

ISSUE: Is segregation of the races reasonable if based upon the established custom, usage and traditions of the people in the state?

HOLDING AND DECISION: (Brown, J.) Yes. Segregation of the races is reasonable if based upon the established custom, usage and traditions of the people in the state. This is a valid exercise of the state's police power. Where this has been the established custom, usage or tradition in the state, it may continue to require such segregation as is reasonable to preserve order and the public peace. Such decisions have been continuously upheld. This is not a badge of "slavery" under the Thirteenth Amendment and it violates no provision of the Fourteenth Amendment. The enforced separation of the races is not a badge of servitude or inferiority regardless of how Plessy (D) and other blacks deem to treat it. The conviction is sustained.

DISSENT: (Harlan, J.) The statute interferes with the personal freedom of individuals to freely associate with others. The Constitution is color-blind. All citizens should and must be treated alike. Blacks are not subordinate or inferior things. They are citizens and are entitled to all of the privileges that this entails. Enforced separation is an impermissible burden on these privileges and freedoms. The conviction should be overturned.

▶ ANALYSIS

Plessy is of importance only for its historical perspective. Later cases borrowed the "separate but equal" phraseology and turned it around 180 degrees. In *Brown v. Board of Education*, 347 U.S. 483 (1954), the Court, 58 years after *Plessy*, held that separate could never be considered equal. It thus expressly overruled *Plessy*.

■═■

Quicknotes

FOURTEENTH AMENDMENT Declares that no state shall make or enforce any law that shall abridge the privileges and immunities of citizens of the United States.

POLICE POWER The power of a government to impose restrictions on the rights of private persons, as long as those restrictions are reasonably related to the promotion and protection of public health, safety, morals and the general welfare.

THIRTEENTH AMENDMENT The constitutional provision that abolished slavery in the United States.

■═■

Korematsu v. United States

Japanese American (D) v. Federal government (P)

323 U.S. 214 (1944).

NATURE OF CASE: Appeal from a conviction for violation of exclusion order No. 34.

FACT SUMMARY: Korematsu (D), an American citizen of Japanese ancestry, was convicted of violating exclusion order No. 34, a World War II decree that ordered all persons of Japanese ancestry to leave the military area of the Western United States.

🏛 RULE OF LAW
Apprehension by the proper military authorities of the gravest imminent danger to the public safety can justify the curtailment of the civil rights of a single racial group.

FACTS: Korematsu (D), an American citizen of Japanese ancestry, was convicted in federal district court for remaining in San Leandro, California, a "military area," contrary to civilian exclusion order No. 34 of the commanding general of the western command. The order directed that after May 9, 1942, all persons of Japanese ancestry should be excluded from the area in order to protect against acts of sabotage and espionage during World War II. Those of Japanese ancestry were to report to and temporarily remain in an assembly center and go under military control to a relocation center for an indeterminate period. Korematsu (D) appealed on grounds that the order denied equal protection.

ISSUE: Can apprehension by the proper military authorities of the gravest imminent danger to the public safety justify the curtailment of the civil rights of a single racial group?

HOLDING AND DECISION: (Black, J.) Yes. Apprehension by the proper military authorities of the gravest imminent danger to the public safety can justify the curtailment of the civil rights of a single racial group. While such a classification is immediately suspect and is subject to the most rigid scrutiny, pressing public necessity can sometimes justify such exclusions. When under conditions of modern warfare the country is threatened, "the power to protect must be commensurate with the threatened danger." Korematsu (D) was excluded because the United States was at war with the Empire of Japan, because the proper military authorities feared invasion of the West Coast and believed security required exclusion, and because Congress, placing its confidence in the military, determined that the military should have that power. Affirmed.

CONCURRENCE: (Frankfurter, J.) This decision only says that the Constitution was not violated, and not that the Court approved of the methods used.

DISSENT: (Murphy, J.) It cannot be reasonably assumed that all persons of Japanese ancestry may have a dangerous tendency to commit enemy acts.

DISSENT: (Jackson, J.) A civil court should not be made to enforce an order that violates constitutional limitations even if it is a reasonable exercise of military authority.

▶ ANALYSIS

This case has received severe and growing criticism over the years. However, Chief Justice Warren expressed the view that in some circumstances the Court will simply not be in a position to reject descriptions by the executive of the degree of military necessity. Where time is of the essence, the Court could only reject the necessity not on grounds of factual unassailability, but for insufficiency. Justice Douglas, 30 years later, wrote, "the decisions were extreme and went to the verge of wartime power . . . It is easy in retrospect to denounce what was done, as there actually was no attempted Japanese invasion of our country . . . but those making plans for the defense of the nation had no such knowledge and were planning for the worst." *De Funis v. Odegaard*, 416 U.S. 312 (1974).

■■■

Quicknotes

EQUAL PROTECTION CLAUSE A constitutional guarantee that no person should be denied the same protection of the laws enjoyed by other persons in like circumstances.

■■■

Brown v. Board of Education

[Parties not identified in casebook excerpt.]

347 U.S. 483 (1954).

NATURE OF CASE: Black minors seek the Court's aid in obtaining admission to the public schools of their community on a nonsegregated basis.

FACT SUMMARY: Black children were denied admission to public schools attended by white children.

🏛 RULE OF LAW
The "separate but equal" doctrine has no application in the field of education and the segregation of children in public schools based solely on their race violates the Equal Protection Clause.

FACTS: Black children had been denied admission to public schools attended by white children under laws requiring or permitting segregation according to race. It was found that the black children's schools and the white children's schools had been or were being equalized with respect to buildings, curricula, qualifications, and salaries of teachers.

ISSUE: Does the "separate but equal" doctrine have application in the field of education and does the segregation of children in public schools based solely on their race violate the Equal Protection Clause?

HOLDING AND DECISION: (Warren, C.J.) The "separate but equal" doctrine has no application in the field of education and the segregation of children in public schools based solely on their race violates the Equal Protection Clause. First of all, intangible as well as tangible factors may be considered. Hence, the fact that the facilities and other tangible factors in the schools have been equalized is not controlling. Segregation of white and black children in public schools has a detrimental effect on the black children because the policy of separating the races is usually interpreted as denoting the inferiority of the black children. A sense of inferiority affects a child's motivation to learn. Segregation tends to deprive black children of some of the benefits they would receive in an integrated school. Any language in *Plessy v. Ferguson* contrary to this is rejected. The "separate but equal" doctrine has no place in the field of education. Separate facilities are inherently unequal. Such facilities deprive black children of their right to equal protection of the laws. Reversed.

▶ ANALYSIS

In *Plessy v. Ferguson*, 163 U.S. 537 (1896), the Court sustained a Louisiana statute requiring "equal, but separate accommodations" for black and white railway passengers. The separate but equal doctrine was born and under it a long line of statutes providing separate but equal facilities were upheld. Justice Harlan was the only dissenter in *Plessy*. He stated, "The arbitrary separation of citizens, on the basis of race, while they are on a public highway . . . cannot be justified upon any legal grounds. The thin disguise of equal accommodations for passengers in railway cars will not mislead anyone, nor atone for the wrong done this day." After the 1954 decision in *Brown v. Board of Education*, the Court found segregation unconstitutional in other public facilities as well. Despite the emphasis on the school context in *Brown*, the later cases resulted in per curiam orders simply citing *Brown*. Facilities that were desegregated included beaches, buses, golf courses and parks.

Quicknotes

EQUAL PROTECTION CLAUSE A constitutional guarantee that no person should be denied the same protection of the laws enjoyed by other persons in like circumstances.

Brown v. Board of Education (II)

[Parties not identified in casebook excerpt.]

349 U.S. 294 (1955).

NATURE OF CASE: Decision to determine the manner in which relief from segregation in public schools is to be accorded.

FACT SUMMARY: In May 1954, the Court decided that racial discrimination in public education is unconstitutional. It requested further arguments on the question of relief.

RULE OF LAW

Court orders must be consistent with equitable principles of flexibility and requiring the defendant to make a prompt and reasonable start toward full racial integration in public schools.

FACTS: These cases were decided in May 1974. The opinions declared that racial discrimination in public education is unconstitutional. They are incorporated here. Because the cases arose under various local conditions and their disposition will involve a variety of local problems, the Court requested additional arguments on the question of relief. All provisions of federal, state, and local laws that permit segregation in public schools must be modified.

ISSUE: Must court orders be consistent with equitable principles of flexibility and requiring the defendant to make a prompt and reasonable start toward full racial integration in public schools?

HOLDING AND DECISION: (Warren, C.J.) Yes. Court orders must be consistent with equitable principles of flexibility and requiring the defendant to make a prompt and reasonable start toward full racial integration in public schools. School authorities have the primary responsibility for assessing and solving the problem of achieving racial integration in the public schools. It will be for courts to consider whether the school authorities' actions are a good faith implementation of the governing constitutional principles. Because of their proximity to local conditions and the possible need for further hearings, the courts that originally heard these cases can best perform this judicial appraisal. In doing so, the courts will be guided by the equitable principles of practical flexibility in shaping remedies and the facility for adjusting and reconciling public and private needs. The courts will require that the defendants make a prompt and reasonable start toward full racial integration in the public schools. Once such a start is made, the courts may determine that additional time is required to carry out the May 1954 ruling. However, the burden rests upon the defendant to determine that such time is necessary and consistent with good faith compliance with the Constitution. The courts may consider problems related to administration, the facilities, school transportation systems and revision of school districts and local laws. They will also consider the adequacy of any plans proposed by the defendants and will retain jurisdiction during the transition period. The cases are remanded to the lower courts to enter orders consistent with this opinion as necessary to insure that the parties to these cases are admitted to public schools on a racially nondiscriminatory basis.

ANALYSIS

After its promulgation of general deliberate speed in *Brown II* in 1955, the court maintained silence about implementation for several years. Enforcement of the desegregation requirement was left largely to lower court litigation. In 1958, the Court broke its silence in *Cooper v. Aaron*, 358 U.S. 1 (1958), where it reaffirmed the *Brown* principles in the face of official resistance in Little Rock, Arkansas. It was not until the early sixties, however, that the Court began to consider the details of desegregation plans. During the late sixties, court rulings on implementation came with greater frequency, specificity, and urgency. Finally, in *Alexander v. Holmes County Board of Education*, 369 U.S. 19 (1969), the Court called for an immediate end to dual school systems.

Quicknotes

EQUAL PROTECTION CLAUSE A constitutional guarantee that no person should be denied the same protection of the laws enjoyed by other persons in like circumstances.

Loving v. Virginia

White man/black woman (D) v. State (P)

388 U.S. 1 (1967).

NATURE OF CASE: Appeal after conviction for violation of state law barring interracial marriage.

FACT SUMMARY: Loving (D), a white man, and Jeter (D), a black woman, both Virginia residents, were married in the District of Columbia. When they returned to Virginia, they were indicted for violating the State's (P) ban on interracial marriage.

🏛 RULE OF LAW
A state law restricting the freedom to marry solely because of racial classification violates the Equal Protection Clause.

FACTS: In June 1958, Loving (D), a white man, and Jeter (D), a black woman, both Virginia residents, were married in the District of Columbia, pursuant to its laws. Shortly after their marriage, the Lovings (D) returned to Virginia and were indicted for violating the state's law barring interracial marriage. They pleaded guilty and were sentenced to one year in jail. The trial judge suspended the sentence for 25 years on the condition that the Lovings (D) leave the state and not return for 25 years. In 1963, they filed a motion to have the judgment vacated and set aside.

ISSUE: Does a state law that prevents marriages between persons solely on the basis of racial classifications violate the Equal Protection Clause?

HOLDING AND DECISION: (Warren, C.J.) Yes. At the very least, the Equal Protection Clause demands that racial classifications, especially those suspect in criminal statutes, be subjected to the most rigid scrutiny. If they are ever to be upheld, they must be shown to be necessary to the accomplishment of some legitimate state objective. Here, there is no question that Virginia's miscegenation statutes rest solely upon distinctions drawn according to race. The statutes proscribe generally accepted conduct if engaged in by members of different races. The fact that the statute prohibits only interracial marriages involving white persons indicates that its aim is to maintain white supremacy. There is patently no legitimate overriding purpose independent of invidious discrimination that justifies the classification. A statute restricting marriage solely because of race violates the Equal Protection Clause. These statutes also deprive the Lovings (D) of liberty without due process. Since marriage is a basic human civil right, to deny this freedom on so insupportable a basis as racial classifications deprives all the state's citizens of liberty without due process of the law. Reversed.

CONCURRENCE: (Stewart, J.) A state criminal statute cannot be constitutionally valid if the proscribed act is prohibited solely because of the alleged perpetrator's race.

▶ ANALYSIS

In *McLaughlin v. Florida*, 379 U.S. 184 (1964), a state law banning habitual nighttime cohabitation between whites and blacks not married to each other was held to violate the Equal Protection Clause, since other nonmarried couples were not subject to prosecution for the same acts. Ordinances establishing ghettos in which blacks must reside were found to violate the clause (*Buchanan v. Warley*, 245 U.S. 60 [1917]), as was judicial enforcement of covenants restricting ownership of land to whites (*Shelley v. Kraemer*, 334 U.S. 1 [1948]). Racial discrimination in the selection of jurors (*Patton v. Mississippi*, 332 U.S. 463 [1947]), hiring blacks for certain occupations, and establishing racial qualifications for public offices (*Anderson v. Martin*, 375 U.S. 399 [1964]) have all been held to violate equal protection.

━━■

Quicknotes

DUE PROCESS CLAUSE Clause found in the Fifth and Fourteenth Amendments to the United States Constitution providing that no person shall be deprived of "life, liberty, or property, without due process of law."

EQUAL PROTECTION CLAUSE A constitutional guarantee that no person should be denied the same protection of the laws enjoyed by other persons in like circumstances.

MISCEGENATION STATUTE Law barring marriage between two persons of different races.

━━■

Yick Wo v. Hopkins

Chinese laundry operator (D) v. City agency (P)

118 U.S. 356 (1886).

NATURE OF CASE: Appeal from conviction of violating a city health and safety ordinance.

FACT SUMMARY: Only Chinese aliens were prosecuted under an ordinance requiring laundries to be constructed out of brick.

🏛 RULE OF LAW
A valid law unevenly and discriminatorily administered violates the Equal Protection Clause of the Constitution.

FACTS: A San Francisco ordinance made it unlawful to operate a laundry without consent of the board of supervisors unless the laundry was constructed of either stone or brick. Under the ordinance, the supervisors denied permission to Chinese aliens but granted it to whites. Yick Wo (D) was arrested for violating the ordinance. He (D) appealed his conviction on the basis that the law was being administered in a discriminatory fashion.

ISSUE: Can a valid law be declared unconstitutional because it is being arbitrarily and discriminatorily applied?

HOLDING AND DECISION: (Matthews, J.) Yes. When, as here, it can be objectively demonstrated that a law is being discriminatorily applied, a court may declare the law unconstitutional. We can decide this case without ever reaching the question of the ordinance's validity (which is seriously in question). Even if valid, the San Francisco Supervisors (P) have applied it in a highly discriminatory and systematic fashion to exclude those of Chinese origin from practicing the laundry business. Such discriminatory treatment violates both the spirit and letter of the Equal Protection Clause and Yick Wo's (D) conviction must be reversed.

▌ *ANALYSIS*

Other examples in this area include the systematic exclusion of blacks from jury panels through the use of the prosecutor's preemptory challenge power or by excluding them from jury rolls. Also, in *Mayor of Philadelphia v. Educational Equality League*, 415 U.S. 605 (1974), the Mayor was charged with discrimination in his appointment of a selection committee for school board members. However, in this case, the proof of discrimination was insufficient to establish a prima facie case and the charges were dismissed. The Court held that mere statistical data concerning population mixtures was insufficient to prove discrimination as a matter of law.

Quicknotes

EQUAL PROTECTION CLAUSE A constitutional guarantee that no person should be denied the same protection of the laws enjoyed by other persons in like circumstances.

■━━■

Washington v. Davis

[Parties not identified in casebook excerpt.]

426 U.S. 229 (1976).

NATURE OF CASE: Action for a declaratory judgment.

FACT SUMMARY: A qualifying test for positions as police officers in the District of Columbia was failed by a disproportionately high number of black applicants (P).

🏛 RULE OF LAW
A law or official governmental practice must have a "discriminatory purpose," not merely a disproportionate effect on one race, in order to constitute "invidious discrimination" under the Fifth Amendment Due Process Clause or the Fourteenth Amendment Equal Protection Clause.

FACTS: In order to be accepted in the District of Columbia Metropolitan Police Department, all applicants had to receive a grade of at least 40 on "Test 21." This test was developed by the Civil Service Commission for use throughout the federal service to test "verbal ability, vocabulary, reading and comprehension." After failing this test, several black applicants (P) brought an action against the Commissioners of the United States Civil Service Commission (D) for a declaratory judgment that "Test 21" was unconstitutional. In this action, the black applicants (P) claimed that "Test 21" was unlawfully discriminatory against blacks, and, therefore, was in violation of the Fifth Amendment's Due Process Clause. After the test was invalidated by the court of appeals, the Commissioners (D) appealed to the Supreme Court.

ISSUE: Does a law or official governmental practice constitute "invidious discrimination" merely because it affects a greater proportion of one race than another?

HOLDING AND DECISION: (White, J.) No. A law or official governmental practice must have a "discriminatory purpose," not merely a disproportionate effect on one race, in order to constitute "invidious discrimination" under the Fifth Amendment's Due Process Clause or the Fourteenth Amendment's Equal Protection Clause. Of course, a disproportionate impact may be relevant as "evidence" of a "discriminatory purpose." However, such impact "is not the sole touchstone of invidious racial discrimination forbidden by the Constitution," and, standing alone, "it does not trigger the rule that racial classifications are to be subjected to the strictest scrutiny." Here, "Test 21" is racially "neutral" on its face (i.e., it is designed to disqualify anyone who cannot meet the requirements of the police training program). As such, it is valid even though it has a disproportionate effect on blacks. Reversed.

CONCURRENCE: (Stevens, J.) The factual support for purposeful discrimination will vary with each case as does the amount of deference owed to the trial court's finding. The best evidence will be the objective circumstances rather than the subjective intentions of the actor. Discriminatory purpose and discriminatory impact are closer than may appear.

▶ ANALYSIS

Generally, classifications based upon race are considered "suspect" and, therefore, subjected to "strict scrutiny" under the Equal Protection Clause or the Due Process Clause (i.e. such classifications must be justified by a "compelling state interest"). However, as this case illustrates, such "strict scrutiny" is only applied when there is "purposeful discrimination." As such, the Court (as here) can avoid applying "strict scrutiny" by finding that any discriminatory impact is merely incidental. Note that here the court also avoided applying the strict standard in Title VII of the Civil Rights Act of 1964 (by saying that only the constitutional issue was raised). Under Title VII, whenever hiring and promotion practices disqualify disproportionate numbers of blacks, the disqualifications must be justified by more than a rational basis (i.e., must be validated in terms of job performance) even if no discriminatory purpose is shown.

▰▰▰

Quicknotes

DUE PROCESS CLAUSE Clause found in the Fifth and Fourteenth Amendments to the United States Constitution providing that no person shall be deprived of "life, liberty, or property, without due process of law."

EQUAL PROTECTION CLAUSE A constitutional guarantee that no person should be denied the same protection of the laws enjoyed by other persons in like circumstances.

INVIDIOUS DISCRIMINATION Unequal treatment of a class of persons that is particularly malicious or hostile.

RATIONAL BASIS REVIEW A test employed by the court to determine the validity of a statute in equal protection actions, whereby the court determines whether the challenged statute is rationally related to the achievement of a legitimate state interest.

Continued on next page.

STRICT SCRUTINY Method by which courts determine the constitutionality of a law, when a law affects a fundamental right. Under the test, the legislature must have a compelling interest to enact the law and measures prescribed by the law must be the least restrictive means possible to accomplish its goal.

■▬■

Grutter v. Bollinger

Law school applicant (P) v. Law school (D)

539 U.S. 306 (2003).

NATURE OF CASE: Appeal in racial discrimination case.

FACT SUMMARY: When Grutter (P), a white Michigan resident, was denied admission to the University of Michigan Law School (the Law School) (D), she sued the latter in federal district court, alleging racial discrimination against her in violation of the Equal Protection Clause on the basis of the Law School's (D) express consideration of race as a factor in the admissions process.

🏛 RULE OF LAW
Student body diversity is a compelling state interest that can justify the use of race in university admissions.

FACTS: To attempt to achieve student body diversity, the University of Michigan Law School (the Law School) (D) admissions committee required admissions officials to evaluate each applicant based on all the information in the file, including a personal statement, letters of recommendation, a student's essay, GPA score, LSAT score, as well as so-called "soft variables." The admissions policy, furthermore, specifically stressed the Law School's (D) longstanding commitment to racial and ethnic diversity. When Grutter (P), a white Michigan resident, applied for admission but was denied, she sued the Law School (D) in federal district court, alleging racial discrimination against her in violation of the Equal Protection Clause. [The district court upheld Grutter's (P) claim. The court of appeals reversed, and Grutter (P) appealed.]

ISSUE: Is student body diversity a compelling state interest that can justify the use of race in university admissions?

HOLDING AND DECISION: (O'Connor, J.) Yes. Student body diversity is a compelling state interest that can justify the use of race in university admissions. Here, the Law School's (D) admissions program bears the hallmarks of a narrowly tailored plan. Truly individualized consideration demands that race be used in a flexible, nonmechanical way. It follows from this mandate that universities cannot establish quotas for members of certain racial groups or put members of those groups on separate admissions tracks. Nor can universities insulate applicants who belong to certain racial or ethnic groups from the competition for admission. Universities can, however, as was done here, consider race or ethnicity more flexibly as a plus factor in the context of individualized consideration of each and every applicant. The Law School's (D) goal of attaining a critical mass of underrepresented minority students does not transform its program into a quota. The

evidence indicated that the Law School (D) engaged in a highly individualized, holistic review of each applicant's file, giving serious consideration to all the ways an applicant might contribute to a "diverse educational environment." Furthermore, evidence showed that the Law School (D) gives substantial weight to diversity factors besides race by frequently accepting nonminority applicants with grades and test scores lower than underrepresented minority applicants. There was no Law School (D) policy, either de facto or de jure, of automatic acceptance or rejection based on any single "soft" variable. Narrow tailoring does not require exhaustion of every conceivable race-neutral alternative. Nor does it require a university to choose between maintaining a reputation for excellence or fulfilling a commitment to provide educational opportunities to members of all racial groups. Affirmed.

CONCURRENCE: (Ginsburg, J.) From today's vantage point, one may hope, but not firmly forecast, that over the next generation's span, progress toward nondiscrimination and genuinely equal opportunity will make it safe to sunset affirmative action.

DISSENT: (Rehnquist, C.J.) Although the Law School (D) claims it must take the steps it does to achieve "critical mass" of underrepresented minority students, its actual program bears no relation to this asserted goal. Stripped of its "critical mass" veil, the Law School's (D) program is revealed as a naked effort to achieve racial balancing.

DISSENT: (Kennedy, J.) Refusal of the Court to apply strict scrutiny that is meaningful will lead to serious consequences. By deferring to the law school's (D) choice of minority admissions programs, courts will lose the talents and resources of the faculties and administrators in devising new and fairer ways to ensure individual consideration.

CONCURRENCE AND DISSENT: (Scalia, J.) Unlike a clear constitutional holding that racial preferences in state educational institutions are impermissible, or even a clear anticonstitutional holding, today's decision seems perversely designed to prolong the controversy and the litigation. The Constitution proscribes government discrimination on the basis of race, and state-provided education is no exception.

CONCURRENCE AND DISSENT: (Thomas, J.) Blacks can achieve in every avenue of American life without the meddling of university administrators. The majority upholds the Law School's (D) racial discrimination not

Continued on next page.

by interpreting the people's Constitution, but by responding to a faddish slogan.

▶ *ANALYSIS*

As seen in *Grutter* and predecessor Supreme Court decisions, not every decision influenced by race is equally objectionable, and "strict scrutiny" is designed to provide a framework for carefully examining the importance and the sincerity of the reasons advanced by the governmental decisionmaker for the use of race in any given context.

■══■

Quicknotes

EQUAL PROTECTION CLAUSE A constitutional provision that each person be guaranteed the same protection of the laws enjoyed by other persons in like circumstances.

■══■

Gratz v. Bollinger

College applicants (P) v. University (D)

539 U.S. 244 (2003).

NATURE OF CASE: Challenge of university's undergraduate affirmative action policies.

FACT SUMMARY: Gratz (P) and other "qualified" white students denied admission as undergraduates to the University of Michigan (D), sued the latter, arguing the admission policy of automatically distributing one-fifth of the points needed to guarantee admission to every single "underrepresented minority" solely because of race, constituted prohibited racial discrimination.

RULE OF LAW

A university admissions policy that automatically distributes one-fifth of the points needed to guarantee admission to every single "underrepresented minority" solely because of race is not narrowly tailored to achieve the interest in educational diversity so as to avoid violation of the Equal Protection Clause of the Fourteenth Amendment.

FACTS: Gratz (P) and other white students who were denied admission as undergraduates to the University of Michigan (the University) (D), although they were deemed "qualified" by the college admissions committee, brought suit against the University (D), arguing that its applicant selection method violated the Equal Protection Clause of the Fourteenth Amendment on the grounds that the University (D) automatically distributes one-fifth of the points needed to guarantee admission to every single "underrepresented minority" solely because of race.

ISSUE: Is a university admissions policy that automatically distributes one-fifth of the points needed to guarantee admission to every single "underrepresented minority" solely because of race, narrowly tailored to achieve the interest in educational diversity so as to avoid violation of the Equal Protection Clause of the Fourteenth Amendment?

HOLDING AND DECISION: (Rehnquist, C.J.) No. A university admissions policy that automatically distributes one-fifth of the points needed to guarantee admission to every single "underrepresented minority" solely because of race, is not narrowly tailored to achieve the interest in educational diversity so as to avoid violation of the Equal Protection Clause of the Fourteenth Amendment. This Court emphasizes the importance of considering each particular applicant as an individual, assessing all of the qualities that an individual possesses, and in turn, evaluating that individual's ability to contribute to the unique setting of higher education. In this regard, the Court does not contemplate that any single characteristic

automatically ensures a specific and identifiable contribution to a university's diversity. Here, the University's (D) admission policy does not provide such individualized consideration; to the contrary, it automatically distributes 20 points to "underrepresented minority" groups, the only consideration being whether the applicant is a member of one of these minority groups. Even if an applicant's extraordinary artistic talent rivaled that of Monet or Picasso, the applicant would receive, at most, five points under the University's (D) admissions system. Clearly, such a system does not offer applicants the individualized selection process. Nor, does the fact that the implementation of a program capable of providing individualized consideration might present administrative challenges render constitutional an otherwise problematic system. The admissions policy violates the Equal Protection Clause of the Fourteenth Amendment.

CONCURRENCE: (O'Connor, J.) The selection index, by setting up automatic, predetermined point allocations for the soft variables, ensures that the diversity contributions of applicants cannot be individually assessed. This is in sharp contrast to the law school's admission plan that enables admissions officers to make nuanced judgments as to the contributions each applicant is likely to make.

CONCURRENCE: (Thomas, J.) A state's use of racial discrimination in higher education admissions is categorically prohibited by the Equal Protection Clause.

CONCURRENCE: (Breyer, J.) The Constitution requires the law respect individuals equally and laws of inclusion are more likely to accomplish that requirement. Government entities may thus distinguish between inclusive and exclusive policies to meet the constitutional goal.

DISSENT: (Stevens, J.) Standing is lacking so the case must be dismissed.

DISSENT: (Souter, J.) On its face, the assignment of specific points does not set race apart from all other weighted considerations. Since college admission is not left entirely to inarticulate intuition, it is hard to see what is inappropriate in assigning some stated value to a relevant characteristic, whether it be reasoning ability, writing style, running speed, or minority race.

DISSENT: (Ginsburg, J.) The stain of generations of racial oppression is still visible in our society, and the determination to hasten its removal remains vital. Here,

Continued on next page.

there has been no demonstration that the University (D) unduly constricts admissions opportunities for students who do not receive special consideration based on race.

▶ *ANALYSIS*

As made clear by the Supreme Court in its *Gratz*, and also *Grutter*, 539 U.S. 306 (2003), decisions, achieving diversity in higher education, whether it be at college level or graduate school, remains as a compelling state interest sufficient to justify some degree of racial preferences without violating the Equal Protection Clause of the Fourteenth Amendment.

■━■

Quicknotes

EQUAL PROTECTION CLAUSE A constitutional guarantee that no person should be denied the same protection of the laws enjoyed by other persons in like circumstances.

■━■

Parents Involved in Community Schools v. Seattle School Dist.

Parents of unadmitted students (P) v. Public school district (D)

551 U.S. 701 (2007).

NATURE OF CASE: Suits challenging school-assignment plans under the Equal Protection Clause.

FACT SUMMARY: Two metropolitan school districts sought to assign students to schools to achieve racial balance.

RULE OF LAW
Racial balance between local high-school districts is not a compelling government interest under the Equal Protection Clause.

FACTS: The Seattle School District (Seattle) (D) and Jefferson County Public Schools in Louisville, Kentucky, (Louisville) (D) both implemented a student assignment plan designed to achieve numerically defined racial balance among the public high schools in each city. [Seattle (D) had never been found to run racially segregated schools.] Louisville (D) was under a desegregation order from 1975 to 2000; the order was dissolved in 2001 when a federal court ruled that Louisville (D) had reached unitary status by largely eliminating the district's earlier racial segregation. After the decree was dissolved, Louisville (D) voluntarily adopted a student-assignment plan that required specific minimum and maximum enrollment percentages for black students. Parents (P) of students who were denied admission in each school district sued their respective district, alleging, in part, violations of the Equal Protection Clause. After the intermediate appellate courts in both cases upheld the assignment plans, the parents (P) petitioned the Supreme Court for further review.

ISSUE: Is racial balance between local high-school districts a compelling government interest under the Equal Protection Clause?

HOLDING AND DECISION: (Roberts, C.J.) No. Racial balance between local high-school districts is not a compelling government interest under the Equal Protection Clause. Because both school districts (D) have apportioned government benefits on the basis of race, the applicable standard of review in these cases is strict scrutiny: Seattle (D) and Louisville (D) must show that their race-based discrimination (1) advances a compelling government interest through (2) means that are narrowly tailored to achieve the intended purpose. The asserted interests in both Seattle (D) and Louisville (D) reduce to nothing more than the goal of numerical racial balance between each district's (D) schools. This Court has consistently found such a purpose illegitimate. *Grutter v. Bollinger*, 539 U.S. 306 (2003), does not control here because *Grutter* involved the specific interests of higher education; it is also

instructive, though, that *Grutter* upheld the law-school admission policy there because racial diversity was only one of a mix of admissions criteria. Here, on the other hand, pure numerical racial balance, by itself, is the government interest, and that interest has never been recognized as valid. The plans at issue here also fail because the school districts (D) have failed to show that they seriously considered other means besides explicit racial classifications. Reversed.

CONCURRENCE: (Thomas, J.) Racial imbalance and racial segregation are not synonymous; it is possible to have racial imbalance through no conscious decision to segregate. Further, forced racial mixing of students may or may not provide educational benefits in general or higher achievement for black students in particular. The color-blind Constitution, then, requires that these student assignment plans be struck down.

CONCURRENCE IN PART: (Kennedy, J.) Contrary to the Chief Justice's plurality opinion, race can be considered as one among several factors in examining school enrollments. General, indirect solutions to problems of racial composition of schools are much better than the crude plans in these cases as ways to address those problems. The United States has special obligations to ensure equal opportunity for all children, and government should be permitted to consider race in its attempts to fulfill that mission. As the plurality correctly notes, though, government may not classify students based solely on race without first making a showing that such a step is necessary.

DISSENT: (Stevens, J.) In his demand of strict equality under the Constitution, the Chief Justice forgets that, before *Brown*, only black students were told where they could and could not go to school. Today's plurality decision rewrites the history of our landmark school-desegregation decision.

DISSENT: (Breyer, J.) These voluntary plans bear striking resemblances to plans that this Court has long required, permitted, and encouraged local school districts to formulate and use. Every branch of government has acknowledged that government may voluntarily use race-conscious plans to address race-based problems even when such plans are not constitutionally obligatory. The plurality overlooks the fact that no case has ever decided that all racial classifications should receive precisely the same scrutiny. Actually, our decisions have applied different standards to assess racial classifications depending on whether the government's purpose was to exclude persons

Continued on next page.

from, or to include persons in, government programs. The plurality's interpretation of strict scrutiny, however, would automatically invalidate all race-conscious government action. The school districts' (D) interest here serves remedial, educational, and democratic purposes; such a multiplicity of concerns means that *Grutter*'s rationale controls here and requires upholding these assignment plans. Even under the strictest scrutiny, though, the plans here pass muster under the Equal Protection Clause because they are more narrowly tailored than the plan approved in *Grutter*. Accordingly, these plans are consistent with equal protection of the laws.

▶ ANALYSIS

Chief Justice Roberts's plurality opinion in *Parents Involved* focuses on the firm percentages used by Seattle (D) and Louisville (D) in making student-assignment decisions. Despite Justice Breyer's objections in dissent, it is difficult to see how such an overtly numerical approach differs from the quota-based systems that the Court consistently has struck down under the Equal Protection Clause. See, e.g., *Regents of the University of California v. Bakke,* 438 U.S. 265, 307 (1978): "If [the University's] purpose is to assure within its student body some specified percentage of a particular group merely because of its race or ethnic origin, such a preferential purpose must be rejected not as insubstantial but as facially invalid."

■▬■

Quicknotes

EQUAL PROTECTION CLAUSE A constitutional provision that each person be guaranteed the same protection of the laws enjoyed by other persons in like circumstances.

STRICT SCRUTINY Method by which courts determine the constitutionality of a law, when a law affects a fundamental right. Under the test, the legislature must have had a compelling interest to enact the law and measures prescribed by the law must be the least restrictive means possible to accomplish its goal.

■▬■

Craig v. Boren

Underage male (P) v. State (D)

429 U.S. 190 (1976).

NATURE OF CASE: Review of judgment holding state liquor law constitutional.

FACT SUMMARY: Craig (P) filed suit challenging an Oklahoma statute that prohibited the sale of "non-intoxicating" 3.2% beer to males under the age of 21.

RULE OF LAW
In order to withstand a constitutional challenge, classifications by gender must serve important governmental objectives and be substantially related to achieving those objectives.

FACTS: Craig (P) brought suit to have two sections of an Oklahoma statute that prohibited the sale of "nonintoxicating" 3.2% beer to males under the age of twenty-one and to females under the age of 18. Craig (P) contended that this gender-based differential constituted a denial to males 18–20 years of age equal protection of the laws in violation of the Fourteenth Amendment. The State of Oklahoma (D) argued that the law was enacted as a traffic safety measure and introduced statistical data demonstrating that males 18–20 years of age were arrested in far greater numbers for drunk driving offenses than females of the same age group. The lower courts upheld the law, and the Supreme Court granted Craig's (P) petition for certiorari.

ISSUE: Must classifications by gender serve important governmental objectives and be substantially related to achieving those objectives in order to withstand a constitutional challenge?

HOLDING AND DECISION: (Brennan, J.) Yes. In order to withstand a constitutional challenge, classifications by gender must serve important governmental objectives and be substantially related to achieving those objectives. Although the protection of the public health and safety are important state goals, the relationship between gender and traffic safety is far too tenuous to satisfy the standard of review in this case. None of the studies cited measured the dangerousness of 3.2% beer as compared with other types of alcohol. Furthermore, the statute only prohibits the sale of the beer to the 18–20-year-old males, but does not prohibit them from consuming it. It has not been demonstrated that the gender-based difference is substantially related to the statutory objective. Reversed.

CONCURRENCE: (Powell, J.) This is an easy case. The statute adopted by the state legislature does not bear a fair and substantial relation to the objective of improving traffic safety.

CONCURRENCE: (Stevens, J.) It is difficult to believe that the statute in question was actually intended to cope with the problem of traffic safety since it has only a minimal effect on access to a not-very-intoxicating beverage and does not prohibit its consumption.

DISSENT: (Rehnquist, J.) The majority's holding is objectionable on two grounds. The first fallacy is its conclusion that men challenging a gender-based statute that treats them less favorably than women may invoke a more stringent standard of judicial review than pertains to most other types of classifications. The second error is the Court's enunciation of this standard, without citation to any source, as "classifications by gender must serve important governmental objectives and must be substantially related to achievement of those objectives." The Equal Protection Clause contains no such language and none of the previous cases have adopted this standard. The Court takes the view that gender discrimination is the same without regard to which gender should bear a heavier burden. The appropriate standard of review is the rational basis test, and the evidence suggests that there are in fact clear differences between the drinking and driving habits of young men and women.

ANALYSIS

Prior to 1971, the Court applied rational basis review to classifications on the basis of gender. Since that time however, and contrary to Justice Rehnquist's assertions in his dissenting opinion, the intermediate scrutiny test as articulated by the majority has been applied. The Court has also applied intermediate scrutiny to classifications on the basis of alienage and illegitimacy.

Quicknotes

CERTIORARI A discretionary writ issued by a superior court to an inferior court in order to review the lower court's decisions; the Supreme Court's writ ordering such review.

EQUAL PROTECTION A constitutional provision that each person be guaranteed the same protection of the laws enjoyed by other persons in life circumstances.

FOURTEENTH AMENDMENT Declares that no state shall make or enforce any law that shall abridge the privileges and immunities of citizens of the United States.

Continued on next page.

INTERMEDIATE SCRUTINY A standard of reviewing the propriety of classifications pertaining to gender or legitimacy, under the Equal Protection Clause of the United States Constitution, that requires a court to ascertain whether the classification furthers an important state interest and is substantially related to the attainment of that interest.

RATIONAL BASIS TEST A test employed by the court to determine the validity of a statute in equal protection actions, whereby the court determines whether the challenged statute is rationally related to the achievement of a legitimate state interest.

United States v. Virginia

Federal government (P) v. State institution (D)

518 U.S. 515 (1996).

NATURE OF CASE: Appeal from final judgment upholding a college's male-only admission policy.

FACT SUMMARY: Virginia Military Institute (D), a state sponsored university, had a policy of excluding women from attending.

🏛 RULE OF LAW
Public schools may not exclude women.

FACTS: Since 1839, Virginia Military Institute (VMI) (D), a Virginia (D) public institution, had been a male-only college that sought to train "citizen-soldiers." In 1990, the Attorney General (P) sued VMI (D) and Virginia (D), claiming that the admission policy violated the Equal Protection Clause. Virginia (D) eventually proposed a remedial plan under which a parallel program would be developed for women. The Virginia Women's Institute for Leadership (VWIL) would be created at Mary Baldwin College. The trial court and an appellate court upheld this remedial plan, but the Attorney General (P) appealed and the Supreme Court granted a writ of certiorari.

ISSUE: May public schools exclude women?

HOLDING AND DECISION: (Ginsburg, J.) No. Public schools may not exclude women. States must show that a sex-based government action serves important governmental objectives and that the discriminatory means employed are substantially related to the achievement of those objectives. There must be an exceedingly persuasive justification for the action. This heightened review standard prevents classifications that perpetuate the legal, social, and economic inferiority of women. While single-sex education may provide benefits to some students, Virginia (D) has not shown that it pursued this option as a means to providing a diversity of educational opportunities. On the other hand, the historical record shows that Virginia (D) has systematically prevented women from obtaining higher education until relatively recently. The fact that women have been successfully integrated into the armed forces and service academies demonstrates that VMI's (D) stature will not be downgraded by admitting women. The proposed VWIL does not qualify as VMI's (D) equal in terms of faculty, facilities, course offerings, and its reputation. Accordingly, since Virginia (D) is unable to provide substantial equal opportunities for women who desire to attend VMI (D), the male-only admission policy is unconstitutional. Reversed.

CONCURRENCE: (Rehnquist, C.J.) The majority decision is correct but there is no basis for stating that states must demonstrate an exceedingly persuasive justification to support sex-based classifications.

DISSENT: (Scalia, J.) The majority sweeps away an institution that has thrived for 150 years and the precedents of this Court to embark on a course of proscribing its own elite opinions on society. Virginia (D) has an important interest in providing education, and single-sex instruction is an approach substantially related to this goal. The proposed VWIL was designed for women and not designed to be exactly equal to VMI (D).

▶ ANALYSIS

Justice Scalia's dissent carries a tone of disgust for the majority opinion. As he did in *Romer v. Evans*, 517 U.S. 620 (1996), Justice Scalia states that the majority seeks to satisfy some unidentified group of antimajoritarian elites. This attitude is unusual for a member of the Supreme Court since dissents are usually restricted to attacks on the majority's legal reasoning.

■━■

Quicknotes

EQUAL PROTECTION CLAUSE A constitutional guarantee that no person should be denied the same protection of the laws enjoyed by other persons in like circumstances.

■━■

Califano v. Webster

[Parties not identified in casebook excerpt.]

430 U.S. 313 (1977).

NATURE OF CASE: Appeal from an action to have § 215 of the Social Security Act declared unconstitutional.

FACT SUMMARY: A district court held that § 215 of the Social Security Act, which allows women to eliminate additional low-earning years from the calculation of their retirement benefits, was violative of the equal protection component of the Due Process Clause of the Fifth Amendment.

 RULE OF LAW
Section 215 of the Social Security Act, which allows women to eliminate additional low-earning years from the calculation of their retirement benefits, does not violate the Fifth Amendment because it works directly to remedy past discrimination.

FACTS: This suit was brought to challenge the constitutionality of § 215 of the Social Security Act, which allows women to eliminate additional low-earning years from the calculation of their retirement benefits. The district court held that, on two grounds, the statutory scheme violated the equal protection component of the Due Process Clause of the Fifth Amendment: (1) that to give women who reached age 62 before 1975 greater benefits than men of the same age and earnings record was irrational, and (2) that the 1972 amendment, under which elapsed years for calculation of retirement benefits no longer depended on sex, was to be construed to apply retroactively, because construing the amendment to give men who reach age 62 in 1975 or later its benefit but denying to older men the same benefit is irrational and therefore unconstitutional.

ISSUE: Does § 215 of the Social Security Act, which allows women to eliminate additional low-earning years from the calculation of their retirement benefits, violate the Fifth Amendment?

HOLDING AND DECISION: (Per curiam) No. Section 215 of the Social Security Act, which allows women to eliminate additional low-earning years from the calculation of their retirement benefits, does not violate the Fifth Amendment because it works directly to remedy past discrimination. To withstand scrutiny under the equal protection component of the Fifth Amendment's Due Process Clause, classifications by gender must serve important governmental objectives and must be substantially related to achievement of those objectives. Reduction of the disparity in economic condition between men and women has been recognized as an important governmental objective. However, the Court must also inquire into the legislative purposes behind such benign gender-based classifications.

The only discernible purpose of § 215's more favorable treatment of women is the permissible one of redressing our society's longstanding disparate treatment of women. That Congress changed its mind in 1972 and equalized the treatment of men and women does not, as the district court concluded, constitute an admission by Congress that its previous policy was invidiously discriminatory. Rather, it marks the recent trend in congressional reforms that legislate directly upon the subject of equal treatment of men and women. The judgment of the district court is reversed.

CONCURRENCE: (Burger, C.J.) This concurring opinion rests not on the distinction drawn by the Court on a case similarity basis but on the reasons stated by Justice Rehnquist in the previous case of Goldfarb in his dissenting opinion.

▌ *ANALYSIS*

In Title VII sex discrimination cases, the standard of proof is not the showing of a motive of purposeful discrimination. Rather, "to establish a prima facie case of discrimination, a plaintiff need only show that facially neutral standards in question select applicants for hire in a significantly discriminatory pattern. Once it is shown that employment standards are discriminatory in effect," the employer must meet the burden of showing that the requirements are manifestly related to the employment. *Dothard v. Rawlinson*, 433 U.S. 321, (1977).

■=■

Quicknotes

DUE PROCESS CLAUSE Clause found in the Fifth and Fourteenth Amendments to the United States Constitution providing that no person shall be deprived of "life, liberty, or property, without due process of law."

INVIDIOUS DISCRIMINATION Unequal treatment of a class of persons that is particularly malicious or hostile.

■=■

Mississippi University for Women v. Hogan

University (D) v. Applicant (P)

458 U.S. 718 (1982).

NATURE OF CASE: Action to declare unconstitutional a gender-based statute.

FACT SUMMARY: Hogan (P) sought to strike down a Mississippi statute that excluded males from enrolling in a state-supported nursing school.

RULE OF LAW
A statute that discriminates against men must meet the same "heightened scrutiny" equal protection analysis as statutes that discriminate against women.

FACTS: The Mississippi University for Women (the University) (D) traditionally barred males from enrolling. Hogan (P) applied to the nursing school and was turned down solely by virtue of his gender.

ISSUE: Must a statute that discriminates against men meet the same "heightened scrutiny" equal protection analysis as statutes that discriminate against women?

HOLDING AND DECISION: (O'Connor, J.) Yes. A statute that discriminates against men must meet the same "heightened scrutiny" equal protection analysis as statutes that discriminate against women. The test that must be applied when a statute involves gender-based discrimination is whether the discriminatory classification serves important governmental objectives and whether the means employed are substantially related to the achievement of those objectives. Thus, the standard is more heightened than the mere "rational basis" standard generally employed in equal protection cases but slightly lower than the "strict scrutiny" applied in cases involving suspect classes or fundamental rights. The fact that the statute discriminates against males rather than females does not lower the standard of judicial review. In the instant case, the University (D) failed to meet either requirement of the heightened scrutiny test. It contended that the all-female requirement was necessary to compensate for past discriminatory practices against women. Yet, the statistics show that over 90% of the members of the nursing profession are women. Clearly, compensation is not necessary in this area. Similarly, the University's (D) second contention that admitting men would tend to adversely affect the women at the school is undermined by the practice of allowing men to audit the classes. As the University (D) has not met its burden of showing that an important governmental objective necessitates the statute in question, the statute must fall. Affirmed.

DISSENT: (Burger, C.J.) It must be emphasized that the Court's opinion is limited to nursing schools and is based largely on the fact that nursing is a predominantly female profession.

DISSENT: (Powell, J.) This is not the type of case in which the Equal Protection Clause was meant to be applied. There is no discrimination involved. Both men and women in Mississippi are provided with a choice regarding the institution of higher learning that they wish to attend. The Court's decision today merely means that one such choice—an all female college—will no longer be available to women.

ANALYSIS

See also *Caban v. Mohammed*, 441 U.S. 380 (1979), where a section of the New York Domestic Relations Law that permitted an unwed mother, but not an unwed father, to prevent the adoption of their child simply by withholding consent, was challenged under the Equal Protection Clause. The Court found that the state had been unable to advance any important interests justifying the gender-based discrimination and, thus, ruled the statute unconstitutional.

■═■

Quicknotes

FUNDAMENTAL RIGHT A liberty that is either expressly or implicitly provided for in the United States Constitution, the deprivation or burdening of which is subject to a heightened standard of review.

HEIGHTENED SCRUTINY A purposefully vague judicial description of all levels of scrutiny more exacting than minimal scrutiny.

RATIONAL BASIS TEST A test employed by the court to determine the validity of a statute in equal protection actions, whereby the court determines whether the challenged statute is rationally related to the achievement of a legitimate state interest.

STRICT SCRUTINY Method by which courts determine the constitutionality of a law, when a law affects a fundamental right. Under the test, the legislature must have a compelling interest to enact the law and measures prescribed by the law must be the least restrictive means possible to accomplish its goal.

SUSPECT CLASSIFICATION A class of persons that have historically been subject to discriminatory treatment; statutes drawing a distinction between persons based on a suspect classification, i.e. race, nationality or alienage, are subject to a strict scrutiny standard of review.

■═■

Romer v. Evans

[Parties not identified in casebook excerpt.]

517 U.S. 620 (1996).

NATURE OF CASE: Appeal of order regarding constitutionality of statewide referendum amending a state constitution.

FACT SUMMARY: A Colorado (D) constitutional amendment, Amendment 2, which struck down local antidiscrimination laws based on sexual orientation, was challenged for being violative of the Equal Protection Clause.

 RULE OF LAW
Colorado's Amendment 2 violates the Equal Protection Clause because it singles out a class of citizens—homosexuals—for disfavored legal status.

FACTS: In 1992, Colorado (D) amended its state constitution by a statewide referendum. Amendment 2, as it was designated, provided that the state and local branches of government were forbidden from enacting any laws or regulations that would protect homosexuals from discrimination. Amendment 2 was challenged in court as unconstitutional for violating the Equal Protection Clause. Colorado (D) responded that Amendment 2 simply denies homosexuals any special rights given to protected classes, such as minorities. The Supreme Court granted certiorari to decide the issue.

ISSUE: Does Colorado's Amendment 2 violate the Equal Protection Clause because it singles out a class of citizens—homosexuals—for disfavored legal status?

HOLDING AND DECISION: (Kennedy, J.) Yes. Colorado's Amendment 2 violates the Equal Protection Clause because it singles out a class of citizens—homosexuals—for disfavored legal status. The Colorado Supreme Court construction of Amendment 2 found that its objective was to repeal existing antidiscrimination ordinances. Accordingly, Amendment 2 places homosexuals in a solitary class, since it withdraws legal protection for discrimination and forbids reinstatement of these policies except by constitutional amendment. Thus, it imposes a special disability on homosexuals, who can now only change the law by amending the state constitution, no matter how local the harm. Generally, legislative classifications are constitutional if they bear a rational relation to a legitimate end. However, Amendment 2 identifies persons by a single trait and denies them protection across the board. Therefore, it violates the principle that the government remain open on impartial terms to all who seek its assistance. Finally, equal protection means that the desire to harm a politically unpopular group is not a legitimate

government interest. Accordingly, Amendment 2 violates the Equal Protection Clause and is unconstitutional.

DISSENT: (Scalia, J.) Amendment 2 only prohibits the special treatment of homosexuals in that they may not obtain preferential treatment without amending the state constitution. Surely, Colorado has the right to be hostile toward homosexuals just as they may have animosity toward murderers or polygamists. Also, since homosexuals are segregated in certain communities, they possess political power much greater than their numbers. Amendment 2 seeks to counter this disproportionate political power. The majority has taken the side of the elites in this culture law.

▶ **ANALYSIS**

Justice Scalia's dissenting opinion is astonishing for its not-at-all disguised animus toward homosexuals, who will no doubt be surprised to find that they are politically powerful. The dissent is also remarkable for its tone of disgust toward the majority. At the heart of the majority decision is the recognition that homosexuality is more of a status (like sex, race, or ethnicity) than a conduct or lifestyle.

■=■

Quicknotes

EQUAL PROTECTION CLAUSE A constitutional guarantee that no person should be denied the same protection of the laws enjoyed by other persons in like circumstances.

■=■

Ambach v. Norwick

[Parties not identified in casebook excerpt.]

441 U.S. 68 (1979).

NATURE OF CASE: Appeal from state citizenship-employment qualification law.

FACT SUMMARY: New York state law required that applicants for employment as teachers in the public school system be American citizens.

🏛 RULE OF LAW
States do not violate the Equal Protection Clause of the Fourteenth Amendment by excluding aliens from the ranks of its public school teachers.

FACTS: New York law required that all applicants for employment as teachers in its public school system be American citizens. Resident aliens who had expressed an unwillingness to obtain United States citizenship would not even be considered for employment. Aliens residing in New York who were members of the applicant pool challenged the law on the grounds that it violated the Equal Protection Clause of the Fourteenth Amendment, and the court of appeals agreed with their position.

ISSUE: Do states violate the Equal Protection Clause of the Fourteenth Amendment by excluding aliens from the ranks of its public school teachers?

HOLDING AND DECISION: (Powell, J.) No. Although classifications based on alienage are inherently suspect and subject to close judicial scrutiny under the Equal Protection Clause of the Fourteenth Amendment, in appropriately defined classes of positions, citizenship may be required as a qualification for office or employment because states have an obligation to preserve "the basic conception of a political community." Here, public school teachers perform tasks "that go to the heart of representative government." Public education, like the police function, fulfills a most fundamental obligation of government to its constituency: it prepares individuals for participation as citizens. Because teachers have much discretion over the way course material is presented to their students, and because they often serve as role models for their students, their belief in the value of American citizenship (as opposed to aliens' continuing primary loyalty to foreign countries) is an essential qualification for their employment. New York's law excluding aliens from teaching in its public schools thus bears a reasonable relationship to its interest in inculcating citizenship values and in perpetuating the American political community and does not violate the Equal Protection Clause of the Fourteenth Amendment. Reversed.

DISSENT: (Blackmun, J.) The New York classification is irrational because it disfavors aliens with excellent overall teaching skills. Further, this Court has previously held that aliens may become attorneys, but surely attorneys inculcate citizenship values as much or more than public school teachers.

▶ ANALYSIS

The rule in this case has been referred to as the "political function" exception to the standard of intermediate scrutiny typically adopted in equal protection cases involving aliens. In *Bernal v. Fainter*, 467 U.S. 216 (1984) (aliens may become notary publics), the Supreme Court per Justice Marshall held that this exception must be narrowly construed to avoid "swallowing up" the "heightened scrutiny" appropriate to "discrete and insular minorities." State laws governing aliens also often run afoul of the Constitution based on the Supremacy Clause. See, e.g., *Toll v. Moreno*, 458 U.S. 1 (1982) (University of Maryland rule flatly denying "in-state" tuition to nonimmigrant aliens with G-4 visas violates the Supremacy Clause).

Quicknotes

EQUAL PROTECTION A constitutional provision that each person be guaranteed the same protection of the laws enjoyed by other persons in life circumstances.

INTERMEDIATE SCRUTINY A standard of reviewing the propriety of classifications pertaining to gender or legitimacy, under the Equal Protection Clause of the United States Constitution, which requires a court to ascertain whether the classification furthers an important state interest and is substantially related to the attainment of that interest.

SUPREMACY CLAUSE Article VI, § 2, of the Constitution, which provides that federal action must prevail over inconsistent state action.

Mathews v. Lucas

Federal government (D) v. Illegitimate children (P)

427 U.S. 495 (1976).

NATURE OF CASE: Due process challenge to federal law.

FACT SUMMARY: The Lucas children (P) challenged the constitutional validity of a provision of the Social Security Act, providing benefits to certain classes of legitimate and illegitimate children, claiming Due Process Clause violations.

 RULE OF LAW
Once a state posits a judicially enforceable right on behalf of children to needed support from the government, there is no constitutionally sufficient justification for denying such an essential right to the child simply because its parents are not married.

FACTS: The Social Security Act provides survivor's benefits to dependent children of the deceased parent at the time of death. Certain classes of legitimate and illegitimate children are presumed to be dependent; other classes of illegitimate children must prove "that the deceased wage earner was the child's parent" and was either living with the child or contributing to his support at the time of death. Illegitimate children (P) who were denied benefits challenged the statute as in violation of the Due Process Clause. The district court concluded the legislation was constitutionally suspect and the Government (D) appealed.

ISSUE: Once a state posits a judicially enforceable right on behalf of children to needed support from the government, is there a constitutionally sufficient justification for denying such an essential right to the child simply because its parents are not married?

HOLDING AND DECISION: (Blackmun, J.) No. Once a state posits a judicially enforceable right on behalf of children to needed support from the government there is no constitutionally sufficient justification for denying such an essential right to the child simply because its parents are not married. Congress's purpose in adopting the presumptions of dependency was to serve administrative convenience. Such approximations must be supported by a showing that the Government's (D) dollar lost to overincluded benefit recipients is returned by a dollar saved in administrative expense avoided. The statutory classifications challenged here are justified as reasonable empirical judgments consistent with a scheme to qualify entitlement to benefits upon a child's dependency upon the parent's death. Here the statute does not broadly discriminate between legitimates and illegitimates without more; the presumption of dependency is withheld only in the absence of any significant indication of the likelihood of actual dependency. Reversed.

DISSENT: (Stevens, J.) The classification is more probably the product of a tradition of thinking of illegitimates, as less deserving persons than legitimates; the tradition should be rejected.

▶ *ANALYSIS*

While the Court recognizes that illegitimacy is "a characteristic determined by causes not within the control of the illegitimate individual," it rejects the notion that illegitimates carry the same "badge" as do race and sex. Thus it concludes that discrimination on the basis of legitimacy does not "command extraordinary protection" as strict scrutiny would entail.

■■■

Quicknotes

DUE PROCESS CLAUSE Clause found in the Fifth and Fourteenth Amendments to the United States Constitution providing that no person shall be deprived of "life, liberty, or property, without due process of law."

EQUAL PROTECTION A constitutional guarantee that no person shall be denied the same protection of the laws enjoyed by other persons in like circumstances.

PRESUMPTION A rule of law requiring the court to presume certain facts to be true based on the existence of other facts, thereby shifting the burden of proof to the party against whom the presumption is asserted to rebut.

STRICT SCRUTINY Method by which courts determine the constitutionality of a law, when a law affects a fundamental right. Under the test, the legislature must have a compelling interest to enact the law and measures prescribed by the law must be the least restrictive means possible to accomplish its goal.

■■■

Cleburne v. Cleburne Living Center, Inc.

City (D) v. Group home (P)

473 U.S. 432 (1985).

NATURE OF CASE: Appeal from decision finding zoning ordinance unconstitutional.

FACT SUMMARY: The City of Cleburne (D) appealed from a court of appeals decision finding that a zoning ordinance that required a special use permit for the operation of a home for the mentally retarded violated the Equal Protection Clause, holding that mental retardation is a quasi-suspect classification deserving heightened scrutiny.

🏛 RULE OF LAW
Classifications based on mental retardation will withstand equal protection review if they are rationally related to a legitimate governmental purpose.

FACTS: The City of Cleburne (D) required a special use permit for the operation of a group home for the mentally retarded. This special permit is not required of apartments, boarding houses, fraternities and sororities, dormitories, hospitals, sanitariums, and many other types of multiple dwellings. Cleburne Living Center (CLC) (P) sought to operate a home for 13 mentally retarded adults, who would be under the supervision of CLC (P) staff members. CLC (P) submitted an application for the permit, which the City of Cleburne (D) denied after a public hearing. CLC (P) brought suit, and the court of appeals found that mental retardation was a quasi-suspect classification subject to heightened scrutiny under the Equal Protection Clause, and that the permit requirement violated the Equal Protection Clause since it did not further a substantial governmental purpose. From this decision, the City of Cleburne (D) appealed.

ISSUE: Will classifications based on mental retardation withstand equal protection review if they are rationally related to a legitimate governmental purpose?

HOLDING AND DECISION: (White, J.) Yes. Classifications based on mental retardation will withstand equal protection review if they are rationally related to a legitimate governmental purpose. In holding that mental retardation was a quasi-suspect classification entitled to more exacting review than normally required of economic and social legislation, the court of appeals erred. The state's interest in dealing with and providing for the mentally retarded is clearly a legitimate one. State and federal legislative response to the plight of the mentally retarded highlights the real and undeniable differences between the mentally retarded and others, and the generally favorable tenor of this legislation indicates that the mentally retarded are not politically powerless. To allow heightened review to

classifications based on mental retardation would open the floodgates to a variety of groups similarly situated who would desire that they be treated differently under equal protection. One should not focus on specifics, but rather on the likelihood that governmental action premised on a particular classification is valid as a general matter. There is no rational basis for believing that the home for the mentally retarded will pose any special threat to the legitimate interests of the City of Cleburne (D) that other permitted uses under the ordinance would not. Negative attitudes toward the presence of the retarded or other unsubstantiated fears of the effect of the home are insufficient to justify their differing treatment in the present case, and therefore the ordinance as applied in this case is invalid. Affirmed in part; reversed in part.

CONCURRENCE: (Stevens, J.) In approaching equal protection cases, if one properly applies the rational basis test, there is no need to inquire into strict scrutiny, or even heightened scrutiny to decide these cases.

CONCURRENCE AND DISSENT: (Marshall, J.) It is important to articulate the facts and principles that justify subjecting this ordinance to the searching review, the heightened scrutiny, that the majority applies in invalidating it, even though the majority claims adherence to the rational basis test. Failure to acknowledge that heightened scrutiny is at work will allow this searching review to be applied in the review of economic and commercial classifications, and provides no principled foundation for determining when more searching inquiry is warranted. The level of scrutiny employed should vary with the interest adversely affected, and the recognized invidiousness of the classification. These considerations lead to the conclusion that classifications with respect to mental retardation should be subjected to heightened review, and the majority should so acknowledge.

▎ANALYSIS

While Justice Stevens, writing the concurrence, differs from Justice Marshall, who wrote the dissent, in the use of certain tests for determining equal protection violations, they both seem to embody the fundamental basis of the so-called sliding scale of review, that would treat state classifications in economic regulation cases with great deference, while treating classifications based on race with a very strong presumption of unconstitutionality. Although Justice Marshall still adheres to the classification of levels of review, his view that the level of scrutiny should

Continued on next page.

vary with the constitutional and societal importance of the interest adversely affected and the recognized invidiousness of the basis upon which the classification is drawn seems to belie any reliance on the strict three-tier system of review in equal protection cases.

■≡■

Quicknotes

QUASI-SUSPECT CLASS   A class of persons that has historically been subject to discriminatory treatment; statutes drawing a distinction between persons based on a quasi-suspect classification, i.e., gender or legitimacy, are subject to an intermediate scrutiny standard of review.

RATIONAL BASIS TEST   A test employed by the court to determine the validity of a statute in equal protection actions, whereby the court determines whether the challenged statute is rationally related to the achievement of a legitimate state interest.

■≡■

Kramer v. Union Free School District

Ineligible voter (P) v. School district (D)

395 U.S. 621 (1969).

NATURE OF CASE: Appeal from dismissal of a complaint to overturn voter eligibility requirements.

FACT SUMMARY: Kramer (P) claimed that Union's (D) School District voter eligibility requirements denied him equal protection of the laws.

🏛 **RULE OF LAW**
Legal classifications must be tailored so that exclusion of a certain class of persons is necessary to achieve an articulated state goal.

FACTS: The New York Education Code provided that in certain school districts residents may vote in a school district election only if they or their spouse own or lease taxable real property within the district, or are parents or have custody of children enrolled in local public schools. Kramer (P), an unmarried man who neither owned nor leased taxable real property, argued that the voter eligibility requirements denied him equal protection. Union (D) argued that the state has a legitimate interest in limiting the right to vote in school district elections and may reasonably conclude that parents are those primarily interested in school affairs. A three-judge federal district court dismissed Kramer's (P) complaint, and he appealed.

ISSUE: Must legal classifications be tailored so that exclusion of a certain class of persons is necessary to achieve an articulated state goal?

HOLDING AND DECISION: (Warren, C.J.) Yes. Legal classifications must be tailored so that exclusion of a certain class of person is necessary to achieve an articulated state goal. As statutes distributing voting rights are at the foundation of representative society, any unjustified discrimination in who may vote undermines the legitimacy of representative government. Thus a statute that allows some to vote while prohibiting others must promote a compelling state interest to be valid. Assuming for purposes of argument that New York can limit the right to vote in school district elections to persons primarily interested in school affairs, that statute does not accomplish that goal. The statute excludes persons who have a distinct and direct interest in school affairs while it includes those whose interest is remote and indirect. Here, Kramer (P), who lives with his parents and pays state and federal taxes, cannot vote, while an unemployed man who pays no taxes, but who rents an apartment in the district, can vote. Reversed.

DISSENT: (Stewart, J.) The statute does not impinge on constitutionally protected rights "for the Constitution of the United States does not confer the right of suffrage upon any one." Accordingly, the "compelling state interest" test should not have been applied. The classification appeared to have been rationally related to a permissible legislative end and should have been upheld.

▶ *ANALYSIS*

It appears that the Court will not be quick to sustain "interest" voting tests but will tend to uphold competency voting tests such as requirements based on age and sanity. It is not a denial of equal protection for the state to deny ex-convicts the right to vote. An interest classification that has been upheld involved only allowing landowners in a water storage district to vote. The district had a very limited purpose, *Salyer Land Co. v. Tulare Lake Basin Water Storage District*, 410 U.S. 719 (1973).

■═■

Quicknotes

EQUAL PROTECTION CLAUSE A constitutional guarantee that no person should be denied the same protection of the laws enjoyed by other persons in like circumstances.

■═■

Reynolds v. Sims

[Party not identified in casebook excerpt.] (D) v. Voter (P)

377 U.S. 533 (1964).

NATURE OF CASE: Appeal from an order requiring reapportionment of a state legislature.

FACT SUMMARY: Sims (P) and other Alabama voters challenged the apportionment of the Alabama legislature, which had not been reapportioned since 1901.

🏛 RULE OF LAW
Equal protection requires that the seats in both houses of a bicameral state legislature must be apportioned on a population basis.

FACTS: The Alabama constitution required that the state legislature be reapportioned every ten years on the basis of population, but no reapportionment had been made since 1901. Sims (P) and other Alabama voters challenged the resultant malapportionment. Using 1960 census figures, only 21.5% of Alabama's total population lived in districts represented by a majority of members of the state senate, and only 25.7% lived in counties that could elect a majority in the lower house. Population variance ratios of up to 41 to 1 existed in the Senate and 16 to 1 in the House. The district court held that equal protection had been violated.

ISSUE: Does equal protection require that the seats in both houses of a bicameral state legislature must be apportioned on a population basis?

HOLDING AND DECISION: (Warren, C.J.) Yes. Equal protection requires that the seats in both Houses of a bicameral state legislature must be apportioned on a population basis. As the right of suffrage is fundamental, strict scrutiny must be given the alleged infringement. Diluting the weight of votes because of place of residence impairs basic constitutional rights just as much as invidious discriminations based upon factors such as economic status. "[To] the extent that a citizen's right to vote is debased, he is that much less a citizen." The federal Congress was not intended as a model of apportionment. The congressional system was born out of compromise between larger and smaller states. But ordering apportionment of both Houses by population will not render bicameralism anachronistic. Its purpose to insure mature and deliberate consideration of legislation is just as important. Districts should be as nearly equal as possible. As for districting guidelines, disparities from a strict population standard based on legitimate considerations incident to the effectuation of a rational state policy are constitutionally permissible. Factors that cannot be considered include historical, economic, or group interests. While reapportionment may be made more

often than every ten years, failure to reapportion at least once every ten years is constitutionally suspect. Affirmed.

DISSENT IN COMPANION CASES: (Stewart, J.) The Court's constitutional rule seems to require elections at large with no geographic districts. It is confusing why the Court claims that a voter in a less populous district will feel "debasement" when all voters are guaranteed two Senators no matter the population of their state. The Constitution should not specify one theory of political thought.

DISSENT: (Harlan, J.) The Court inexplicably ignores the Fourteenth Amendment in its analysis. The legislative history clearly establishes the adopters' belief that the Equal Protection Clause did not interfere with the states' ability to district their legislatures. With the decision in this case, courts are given the authority in most states to control the legislative apportionment. Now the states may only consider numbers and political subdivisions when determining districts. Nothing in the Constitution allows for such a result.

▶ ANALYSIS

By 1968, 37 states had complied with the decision that was considered to be one of the great successes of the Warren Court. However, various studies on the effect of the decision on state policy and the responsiveness of state legislatures have been conflicting. One thing is clear, rural low population areas no longer dominate the high population urban areas that were grossly unrepresented prior to reapportionment.

■■■

Quicknotes

APPORTIONMENT The division of property costs in proportion to the parties' respective interests therein.

BICAMERAL LEGISLATION In order for a bill to become a law, it must pass both houses of Congress (bicameralism), be presented to the President (presentment), and receive his approval by signature.

EQUAL PROTECTION CLAUSE A constitutional guarantee that no person should be denied the same protection of the laws enjoyed by other persons in like circumstances.

INVIDIOUS DISCRIMINATION Unequal treatment of a class of persons that is particularly malicious or hostile.

Continued on next page.

STRICT SCRUTINY Method by which courts determine the constitutionality of a law, when a law affects a fundamental right. Under the test, the legislature must have a compelling interest to enact the law and measures prescribed by the law must be the least restrictive means possible to accomplish its goal.

■▬■

Davis v. Bandemer

State (D) v. Democrats (P)

478 U.S. 109 (1986).

NATURE OF CASE: Challenge to state legislature's redistricting plan.

FACT SUMMARY: Democrats challenged Indiana's 1981 redistricting plan adopted by the Republican-controlled legislature.

🏛 RULE OF LAW
To constitute an equal protection violation, redistricting must have the effect of consistently degrading a voter's or group of voters' influence.

FACTS: In 1981, the Republican-controlled Indiana state legislature enacted a redistricting plan that had the intent of creating numerous "safe" Republican districts. State Democrats challenged this on the basis that this constituted a dilution of the voting rights of Democratic voters. The 1982 election resulted in a somewhat smaller percentage of Democratic legislators than the overall percentage of Democratic votes. The district court found this persuasive evidence that the redistricting plan did discriminate against Democrats, and it held the plan invalid.

ISSUE: To constitute an equal protection violation, must redistricting have the effect of consistently degrading a voter's or group of voters' influence?

HOLDING AND DECISION: (White, J.) Yes. To constitute an equal protection violation, redistricting must have the effect of consistently degrading a voter's or group of voters' influence. The mere fact that such a plan makes it harder for a group to elect a representative does not make the plan infirm. It is only when the electoral system is arranged in a manner that will degrade a voter's influence on the political process as a whole that a constitutional violation occurs. Here, the results of one election showed a slightly lower percentage of Democratic legislators than the percentage of Democratic votes, and this does not meet the evidentiary burden of consistent exclusion from the political process. Reversed.

CONCURRENCE AND DISSENT: (Powell, J.) When districts are arbitrarily drawn to dilute the voting strength of a certain group, the plan should be invalidated.

CONCURRENCE IN PART: (O'Connor, J.) This was a nonjusticiable question, as it was political in nature.

▶ ANALYSIS

A side issue, one raised by Justice O'Connor, was whether the controversy was justiciable. The plurality held that a nonjusticiable controversy existed when the question called for nonjudicial discretion, involved undue interference with other branches of government, or would subject the government to lack of respect abroad. Justice O'Connor's dissent contended that redistricting was a political matter best left alone by the courts.

Quicknotes

EQUAL PROTECTION CLAUSE A constitutional guarantee that no person should be denied the same protection of the laws enjoyed by other persons in like circumstances.

JUSTICIABILITY An actual controversy that is capable of determination by the court.

REDISTRICTING Legal requirement that, subsequent to each decennial census, voting districts must be redrawn in response to changes in population that have taken place since the previous census in order to ensure adequate representation in elected government.

Vieth v. Jubelirer

Challengers to districting map (P) v. Pennsylvania (D)

541 U.S. 267 (2004).

NATURE OF CASE: Appeal.

FACT SUMMARY: Vieth (P) and others challenged a map drawn by the Pennsylvania General Assembly (D) establishing districts for the election of congressional representatives, arguing that the districting constituted an unconstitutional political gerrymander.

RULE OF LAW

Since no constitutional provision provides a judicially enforceable limit on political considerations states and Congress may consider when districting, gerrymandering claims are nonjusticiable.

FACTS: Vieth (P) and others challenged a map drawn by the Pennsylvania General Assembly (D) establishing districts for the election of congressional representatives, on the ground that the districting constituted an unconstitutional political gerrymander.

ISSUE: Since no constitutional provision provides a judicially enforceable limit on political considerations states and Congress may consider when districting, are gerrymandering claims nonjusticiable?

HOLDING AND DECISION: (Scalia, J.) Yes. Since no constitutional provision provides a judicially enforceable limit on political considerations states and Congress may consider when districting, gerrymandering claims are nonjusticiable. "Fairness" is not a judicially manageable standard. Some criterion more solid and more demonstrably met than that is necessary to enable the state legislatures to discern the limits of their districting discretion, to meaningfully constrain the discretion of the courts, and to win public acceptance for the courts' intrusion into a process that is the very foundation of democratic decision-making. The very fact so many different standards have been proposed goes a long way to establishing that there is no constitutionally discernable standard. The issue is not whether severe partisan gerrymanders violate the Constitution, but whether it is for the courts to say when a violation has occurred and to design a remedy. Political gerrymanders are not new to the American scene. In fact, since 1980, no fewer than five bills have been introduced by Congress to regulate gerrymandering in congressional districting. Nevertheless, a reality of life is that some intent to gain political advantage is inescapable whenever political bodies devise a district plan. We decline to adjudicate these political gerrymandering claims.

CONCURRENCE: (Kennedy, J.) While the Court is correct to refrain from directing this substantial intrusion into the Nation's political life, one should not foreclose all possibility of judicial relief if some limited and precise rationale were found to correct an established violation of the Constitution in some redistricting cases. That no standard for review of gerrymandering cases has here emerged should not be taken to prove that no standard could exist. Allegations of unconstitutional bias in apportionment are most serious claims.

DISSENT: (Stevens, J.) Several standards for identifying impermissible partisan influence are available to judges who have the will to enforce them. What is clear is that it is not the unavailability of judicially manageable standards that drives today's decision. It is, instead, a failure of judicial will to condemn even the most blatant violations of a state legislature's fundamental duty to govern impartially.

DISSENT: (Souter, J.) It is common sense to break down a large and intractable issue, such as gerrymandering, into discrete fragments as a way to get a handle on the larger one, and there are indeed elements tractable in both theory and practice.

DISSENT: (Breyer, J.) Unjustified political factors cannot be used to entrench a party in power despite having only minority support. Legislative boundary drawing may otherwise consider politics.

▶ ANALYSIS

In *Vieth*, the Supreme Court makes clear its position that the regular insertion of the judiciary into districting, with the delay and uncertainty that brings to the political process and the partisan enmity it brings upon the courts, is not worth the benefit to be achieved—an accelerated (by some unknown degree) effectuation of the majority will.

Quicknotes

GERRYMANDERING To create a civil division of an unusual shape for an improper purpose such as redistricting a state so that a maximum number of the elected representatives will be of a particular political party.

JUSTICIABILITY An actual controversy that is capable of determination by the court.

Mobile v. Bolden

Municipality (D) v. Black citizens (P)

446 U.S. 55 (1980).

NATURE OF CASE: Federal class action challenging the constitutionality of election procedures.

FACT SUMMARY: Bolden (P) brought a class action suit alleging that the practice of electing Mobile, Alabama's (D) city commissioners at-large was unconstitutional in that it unfairly diluted black voting strength.

RULE OF LAW
An at-large electoral scheme violates the Fourteenth Amendment Equal Protection Clause only when it is proven that it was conceived or operated as a purposeful device to further racial discrimination.

FACTS: In bringing a federal class action suit on behalf of himself and other black citizens of Mobile, Alabama (D), Bolden (P) claimed that the practice of electing city commissioners at-large unfairly diluted the voting strength of blacks and thus violated both the Fourteenth and Fifteenth Amendments. He noted that no black had ever been elected despite a large black population in certain areas of Mobile (D). After finding the practice did so violate the Constitution, the district court ordered that the city commission be done away with and that there be instead a mayor and city council with members elected from single-member districts. The court of appeals affirmed.

ISSUE: Does an at-large electoral scheme violate the Fourteenth Amendment Equal Protection Clause only when it is proven that it was conceived or operated as a purposeful device to further racial discrimination?

HOLDING AND DECISION: (Stewart, J.) Yes. An at-large electoral scheme violates the Fourteenth Amendment Equal Protection Clause only when it is proven that it was conceived or operated as a purposeful device to further racial discrimination. A simple showing that the group allegedly discriminated against has not elected representatives in proportion to its numbers is not enough to prove such a purpose, although it may afford some evidence of a discriminatory purpose. Nothing in the Constitution guarantees this type of proportional representation. In this case, there simply has not been sufficient evidence to prove that the discriminatory purpose necessary to find an equal protection violation occurred. Reversed.

CONCURRENCE: (Blackmun, J.) Assuming intent is a prerequisite applicable in this case, I would view the district court's findings as amply supportive of an inference of purposeful discrimination. However, the district court did not exercise proper judicial discretion in deciding to dismantle Mobile's (D) commission form of government and replace it with a mayor-council system. It could have

taken less drastic action by restructuring the existing system to remedy the vote dilution problem, e.g., allowing continued at-large elections for commissioners but imposing district residency requirements.

CONCURRENCE: (Stevens, J.) While state action inhibiting an individual's right to vote should be tested by the strictest of constitutional standards, state action affecting the political strength of various groups that compete for leadership in a democratically governed community is in a different category and must be judged by a standard that allows the political process to function effectively. No case has established a constitutional right to proportional representation for racial minorities. A proper test of the constitutionality of this at-large electoral scheme should focus on its objective effects rather than the subjective motivation behind it. A political decision that is supported by valid and articulable justifications, as is the at-large electoral scheme in Mobile (D), cannot be invalid simply because some participants in the decision-making process were motivated by a purpose to disadvantage a minority group.

DISSENT: (Brennan, J.) Discriminatory purpose was clearly shown here. In any case, proof of discriminatory impact is sufficient.

DISSENT: (White, J.) The facts here lead to a proper inference of invidious discriminatory purpose.

DISSENT: (Marshall, J.) Prior vote-dilution decisions establish that a showing of discriminatory impact is sufficient to justify the invalidation of a multimember districting scheme and that this standard they adopted was unaffected by the subsequent cases in which this Court held a showing of purposeful discrimination was required. The vote-dilution cases were premised on the fundamental interest in voting protected by the Fourteenth Amendment, while the "purposeful discrimination" cases responded to facially neutral classifications having a racially discriminatory impact and challenged on the ground that such classifications based on race are "constitutionally suspect." Thus, the vote dilution cases involved the fundamental-interest branch rather than the antidiscrimination branch of the Equal Protection Clause. Quite simply, the "purposeful discrimination" requirement arose in cases premised on a rationale wholly apart from that underlying the constitutional challenge in this and other vote-dilution cases. It therefore does not apply here. Even if it did, and proof of discriminatory intent were necessary to support a vote-dilution claim, the common-law presumption that every man is taken to contemplate the probable consequences of his acts applies and discriminatory

Continued on next page.

intent may be inferred on that basis. It would then be the burden of Mobile (D) to disprove such intent.

▶ *ANALYSIS*

It is important to remember that the "purpose" requirement is a constitutional one and that Congress can, and at times has, legislatively mandated that discriminatory "effect" be sufficient to establish a prima facie claim of a statutory violation. For example, Congress decided to impose an "effect" requirement in the Voting Rights Acts of 1965, meaning discriminatory effect would support a finding of a statutory violation even though it would not support a claim for violation of the Constitution.

Quicknotes

EQUAL PROTECTION CLAUSE A constitutional guarantee that no person should be denied the same protection of the laws enjoyed by other persons in like circumstances.

INVIDIOUS DISCRIMINATION Unequal treatment of a class of persons that is particularly malicious or hostile.

VOTE DILUTION Specific voting practices or regulations that deprive minority voters of representation. Historically, voting strength has been unconstitutionally diluted on the basis of race as well as population inequality; the one-person, one-vote guarantee is based in the Equal Protection Clause of the Fourteenth Amendment, which also held that voting power must be apportioned equally among the electorate based upon population.

Shaw v. Reno

[Parties not identified in casebook excerpt.]

509 U.S. 630 (1993).

NATURE OF CASE: Appeal of dismissal of action to invalidate a reapportionment plan.

FACT SUMMARY: Shaw (P) alleged that a North Carolina reapportionment plan that included one majority-black district with boundary lines of dramatically irregular shape constituted unconstitutional racial gerrymandering.

RULE OF LAW
An allegation that a reapportionment scheme is so irrational on its face that it can be understood only as an effort to segregate voters based on race without sufficient justification states a cognizable claim under the Fourteenth Amendment.

FACTS: North Carolina, after becoming entitled to a twelfth seat in the U.S. House of Representatives as a result of the 1990 census, enacted a reapportionment plan that included one majority-black district with boundary lines of dramatically irregular shape. Shaw (P) sued, alleging the creation of the irregular district was unconstitutional racial gerrymandering under the Fourteenth Amendment. The district court dismissed the action for failure to state a cognizable claim. Shaw (P) appealed to the Supreme Court.

ISSUE: Does an allegation that a reapportionment scheme is so irrational on its face that it can be understood only as an effort to segregate voters based on race without sufficient justification state a cognizable claim under the Fourteenth Amendment?

HOLDING AND DECISION: (O'Connor, J.) Yes. An allegation that a reapportionment scheme is so irrational on its face that it can be understood only as an effort to segregate voters based on race without sufficient justification states a cognizable claim under the Fourteenth Amendment. The Fourteenth Amendment requires that legislation that is unexplainable on grounds other than race be narrowly tailored to further a compelling governmental interest, even if facially race neutral. An example of such unexplainable legislation would be a reapportionment plan so highly irregular on its face that it rationally cannot be understood as anything other than an effort to segregate voters on the basis of race. Such a plan perpetuates impermissible racial stereotypes by reinforcing the perception that members of the same racial group, regardless of age or economic status, share the same political ideology. Shaw's (P) complaint alleged that the North Carolina plan is such a plan and thus stated a cognizable claim. This Court's decision in *United Jewish Organizations of Williamsburgh, Inc. v. Carey*, 430 U.S. 144 (1977), cited by Shaw (P), where a Hasidic community, which had

been split between two districts under a reapportionment plan, challenged the redistricting was not on point here and therefore not controlling. Reversed.

DISSENT: (White, J.) Shaw (P) failed to state a claim because no cognizable injury is alleged. There is neither an outright deprivation of the right to vote nor a demonstration that the challenged action had the intent and effect of unduly diminishing a group's influence on the political process.

DISSENT: (Stevens, J.) Boundaries are permissibly drawn to provide for adequate representation for a variety of groups. It is no less permissible to provide for the adequate representation of the very group that inspired the Equal Protection Clause.

DISSENT: (Souter, J.) There is no justification for treating the narrow category of bizarrely shaped district claims differently from other districting claims.

ANALYSIS

Though the holding of *Shaw* is limited, the Court spoke extensively in dicta about what constituted sufficient justification for race-based districting. If on remand the plan was found to in fact be racial gerrymandering, the plan must then be found narrowly tailored to further a compelling governmental interest. This high level of scrutiny is imposed because the Court believes racial classifications with respect to voting rights "carry particular dangers" such as "Balkanizing" citizens into competing racial factions, thus moving the country away from the goal of a political system in which race is irrelevant.

Quicknotes

EQUAL PROTECTION CLAUSE A constitutional guarantee that no person should be denied the same protection of the laws enjoyed by other persons in like circumstances.

FOURTEENTH AMENDMENT 42 U.S.C. § 1983 Defamation by state officials in connection with a discharge implies a violation of a liberty interest protected by the due process requirements of the U.S. Constitution.

GERRYMANDERING To create a civil division of an unusual shape for an improper purpose such as redistricting a state with unnatural boundaries, isolating members of a

Continued on next page.

particular political party, so that a maximum number of the elected representatives will be of that political party.

REAPPORTIONMENT PLAN The alteration of a voting districts' boundaries or composition to reflect the population of that district.

■━━■

Bush v. Gore

Presidential candidate (D) v. Presidential candidate (P)

531 U.S. 98 (2000).

NATURE OF CASE: Suit seeking stay of state supreme court order.

FACT SUMMARY: Bush (D) sought a stay of the Florida Supreme Court's order permitting a manual recount of ballots in the 2000 presidential election.

> ## 🏛 RULE OF LAW
> Having once granted the right to vote on equal terms, the state may not, by later arbitrary and disparate treatment, value one person's vote over that of another.

FACTS: After a machine count and recount of ballots in the 2000 Florida presidential election, Gore (P) trailed Bush (D) by less than 1,000 votes. Gore (P) sought further recounts in certain Florida counties. This Court vacated a decision of the Florida Supreme Court extending the deadline for the completion of recounts. The Florida Supreme Court ordered a manual recount of all "undervotes"— those ballots on which the machine did not record any presidential choice. Bush (D) sought a stay of the Florida Supreme Court ruling. The United States Supreme Court stayed the Florida Supreme Court's order three days before the statutory deadline for the completion of proceedings bearing on the final certification of the state's electors.

ISSUE: Having once granted the right to vote on equal terms, may the state, by later arbitrary and disparate treatment, value one person's vote over that of another?

HOLDING AND DECISION: (Per curiam) No. Having once granted the right to vote on equal terms, the state may not, by later arbitrary and disparate treatment, value one person's vote over that of another. The right to vote is protected both in its allocation as well as its exercise. The recount mechanism implemented here does not satisfy the minimum requirement for non-arbitrary treatment of voters necessary to secure the fundamental right. The standards for accepting or rejecting contested ballots vary not only from county to county but within the county from team to team of recounters. Since any recount seeking to meet the December 12 date will be unconstitutional without substantial additional work, the decision of the Florida Supreme Court ordering the recount to proceed is reversed.

DISSENT: (Stevens, J.) While the use of differing substandards for determining voter intent in different counties employing similar voting systems may raise serious concerns, those concerns are alleviated by the fact that a single impartial magistrate will ultimately adjudicate all objections arising from the recount process.

DISSENT: (Souter, J.) The case should be remanded to the Florida courts with instructions to establish uniform standards in any further recounting.

DISSENT: (Ginsburg, J.) The recount could yield a result as fair or precise than the certification that proceeded that recount.

DISSENT: (Breyer, J.) In a system that allows counties to use different types of voting systems, voters arrive at the polls with an unequal chance that their votes will be counted.

▶ ANALYSIS

The Court here does not challenge the Florida Supreme Court's authority to resolve election disputes or to define a legal vote or order a manual recount. The Court rejects the standard employed, which was the "intent of the voter," and the absence of specific standards to ensure its equal application.

■═■

Quicknotes

DUE PROCESS CLAUSE Clause found in the Fifth and Fourteenth Amendments to the United States Constitution providing that no person shall be deprived of "life, liberty, or property, without due process of law."

EQUAL PROTECTION A constitutional guarantee that no person shall be denied the same protection of the laws enjoyed by other persons in like circumstances.

■═■

Shapiro v. Thompson

[Parties not identified in casebook excerpt.]

394 U.S. 618 (1969).

NATURE OF CASE: Appeal from decisions holding residency requirements for welfare applicants unconstitutional.

FACT SUMMARY: Statutory provisions deny welfare assistance to residents who have not resided within their jurisdiction for at least one year.

▥ RULE OF LAW
Any classification that serves to penalize the exercise of a constitutional right is unconstitutional unless it is shown to be necessary to promote a compelling governmental interest, rather than merely shown to be rationally related to a legitimate purpose.

FACTS: A three-judge district court held unconstitutional certain state and District of Columbia statutory provisions. The provisions deny welfare assistance to residents of the state or district who have not resided within their jurisdictions for at least one year immediately preceding their applications for such assistance.

ISSUE: Is any classification that serves to penalize the exercise of a constitutional right unconstitutional unless it is shown to be necessary to promote a compelling governmental interest, rather than merely shown to be rationally related to a legitimate purpose?

HOLDING AND DECISION: (Brennan, J.) Yes. Any classification that serves to penalize the exercise of a constitutional right is unconstitutional unless it is shown to be necessary to promote a compelling governmental interest, rather than merely shown to be rationally related to a legitimate purpose. The states justify the waiting period requirement as a protective device to preserve the fiscal integrity of their public assistance programs, by discouraging needy families from entering their jurisdictions. However, this act of inhibiting migration by needy persons into the state is constitutionally impermissible, since the right to travel from state to state is protected by the Constitution from laws or regulations that would unreasonably burden such movement. If a law has no other purpose than to chill the assertion of a constitutional right by penalizing those who choose to exercise them, it is patently unconstitutional. Further, the statutes create two classes of persons, different only in that one class has been in the area for one year. A state has a valid interest in preserving the fiscal integrity of its programs. But it cannot accomplish this purposefully invidious discrimination between classes of its citizens. The saving of welfare costs cannot be an independent ground for invidious classification. The states also assert that the waiting period serves

certain administrative goals. They contend that a mere showing of a rational relationship and these permissible state goals will justify the classification. This is not true. As stated above, the right to travel is a constitutional right. Any classification that serves to penalize the exercise of a constitutional right is unconstitutional unless it is shown to be necessary to promote a compelling governmental interest. All of the administrative arguments advanced are either unfounded, irrational, or may be accomplished by a less drastic means. The district court's judgment is affirmed.

DISSENT: (Warren, C.J.) This case is not based merely on the state residency requirements that were enacted by the states solely on their own authority. The Congress has authorized this type of requirement for the District of Columbia, so the real question is whether Congress may authorize this type of legislation under the commerce power. Since numerous other restrictions on interstate commerce have been sanctioned by this Court, the insubstantial restriction imposed here is certainly justified by the rational justification advanced for it.

DISSENT: (Harlan, J.) The equal protection argument accepted by the majority has, in reality, two branches. Since any departure from equal protection requires a compelling governmental interest as justification under this theory, there are actually two separate types of equal protection violations. The "suspect classification" branch is well-founded in the racial groupings from which the Fourteenth Amendment sprang. But the other branch is far more troubling, since it looks to "fundamental rights." But the traditional equal protection approach required only that the state show a rational justification for its acts. To now require a "compelling interest" in these cases is to create in this Court a super legislature somehow imbued with a special intelligence and expertise in regulating the internal affairs of the states. Using the traditional, and proper, approach to equal protection, there are perfectly adequate rational justifications for the states to impose a welfare residency requirement and this Court has no authority to create new "fundamental rights" as it has done in this case.

▶ ANALYSIS

Many agreed with Justice Harlan's dissent that the Court was simply resurrecting the judicial intervention of substantive due process under the guise of a new stricter equal protection test. One commentator warned, "Looming down the path is the spectre of economic due process, of judges riding to the rescue of Oklahoma's opticians or the

Continued on next page.

Railway Express Agency." Supporters of the new doctrine answered that it was limited to minorities that seem permanently voiceless and invisible and whom the power structure in the political process tends to ignore. Subsequent decisions have shown the Court to be willing to expand the number of suspect classifications to include national origin and sex as well as race.

■━■

Quicknotes

COMPELLING GOVERNMENT INTEREST Defense to an alleged Equal Protection Clause violation that a state action was necessary in order to protect an interest that the government is under a duty to protect.

SUBSTANTIVE DUE PROCESS A constitutional safeguard limiting the power of the state, irrespective of how fair its procedures may be; substantive limits placed on the power of the state.

SUSPECT CLASSIFICATION A class of persons that has historically been subject to discriminatory treatment; statutes drawing a distinction between persons based on a suspect classification, i.e., race, nationality or alienage, are subject to a strict scrutiny standard of review.

■━■

Saenz v. Roe

New state resident (P) v. State (D)

526 U.S. 489 (1999).

NATURE OF CASE: Appeal from an order enjoining implementation of a state statute.

FACT SUMMARY: When California (D) discriminated against citizens who had resided in the state for less than one year in distributing welfare benefits, the state statute was challenged and held to be unconstitutional.

🏛 RULE OF LAW
Durational residency requirements violate the fundamental right to travel by denying a newly arrived citizen the same privileges and immunities enjoyed by other citizens in the same state, and are therefore subject to strict liability.

FACTS: In 1992, California (D) enacted a statute limiting the maximum first year welfare benefits available to newly arrived residents to the amount they would have received in the state of their prior residence. Saenz (P) and other California residents who were eligible for such benefits challenged the constitutionality of the durational residency requirement, alleging their right to travel was violated. The district court preliminarily enjoined implementation of the statute and the court of appeals affirmed. Congress enacted the Personal Responsibility and Work Opportunity Reconciliation Act of 1996, which expressly authorized states to apply the rules (including benefit amounts) of another state if the family has resided in the state for less than twelve months. California (D) appealed, alleging that the statute should be upheld if it has a rational basis, and that the state's (D) legitimate interest in saving over $10 million a year satisfied that test.

ISSUE: Do durational residency requirements violate the fundamental right to travel by denying a newly arrived citizen the same privileges and immunities enjoyed by other citizens in the same state, and are they thus subject to strict liability?

HOLDING AND DECISION: (Stevens, J.) Yes. Durational residency requirements violate the fundamental right to travel by denying a newly arrived citizen the same privileges and immunities enjoyed by other citizens in the same state, and are therefore subject to strict liability. The first sentence of Article IV, § 2, provides that the citizens of each state shall be entitled to all privileges and immunities of citizens in the several states. The right of a newly arrived citizen to the same privileges and immunities enjoyed by other citizens of the same state is protected not only by the new arrival's status as a state citizen, but also by her status as a citizen of the United States. The Citizenship Clause of the Fourteenth Amendment protects all citizens' right to

choose to be citizens of the state wherein they reside. Neither mere rationality nor some intermediate standard of review should be used to judge the constitutionality of a state rule that discriminates against some of its citizens because they have been domiciled in the state for less than a year. The state's legitimate interest in saving money provides no justification for its decision to discriminate among equally eligible citizens. Affirmed.

DISSENT: (Rehnquist, C.J.) The right to travel and the right to become a citizen are distinct, and one is not a "component" of the other. If states can require an individual to reside in-state for a year before exercising the right to educational benefits, the right to terminate a marriage, or the right to vote in primary elections that all other state citizens enjoy, then it may surely do the same for welfare benefits. California has reasonably exercised its power to protect state resources through an objective, narrowly tailored residence requirement. There is nothing in the Constitution that should prevent the enforcement of that requirement.

DISSENT: (Thomas, J.) The majority attributes a meaning to the Privileges or Immunities Clause that likely was unintended when the Fourteenth Amendment was enacted and ratified. At that time, people understood "privileges or immunities of citizens" to be their fundamental right, rather than every public benefit established by positive law.

▶ ANALYSIS

The court in this case found that a state violated the Privileges and Immunities Clause when it discriminated against citizens who had been residents for less than one year. Justice Thomas's dissent alleged that this was contrary to the original understanding at the time the Fourteenth Amendment was enacted. Chief Justice Rehnquist's dissent went on to point out that a welfare subsidy is as much an investment in human capital as is a tuition subsidy and their attendant benefits are just as portable.

■■■

Quicknotes

FOURTEENTH AMENDMENT Declares that no state shall make or enforce any law that shall abridge the privileges and immunities of citizens of the United States.

Continued on next page.

FUNDAMENTAL RIGHT A liberty that is either expressly or implicitly provided for in the United States Constitution, the deprivation or burdening of which is subject to a heightened standard of review.

PRIVILEGED AND IMMUNITIES CLAUSE OF ARTICLE IV, § 2 A provision in the Fourteenth Amendment to the United States Constitution recognizing that any individual born in any of the United States is entitled to both state and national citizenship and guaranteeing such citizens the privileges and immunities thereof.

RATIONAL BASIS REVIEW A test employed by the court to determine the validity of a statute in equal protection actions, whereby the court determines whether the challenged statute is rationally related to the achievement of a legitimate state interest.

RIGHT TO TRAVEL Constitutional guarantee affording the privileges and benefits of one state to citizens of another residing therein for the statutory period.

STRICT SCRUTINY Method by which courts determine the constitutionality of a law, when a law affects a fundamental right. Under the test, the legislature must have a compelling interest to enact law and measures prescribed by the law must be the least restrictive means possible to accomplish a goal.

M.L.B. v. S.L.J.

Mother (P) v. State (D)

519 U.S. 102 (1996).

NATURE OF CASE: Appeal from decree terminating parental rights.

FACT SUMMARY: A Mississippi court dismissed M.L.B.'s (P) appeal of the termination of her parental rights to her two minor children when she was unable to pay the required record preparation fees.

🏛 **RULE OF LAW**
A state may not condition appeals from trial court decrees terminating parental rights on the affected parent's ability to pay record preparation fees.

FACTS: A Mississippi court ordered M.L.B.'s (P) parental rights to her two minor children terminated. M.L.B. (P) sought to appeal the termination decree, but the state required that she pay in advance over $2,000 in record preparation fees. Because M.L.B. (P) did not have the money to pay the fees, her appeal was dismissed. The Supreme Court granted certiorari to determine whether the Due Process and Equal Protection Clauses of the Fourteenth Amendment permitted such appeals to be conditioned on the ability to pay certain fees.

ISSUE: May a state condition appeals from trial court decrees terminating parental rights on the affected parent's ability to pay record preparation fees?

HOLDING AND DECISION: (Ginsburg, J.) No. A state may not condition appeals from trial court decrees terminating parental rights on the affected parent's ability to pay record preparation fees. Fee requirements are generally examined only for their rationality. While the Court has not prohibited state controls on every type of civil action, it has consistently distinguished those involving intrusions on family relationships. However, the stakes for M.L.B. (P), i.e., the forced dissolution of her parental rights, are far greater than any monetary loss. Mississippi's interest, on the other hand, in offsetting the costs on its court system, is purely financial. Decrees forever terminating parental rights fit in the category of cases in which a state may not "bolt the door to equal justice." Reversed.

DISSENT: (Thomas, J.) The majority's new-found constitutional right to free transcripts in civil appeals cannot be effectively restricted to this case. M.L.B. (P) requested relief under both the Due Process and Equal Protection Clauses, yet the majority does not specify the source of relief it has granted. Mississippi's transcript rule reasonably obliges all potential appellants to bear the cost of availing themselves of a service that the state is not constitutionally required to provide. The Equal Protection Clause is not a panacea for all perceived social and economic inequity.

▶ **ANALYSIS**

While the majority's rationale in granting M.L.B. (P) relief may have been vaguely articulated, as the dissent has alleged, it would seem that the issues at stake here go beyond simple textual analysis. It is not merely M.L.B.'s (P) rights that must be considered, but the impact that the termination of those rights will have on her two minor children. It will likely not be as great of a problem as the dissent suggests to limit the application of this holding to similarly situated parents.

■■■

Quicknotes

DUE PROCESS CLAUSE Clause found in the Fifth and Fourteenth Amendments to the United States Constitution providing that no person shall be deprived of "life, liberty, or property, without due process of law."

EQUAL PROTECTION CLAUSE A constitutional guarantee that no person should be denied the same protection of the laws enjoyed by other persons in like circumstances.

■■■

San Antonio Ind. School District v. Rodriguez

School district (D) v. Students (P)

411 U.S. 1 (1973).

NATURE OF CASE: Appeal from a finding that a school tax finance plan denies equal protection.

FACT SUMMARY: Rodriguez (P) argued that the Texas Public School finance system denied equal protection because students who lived in districts with a low property tax base received a lower quality education than students who lived in high property tax base districts.

RULE OF LAW
School finance systems based upon deferring property tax rates in different school districts do not violate equal protection.

FACTS: Rodriguez (P) brought this class action on behalf of school children throughout Texas who are members of minority groups or who are poor and reside in school districts having a low property tax base. Texas finances its public schools through a system of state and local funding. The local funds are apportioned to reflect each district's relative taxpaying ability. Rodriguez (P) resides in Edgewood, one of seven school districts in the San Antonio metropolitan area. Edgewood has the lowest property value and highest tax rate of the seven districts and spends $356 per pupil. Alamo Heights, the most affluent of the seven, has the highest property value and the lowest tax rate and spends $594 per pupil. The district court found wealth to be a suspect classification and education to be a fundamental interest and held that the Texas system discriminates on the basis of wealth in the way education is provided. San Antonio (D) appealed.

ISSUE: Do school finance systems based upon differing property tax rates in different school districts violate equal protection?

HOLDING AND DECISION: (Powell, J.) No. School finance systems based upon differing property tax rates in different school districts do not violate equal protection. The wealth discrimination alleged here is unlike any other the Court has discussed. This is not a case where poor persons are denied a desired benefit; they are receiving a lower quality version of that desired benefit. Equal protection does not require absolute equality or precisely equal advantages. As for a suspect class, the alleged discriminatory system has none of the traditional characteristics of suspectness, and it must therefore be concluded that the Texas system does not operate to the peculiar disadvantage of any suspect class. As for a fundamental interest, the determination of whether education is fundamental lies in assessing whether there is a right to education explicitly or implicitly guaranteed by the Constitution. Education is not explicitly guaranteed and no basis exists for finding it to be implicitly guaranteed. The action is a direct attack on Texas' method of raising and disbursing tax revenues, and the Court has traditionally disliked interfering with a state's fiscal policies under the Equal Protection Clause. Further, no scheme of taxation has ever been devised completely free of some discriminatory impact. The existence of some inequality in the state's manner of achieving its goal is not alone a sufficient basis for striking down an entire system. Any local taxation scheme requires creation of inevitably arbitrary jurisdictional boundaries. "Moreover, if local taxation for local expenditure is an unconstitutional method of providing for education then it may be an equally impermissible means of providing other necessary (local) services." This decision does not approve of the status quo or deny the need for tax law reform, but any change must come from the legislature, not the courts. Reversed.

DISSENT: (Brennan, J.) A right is not fundamental if it is explicitly or implicitly found in the Constitution; "'Fundamentality' is . . . a function of the right's importance in terms of the effectuation of those rights that are in fact constitutionally guaranteed."

DISSENT: (White, J.) "Requiring the state to establish only that unequal treatment is in furtherance of a permissible goal, without also requiring the state to show that the means chosen to effectuate that goal are rationally related to its achievement, makes equal protection analysis no more than an empty gesture."

DISSENT: (Marshall, J.) The issue was not whether Texas was doing its best to lessen the worst aspects of a discriminatory scheme, but whether the scheme itself was unconstitutionally discriminatory. Educational quality depends on what the state can first give the child, and not upon what the child is able to do with what he receives. Equal protection does not look to minimal sufficiency but to unjustifiable inequalities of state action. Furthermore, strict scrutiny is not only given to established rights found in the text of the Constitution itself.

▌ ANALYSIS

In applying "traditional equal protection analysis," the Court per Justice Brennan held that a food stamp act provision that prevented anyone in a household containing an individual unrelated to any other household member as lacking any rational basis, *U.S. Department of Agriculture v. Moreno*, 413 U.S. 528 (1973). In another equal protection

Continued on next page.

case, the Court per Justice Douglas upheld a zoning ordinance that defined a "family" as persons related by blood, adoption, or marriage, or no more than two unrelated persons living together—this was rational, *Village of Belle Terre v. Boraas*, 416 U.S. 1 (1974). The cases reached opposite conclusions as to rationality without broadening the scope of fundamental rights.

■═■

Quicknotes

EQUAL PROTECTION CLAUSE A constitutional guarantee that no person should be denied the same protection of the laws enjoyed by other persons in like circumstances.

SUSPECT CLASSIFICATION A class of persons that has historically been subject to discriminatory treatment; statutes drawing a distinction between persons based on a suspect classification, i.e., race, nationality or alienage, are subject to a strict scrutiny standard of review.

■═■

The Concept of State Action

Quick Reference Rules of Law

Jackson v. Metropolitan Edison Co.

Power consumer (P) v. Utility (D)

419 U.S. 345 (1974).

NATURE OF CASE: Action seeking damages and injunctive relief from termination of power.

FACT SUMMARY: Jackson (P) contended that Metropolitan Edison Co.'s (D) shutting off of her power constituted "state action" in violation of the Fourteenth Amendment's guarantee of due process of law.

🏛 RULE OF LAW
The actions of a private business are not necessarily converted into "state action" because it is a monopoly, it is subject to extensive and detailed state regulation, or it is a business providing an essential service and is thus "affected with the public interest."

FACTS: Metropolitan Edison Co. (Metropolitan) (D) cut off the power to Jackson's (P) home (for delinquency in payments) in a manner she claimed violated the Fourteenth Amendment's guarantee of due process of law. Jackson (P) sought damages for the termination and an injunction requiring Metropolitan (D) to continue providing power until she was afforded notice, a hearing, and an opportunity to pay the amounts due. Her main argument was that Metropolitan's (D) termination was "state action" inasmuch as it was a monopoly sanctioned by the state, it was subject to extensive and detailed state regulation, it provided an essential public service, and it was a business "affected with the public interest." She appealed an adverse decision.

ISSUE: Do the actions of a private business necessarily become "state actions" because it is a monopoly, it is subject to state regulation, it provides an essential service, or it is "affected with the public interest?"

HOLDING AND DECISION: (Rehnquist, J.) No. Actions taken by a private business do not necessarily become "state actions" simply because it is a monopoly, it is subject to extensive and detailed state regulation, it provides an essential service, or it is a business "affected with the public interest." The first two factors deserve consideration in determining whether there is a sufficiently close nexus between the state and the challenged action of the regulated entity so the action of the latter may be fairly treated as that of the state itself. However, in this case, no such close nexus exists. As for the argument that Metropolitan (D) performs a "public function" by providing an essential public service, the supplying of utility service is not traditionally the exclusive prerogative of the state. Finally, we decline the invitation to expand the doctrine that state action can be found when business performs a public function into a broad principle that all businesses

"affected with the public interest" are state actors in all their actions. Too many businesses are arguably "affected with the public interest" (because they provide arguably essential goods and services) to make such a position tenable. Finally, the fact that the state did not overturn the termination practice of Metropolitan (D) is not the same as the state ordering such a practice be followed and thus putting its own weight on the side of the practice and turning it into "state action." Affirmed.

DISSENT: (Marshall, J.) Today, the Court erroneously takes a major step in repudiating the line of state action cases that have repeatedly relied on several factors clearly presented in this case: a state-sanctioned monopoly; an extensive pattern of cooperation between the "private" entity and the state; and a service uniquely public in nature.

▶ ANALYSIS

A similar "state action" argument was made when a television network declined to accept any "editorial advertisements," having already complied with the fairness doctrine. *Columbia Broadcasting System v. Democratic National Committee*, 412 U.S. 94 (1973). Three of the justices concluded the broadcaster's refusal did not constitute "state action" for First Amendment purposes; two concluded it did; three declined to decide the issue, assumed governmental action, and concluded the ban did not violate the First Amendment; and one assumed it was not state action and concurred in the result that the ban was permissible.

■=■

Quicknotes

DUE PROCESS CLAUSE Clauses found in the Fifth and Fourteenth Amendments to the United States Constitution providing that no person shall be deprived of "life, liberty, or property, without due process of law."

STATE ACTION Actions brought pursuant to the Fourteenth Amendment claiming that the government violated the plaintiff's civil rights.

■=■

Shelley v. Kraemer

African-American property buyer (D) v. Neighboring property owner (P)

334 U.S. 1 (1948).

NATURE OF CASE: Action to enforce a restrictive covenant in the sale of real property.

FACT SUMMARY: Kraemer (P) sought to void a sale of real property to Shelley (D), relying on a racially restrictive covenant.

🏛 RULE OF LAW
Judicial enforcement of a private racially restrictive covenant is considered state action for Fourteenth Amendment purposes.

FACTS: Property owners signed restrictive covenants, which provided in part that the property could not be used or occupied by anyone other than a member of the Caucasian race for a period of up to 50 years. Shelley (D), an African-American, purchased a parcel of land subject to the restrictive covenant. Kraemer (P), an owner of other property subject to the terms of the restrictive covenant, sued to enjoin Shelley (D) from taking possession of the property and to divest title from Shelley (D). The trial court held for Kraemer (P) and Shelley (D) appealed.

ISSUE: Is judicial enforcement of a private racially restrictive covenant considered state action for Fourteenth Amendment purposes?

HOLDING AND DECISION: (Vinson, C.J.) Yes. Judicial enforcement of a private racially restrictive covenant is considered state action for Fourteenth Amendment purposes. Because the restrictive covenants did not involve any action by the state legislature or city council, the restrictive covenant itself did not violate any rights protected by the Fourteenth Amendment, since it was strictly a private covenant. But the judicial enforcement of the covenant did qualify as state action. From the time of the adoption of the Fourteenth Amendment until the present, the Court has consistently ruled that the action of the states to which the amendment has reference includes action of state courts and state judicial officers. In this case, because there was a willing buyer and seller, Shelley (D) would have been able to enforce the restrictive covenants only with the active intervention of the state courts. The court rejected Kraemer's (P) argument that since the state courts would enforce restrictive covenants excluding white persons from ownership of property that there was no denial of equal protection. The court stated that equal protection of the law is not achieved through indiscriminate imposition of inequalities. As to Kraemer's (P) contention that he was being denied equal protection of the laws because his restrictive covenant was not being enforced, the court stated that the Constitution does not confer the right to demand action by the state that would result in the denial of equal protection of the laws to other individuals. Therefore, in granting judicial enforcement of the restrictive agreement, the state has denied Shelley (D) equal protection of the laws and the action of the state courts cannot stand. The Court noted that the enjoyment of property rights, free from discrimination by the states, was among the objectives sought to be effectuated by the framers of the Fourteenth Amendment. Reversed.

▶ ANALYSIS

The Court in its post-*Shelley v. Kraemer* decisions has given this decision a fairly narrow reading. A broad reading of this case requires that whenever a state court enforces a private racial restrictive covenant that such action constitutes state action that is forbidden by the Fourteenth Amendment. In cases where the ruling in this case could have been found to be applicable, the Court has used a different rationale. Some of the Court's statements suggest that more state involvement than even-handed enforcement of private biases was necessary to find unconstitutional state action. Justice Black, in a dissenting opinion, stated that the decision in this case only is applicable in cases involving property rights.

■■■

Quicknotes

EQUAL PROTECTION CLAUSE A constitutional guarantee that no person should be denied the same protection of the laws enjoyed by other persons in like circumstances.

FOURTEENTH AMENDMENT Declares that no state shall make or enforce any law that shall abridge the privileges and immunities of citizens of the United States.

RESTRICTIVE COVENANT A promise contained in a deed to limit the uses to which the property will be made.

STATE ACTION Actions brought pursuant to the Fourteenth Amendment claiming that the government violated the plaintiff's civil rights.

■■■

Reitman v. Mulkey

Property owner (D) v. Prospective tenant (P)

387 U.S. 369 (1967).

NATURE OF CASE: Action for injunctive relief and damages under §§ 51 and 52 of the California Civil Code.

FACT SUMMARY: Reitman (D) refused to rent the Mulkeys (P) an apartment on account of their race.

RULE OF LAW
If the ultimate effect of a state constitution or statute is to encourage racial discrimination, it violates the Equal Protection Clause of the Fourteenth Amendment and is unconstitutional.

FACTS: A state measure, § 26 prevented the state from denying or limiting the right of any person to sell, lease, or rent his property to such persons as he, in his absolute discretion, chooses. The Mulkeys (P) sued under §§ 51 and 52 of the California Civil Code that provided that all persons are free and equal and are entitled to the full and equal accommodations, advantages, facilities, privileges, or services in all business establishments of every kind whatsoever. The Mulkeys (P) claimed that they were denied a lease based on their race. The California Supreme Court held § 26 invalid as a violation of the Fourteenth Amendment equal protection clause.

ISSUE: If the ultimate effect of a state constitution or statute is to encourage racial discrimination, does it violate the Equal Protection Clause of the Fourteenth Amendment?

HOLDING AND DECISION: (White, J.) Yes. If the ultimate effect of a state constitution or statute is to encourage racial discrimination, it violates the Equal Protection Clause of the Fourteenth Amendment and is unconstitutional. The Court gave great deference to the reasoning and conclusion of the California Supreme Court when that court invalidated § 26. While the states are not required to affirmatively forbid racial discrimination, they cannot foster it. Prior to the passage of § 26 as a state constitutional amendment, the state had several statutes forbidding racial discrimination in the sale or rental of private housing units. As Justice Stewart pointed out in his concurring opinion in *Burton v. Wilmington Parking Authority*, 365 U.S. 715 (1961), the state may not authorize discrimination. By abandoning its open housing statutes in favor of a supposed position of neutrality, the state has encouraged private discrimination. If California's position had always been neutral and § 26 was merely a codification of that position, no issue would be presented. But the California Supreme Court determined that the effect of § 26 was to place the state in the position of sanctioning and encouraging private discrimination. While this court undertakes no definite definition of that which would always constitute state action, there is no reason why it should reject the conclusions of the California court. Affirmed.

DISSENT: (Harlan, J.) This case presents no violation of the Fourteenth Amendment since § 26 merely put the state in a neutral position in the area of private discrimination affecting the sale or rental of private residential property. The majority opinion was solely based on a conclusion of law and did not attempt to find any facts that pointed out that § 26 actually did involve state discriminatory actions. For there to be state action sufficient to bring the Fourteenth Amendment into operation, there must be some affirmative and purposeful state action that actively fosters discrimination. There is no such action in this case.

ANALYSIS

This case has been criticized because of the reasoning behind the Court's decision. Many writers felt that § 26 was properly adopted and was within the power of the voters to adopt. Regardless of the views of the critics, the court expanded the state action concept by this decision. The state cannot make lawful that which it has previously held to be discriminatory and unlawful. It was clear in this case that state action was involved, but this case does little to indicate the scope of involvement necessary by the state to make private actions state actions.

■■■

Quicknotes

ARTICLE I, § 26 An amendment to the California state constitution passed in 1967; it provided that property owners were free to sell or rent to whomever they choose. It was proposed in the form of an initiative for the purpose of repealing fair housing legislation previously passed by the Legislature.

STATE ACTION Actions brought pursuant to the Fourteenth Amendment claiming that the government violated the plaintiff's civil rights.

■■■

Moose Lodge v. Irvis

Private club (D) v. Black guest (P)

407 U.S. 163 (1972).

NATURE OF CASE: Constitutional challenge against racial discrimination in a private club.

FACT SUMMARY: The Moose Lodge (D) refused to serve liquor to the black guest of a member solely on the basis of his race.

> 🏛 **RULE OF LAW**
> Merely granting a liquor license to a private club that engages in discriminatory practices is not sufficient state action to invoke the Fourteenth Amendment.

FACTS: Irvis (P), a black, was invited to the Moose Lodge (the Lodge) (D) by a member. The Lodge (D) refused to serve liquor to Irvis (P) solely because he was black. Irvis (P) brought an action in federal district court alleging that the state was authorizing and furthering discrimination. Irvis (P) requested the Court to enjoin the Lodge's (D) discriminatory practices. Irvis's (P) claim of state action under the Fourteenth Amendment was based solely upon the granting of a liquor license to the Lodge (D). The district court found state action present based on the state's total control over the granting of licenses, its use of its police powers to regulate the Lodge's (D) physical facilities, and its licensing requirements including the submission of a list of names and addresses of all members.

ISSUE: Is the issuance of a liquor license alone sufficient state action to invoke the Fourteenth Amendment?

HOLDING AND DECISION: (Rehnquist, J.) No. For state action to be found it must be shown that the state, through an exercise of its power and authority, encouraged or fostered discrimination. Merely granting a permit enabling a private club to serve liquor to its members and their guests is essentially neutral conduct. It cannot be said that such conduct either fosters or encourages discriminatory practices. It also cannot be said that the state is lending either its prestige or support to a discriminatory group. Merely regulating the physical aspects of the club or granting a liquor license is not sufficient state action to invoke the prohibitions of the Fourteenth Amendment. The case might be decided contra if the rules and bylaws of the club required racial discrimination. Here they do not. The decision of the district court is reversed.

DISSENT: (Douglas, J.) Where the state grants a limited resource (e.g., small quota of liquor licenses as here) to a racially discriminatory private group, it is lending its prestige to the group and is fostering and encouraging discrimination.

DISSENT: (Brennan, J.) Merely granting the license was sufficient involvement. When the state grants the permit and regulates the operation, the state becomes entangled in the business.

▶ ANALYSIS

Granting a lease in a public facility has been held to be sufficient governmental involvement to invoke the Fourteenth Amendment. *Burton v. Wilmington Parking Authority*, 365 U.S. 715 (1961). Another example of state action is where a private discriminatory facility contracts with the police to hire deputies to enforce the discriminatory practices. (*Griffin v. Maryland*, 378 U.S. 130 [1964]).

■▬■

Quicknotes

FOURTEENTH AMENDMENT Declares that no state shall make or enforce any law that shall abridge the privileges and immunities of citizens of the United States.

POLICE POWER The power of a government to impose restrictions on the rights of private persons, as long as those restrictions are reasonably related to the promotion and protection of public health, safety, morals and the general welfare.

STATE ACTION Actions brought pursuant to the Fourteenth Amendment claiming that the government violated the plaintiff's civil rights.

■▬■

Rendell-Baker v. Kohn

Vocational counselor (P) v. Private school official (D)

457 U.S. 830 (1982).

NATURE OF CASE: Appeal from discharge by private school.

FACT SUMMARY: Rendell-Baker (P) was discharged by a publicly supported private school and claimed her discharge constituted state action.

🏛 RULE OF LAW
A state normally can be held responsible for a private decision only when it has exercised coercive power or has provided such significant encouragement, either overt or covert, that the choice must in law be deemed to be that of the state.

FACTS: New Perspectives is a private school that specializes in dealing with students who have experienced difficulty completing public high schools. In recent years, nearly all of the students at the school have been referred to it by the Brookline or Boston school committees, or by the Drug Rehabilitation Division of the Massachusetts Department of Mental Health. Between 90 and 99% of the school's budget has been provided in recent years by public funds. To be eligible for tuition funding under Massachusetts law, the school is required to maintain written job descriptions and written statements describing personnel standards and procedures, but they impose few specific requirements. Rendell-Baker (P) was a vocational counselor hired with funds distributed by the State Committee on Criminal Justice, which must approve the school's initial hiring decisions. Rendell-Baker (P) and five teachers at the school alleged that Kohn (D) violated 42 U.S.C. § 1983 by discharging them because of their exercise of the First Amendment right of free speech and without due process under the Fourteenth Amendment.

ISSUE: Can a state normally be held responsible for a private decision only when it has exercised coercive power or has provided such significant encouragement, either overt or covert, that the choice must in law be deemed to be that of the state?

HOLDING AND DECISION: (Burger, C.J.) Yes. A state normally can be held responsible for a private decision only when it has exercised coercive power or has provided such significant encouragement, either overt or covert, that the choice must in law be deemed to be that of the state. The school is like many private contractors, whose acts do not become those of the state even though they may be totally engaged in performing public contracts. Although the school was extensively regulated, the regulators showed little interest in the school's personnel policies, and the decision to discharge Rendell-Baker (P) was not compelled or influenced by any state regulation. The fact that a private entity performs a function that serves the public does not make its acts state action. Affirmed.

DISSENT: (Marshall, J.) Since the school is funded almost entirely by the state, is closely supervised by the state, and exists solely to perform the state's statutory duty to educate children with special needs—since the school is really an arm of the state—its personnel decisions may appropriately be considered state action.

⬤ ANALYSIS

The Court in *Rendell-Baker* analogized the school to the nursing homes that it decided in *Blum v. Yaretsky*, 457 U.S. 991 (1982), were not state actors for the purpose of determining whether decisions regarding transfer of patients could be fairly attributed to the state. As in *Rendell-Baker*, Justices Brennan and Marshall dissented. Justice Brennan wrote that for many nursing home patients, "the nursing home operator is the immediate authority, the provider of food, clothing, shelter, and health care, and, in every significant respect, the functional equivalent of the State."

Quicknotes

DUE PROCESS CLAUSE Clauses found in the Fifth and Fourteenth Amendments to the United States Constitution providing that no person shall be deprived of "life, liberty, or property, without due process of law."

STATE ACTION Actions brought pursuant to the Fourteenth Amendment claiming that the government violated the plaintiff's civil rights.

Flagg Bros., Inc. v. Brooks

Storage company (D) v. Evictee (P)

436 U.S. 149 (1978).

NATURE OF CASE: Constitutional challenge to state law and for damages and injunctive relief.

FACT SUMMARY: Flagg Brothers (D) threatened to sell Brooks' (P) furniture which had been stored with it by the marshals.

🏛 RULE OF LAW
A mere grant of a private remedy to resolve commercial disputes is not state action.

FACTS: Brooks' (P) furniture was brought to Flagg Brothers (D) by marshals for storage pursuant to a decree of eviction. Brooks (P) would not pay the storage charges and Flagg (D) threatened to sell the furniture pursuant to the statutory authority given to warehousemen to sell stored goods for the payment of charges through a private, nonjudicial sale. Brooks (P) brought an action under 42 U.S.C. § 1983 seeking damages, injunctive relief and a declaration that the statute violated the Due Process and Equal Protection Clauses of the Fourteenth Amendment. The district court dismissed, finding no state action. It was reversed on appeal on the ground that the state had conveyed a portion of its sovereign powers to warehousemen by statute. Flagg (D) alleged that a mere grant of authority to settle commercial disputes privately does not constitute state action.

ISSUE: Does the grant of authority to settle commercial disputes privately constitute state action?

HOLDING AND DECISION: (Rehnquist, J.) No. Before a claim under § 1983 is cognizable it must first be established that plaintiff has been deprived of a constitutionally secured right under color of statute. First, neither party has argued or established that Brooks (P) has suffered the deprivation of any right secured under the constitution. Where the alleged deprivation is performed by a private party, it must be established that the actions are attributable to the state. We do not find that state action is present where there is merely a grant of authority to resolve commercial disputes through private means. This is not an area that is exclusively under the control of the government, such as voting. Commercial disputes have been solved through private means for centuries. Moreover, if the state was neutral, the matter of a private sale would still have to be decided by the courts. This is not a case involving the delegation of an exclusive public function to a private party. Mere approval of a nonjudicial method of handling private disputes is far different than ordering conduct by statute. New York has not compelled the sale, merely permitted it to be held as an alternative to other available methods or recovery. There is no state action present and the action must be dismissed. Reversed.

DISSENT: (Stevens, J.) The sole power under which Flagg (D) could sell the property was supplied by the state. Where the state authorizes self-help, it has conveyed a portion of its judicial power to private individuals. Our prior decisions have not required that the power conveyed be "exclusive" as is now required by the majority. We have previously held that there is state action present where the state has conveyed a right to private parties that has been traditionally held by it.

▌ *ANALYSIS*

Where enforcement by the state is present, the Court has no problem finding state action, e.g., enforcement of discriminatory covenants. In *Paul v. Davis*, 424 U.S. 693 (1976), the court found no damage to constitutionally protected rights where Paul's reputation was injured when his name was erroneously placed on the police's known shoplifters list. No specific constitutionally protected right was found.

■=■

Quicknotes

DUE PROCESS CLAUSE Clauses found in the Fifth and Fourteenth Amendments to the United States Constitution providing that no person shall be deprived of "life, liberty, or property, without due process of law."

EQUAL PROTECTION CLAUSE A constitutional guarantee that no person should be denied the same protection of the laws enjoyed by other persons in like circumstances.

STATE ACTION Actions brought pursuant to the Fourteenth Amendment claiming that the government violated the plaintiff's civil rights.

■=■

DeShaney v. Winnebago County Dept. of Social Services

Mother of abused child (P) v. State agency (D)

489 U.S. 189 (1989).

NATURE OF CASE: Appeal from summary dismissal of civil rights action for deprivation of liberty without due process.

FACT SUMMARY: Winnebago Department of Social Services (D) suspected that DeShaney's (P) son, Joshua, who lived with her former husband, was being repeatedly beaten by his father but did nothing to permanently take Joshua out of his father's custody.

🏛 RULE OF LAW
A state's failure to protect an individual against private violence does not violate the substantive due process or liberty rights of the victim.

FACTS: DeShaney's (P) son, Joshua, lived with her former husband. Upon Joshua's father's divorce from his second wife, the Winnebago Department of Social Services (DSS) (D) first learned from the wife that Joshua had been hit by his father, "causing marks." The DSS (D) interviewed the father, who denied the accusations, and took no action. A year later, the boy was admitted to the emergency room of a local hospital with multiple bruises and abrasions; upon notification by Joshua's physician, DSS (D) obtained an order of juvenile court placing Joshua in the hospital's custody. However, upon Joshua's release, the court decided there was insufficient evidence to retain Joshua in its custody. DSS (D), however, enrolled Joshua in a preschool program, provided his father with counseling, and encouraged the father's live-in girlfriend to move out. A month later, Joshua re-entered the emergency room with suspicious injuries, but the DSS (D) caseworker decided there was no basis for action. However, the caseworker repeatedly visited Joshua's home over the next six months and observed many suspicious head injuries. The caseworker also noticed that Joshua had not been enrolled in school and that the girlfriend had not moved out, but took no action although he thought the father may have been abusing Joshua. Once more, Joshua entered the emergency room with injuries his attending doctors believed were caused by child abuse. The caseworker tried to visit Joshua but was told he was too ill to be seen. The DSS (D) again took no action. Finally, the father beat Joshua so badly that he was sent into a life-threatening coma. His brain damage was so severe that he was expected to spend the rest of his life in an institution for the mentally retarded. By now Joshua was four years old. His father was subsequently convicted of child abuse. DeShaney (P) filed a § 1983 action alleging that DSS (D) had deprived Joshua of liberty without due process by failing to intervene to protect him against the risk of violence at his father's

hands, about which they knew or should have known. The district court granted summary judgment for DSS (D), which was affirmed by the seventh circuit. DeShaney (P) appealed.

ISSUE: Does a state's failure to protect against an individual against private violence violate the substantive due process or liberty rights of the victim?

HOLDING AND DECISION: (Rehnquist, C.J.) No. A state's failure to protect an individual against private violence does not violate the substantive due process or liberty rights of the victim. The Due Process Clause is phrased as a limitation on the state's power to act, not as a guarantee of certain minimal levels of safety and security. No affirmative right to government aid exists even where such aid may be necessary to secure life, liberty, or property interests of which the government itself may not deprive the individual. Here the violence committed against Joshua was at the hands of a private—not state—actor, his father. Merely because DSS (D) once took Joshua into its custody did not create a continuing duty to assume responsibility for Joshua's safety and general well-being; after all, DSS (D) returned Joshua to his father's custody. DeShaney (P) and Joshua are left to their state tort remedies, if any. Affirmed.

DISSENT: (Brennan, J.) A state's knowledge of an individual's predicament and its expressions of intent to help can amount to a limitation on an individual's freedom to act on his own behalf or to obtain help from others. Here, Wisconsin established a child-welfare system specifically designed to help children like Joshua; it invited and directed private citizens to depend on DSS (D) to protect children from abuse. DSS (D) had the ultimate decision-making authority regarding whether to disturb Joshua's living arrangements; private citizens felt no further obligation once they had reported Joshua's abuse to DSS (D). Therefore, DSS (D) did not "stand by and do nothing" with respect to Joshua. It actively intervened, acquired knowledge that Joshua was in danger, and confined Joshua to his father's home. This "inaction" was an abuse of power as egregious as "action." Oppression resulted because Wisconsin undertook a vital duty and then ignored it.

DISSENT: (Blackmun, J.) Wisconsin here actively intervened in Joshua's life, thus triggering a fundamental duty to aid the boy once it learned of the severe danger to which he was exposed. DSS (D) placed Joshua in a dangerous predicament despite knowledge of what his father was doing to him and essentially did nothing.

Continued on next page.

▶ *ANALYSIS*

In footnote 9 of the majority opinion, Rehnquist observes that had Joshua been removed from "free society and placed . . . in a foster home," an affirmative duty to protect might have arisen, thus appearing to create a "custodial exception" from the rule in this case. This duty was analogous to that created when an accused criminal is incarcerated or imprisoned. See *Youngberg v. Romero*, 457 U.S. 307 (1982), and *Estelle v. Gamble*, 429 U.S. 97 (1976). However, this "sterile formalism" was rejected by the dissent, which reasoned that given Wisconsin's self-assumed role as protector of children from abuse, DSS (D) was responsible for Joshua's placement once it learned Joshua was the subject of abuse. Accordingly, DSS (D) affirmatively "decided" to "place" him with his father, and the *Youngberg/Estelle* duty arose just as effectively as if DSS (D) had physically removed Joshua from his father's custody.

■═■

Quicknotes

DUE PROCESS CLAUSE Clauses found in the Fifth and Fourteenth Amendments to the United States Constitution providing that no person shall be deprived of "life, liberty, or property, without due process of law."

STATE ACTION Actions brought pursuant to the Fourteenth Amendment claiming that the government violated the plaintiff's civil rights.

■═■

Congressional Enforcement of Civil Rights

Quick Reference Rules of Law

Jones v. Alfred H. Mayer Co.

African-American home buyer (P) v. Home seller (D)

392 U.S. 409 (1968).

NATURE OF CASE: Action for injunctive and other relief to deal with refusal of property owners to sell to blacks.

FACT SUMMARY: Jones (P) brought suit in federal district court against the Alfred H. Mayer Co. (D) alleging that Mayer (D) refused to sell a home to him for the sole reason that Jones (P) is a black person.

🏛 RULE OF LAW
Congress, pursuant to the authority vested in it by the Thirteenth Amendment, which clothes "Congress with power to pass all laws necessary and proper for abolishing all badges and incidents of slavery, may validly bar all racial discrimination, private as well as public, in the sale or rental of property."

FACTS: Relying upon 42 U.S.C. § 1982 (all citizens have the same right to inherit, purchase, lease, hold, and convey real and personal property as is enjoyed by white citizens), Jones (P) brought suit in federal district court against the Alfred H. Mayer Co. (D) alleging that Mayer (D) refused to sell a home to him for the sole reason that Jones (P) is a black person.

ISSUE:
(1) Does purely private discrimination, unaided by any action on the part of the state, violate 42 U.S.C. § 1982 if its effect were to deny a citizen the right to rent or buy property solely because of his race or color?
(2) Does Congress have the power under the Constitution to do what 42 U.S.C. § 1982 purports to do?

HOLDING AND DECISION: (Stewart, J.)
(1) Yes. 42 U.S.C. § 1982 is only a limited attempt to deal with discrimination in a select area of real estate transactions, even though, on its face, § 1982 appears to prohibit all discrimination against blacks in the sale or rental of property. If § 1982, originally enacted as § 1 of the Civil Rights Act of 1866, had been intended to grant nothing more than an immunity from governmental interference, then much of § 2 of the 1866 Act, which provides for criminal penalties where a person has acted "under color" of any law, would have been meaningless. The broad language of § 1982 was intentional. Congress, in 1866, had before it considerable evidence showing private mistreatment of blacks. The focus of Congress, then, was on private groups (e.g., the KKK) operating outside the law.
(2) Yes. At the very least, the Thirteenth Amendment includes the freedom to buy whatever a white man can buy and the right to live wherever a white man can live. Reversed.

DISSENT: (Harlan, J.) The term "right" in § 1982 operates only against state-sanctioned discrimination. There is a difference between depriving a man of a right and interfering with the enjoyment of that right in a particular case. The enforcement provisions of the 1866 Act talk about "law, statute, ordinance, regulation or custom." As for legislative history, residential racial segregation was the norm in 1866. The Court has always held that the Fourteenth Amendment reaches only "state action."

▶ ANALYSIS

In *Sullivan v. Little Hunting Park, Inc.*, 396 U.S. 229 (1969), the Court invalidated a refusal by a homeowner's association to permit a member to assign his recreation share to an African-American. Once again, Harlan in dissent questioned whether the Court should expand a century-old statute to encompass today's real estate transactions. After these two cases, it is questionable whether the Court will place any limits on its reading of the Thirteenth Amendment when reviewing legislation aimed at private discrimination.

Quicknotes

INJUNCTIVE RELIEF A court order issued as a remedy, requiring a person to do, or prohibiting that person from doing, a specific act.

THIRTEENTH AMENDMENT The constitutional provision that abolished slavery in the United States.

Katzenbach v. Morgan

State (D) v. Voters (P)

384 U.S. 641 (1966).

NATURE OF CASE: Challenge to constitutionality of federal statute.

FACT SUMMARY: As part of the Voting Rights Act, Congress inserted a provision that prohibited restrictions on the right to register to vote based on the applicant's inability to read and write English where the applicant had at least a sixth-grade education in a Puerto Rican school where instruction was primarily in Spanish. New York had a statutory requirement of an ability to read and write English as a prerequisite to voter registration.

🏛 **RULE OF LAW**
A federal statute enacted pursuant to the Enabling Clause of the Fourteenth Amendment supersedes any state constitutional or statutory provision that is in conflict with the federal law.

FACTS: New York had a statute that required all persons seeking to register to vote be able to read and write the English language. In the Voting Rights Act of 1965, Congress inserted a provision that prohibited a requirement of ability to read and write English where the person seeking to vote had completed at least a sixth-grade education in Puerto Rico where the language of instruction is primarily Spanish. This suit was instituted by a group of registered voters in New York who challenged that provision of the federal statute insofar as it would prohibit enforcement of the New York requirement. At issue were the several hundred thousand Puerto Rican immigrants in New York who were prevented from voting by the New York statute, but who would be qualified under the federal law. The Attorney General of New York filed a brief in which he argued that the federal legislation would supersede the state law only if the state law were found to violate the provisions of the Fourteenth Amendment without reference to the federal statute. Also advanced was the argument that the federal statute violated the Equal Protection Clause of the Fourteenth Amendment, since it discriminated between non-English-speaking persons from Puerto Rico and non-English-speaking persons from other countries.

ISSUE: Does a federal statute enacted pursuant to the Enabling Clause of the Fourteenth Amendment supersede a conflicting state law by reason of the Supremacy Clause of the U.S. Constitution?

HOLDING AND DECISION: (Brennan, J.) Yes. A federal statute enacted pursuant to the Enabling Clause of the Fourteenth Amendment supersedes any state constitutional or statutory provision that is in conflict with the federal law. There is no need to determine whether the New York English literacy law is violative of the Fourteenth Amendment Equal Protection Clause in order to validate the federal law respecting voter qualifications. If Congress were limited to restricting only those state laws that violated the amendment, there would be no need for the federal law, since the state law could be invalidated in the courts. Rather, the test must be whether the federal legislation is appropriate to enforcement of the Equal Protection Clause. Section 5 of the Fourteenth Amendment is to be read to grant the same powers as the Necessary and Proper Clause of Article 1, § 8. Therefore, the federal statute must be examined to see whether it is "plainly adapted to that end" and whether it is not prohibited by but is consistent with "the letter and spirit of the Constitution." It was well within congressional authority to say that the need to vote by the Puerto Rican community warranted intrusion upon any state interest served by the English literacy test. The federal law was "plainly adapted" to furthering the aims of the Fourteenth Amendment. There is a perceivable basis for Congress to determine that this legislation was a proper way to resolve an inequity resulting from Congress's evaluation that an invidious discrimination existed. As to the contention that the federal law itself violates the Equal Protection Clause, the law does not restrict anyone's voting rights, but rather extends the franchise to a previously ineligible group. This was a reform measure and, as we have previously held, Congress need not correct an entire evil with one law but may "take one step at a time, addressing itself" to that problem that seems most pressing. We hold, therefore, that the federal law was a proper exercise of the powers granted Congress by the Fourteenth Amendment and that the Supremacy Clause prevents enforcement of the New York statute insofar as it is inconsistent with the federal law. Reversed.

DISSENT: (Harlan, J.) The majority has confused the question of legislative enforcement power with the area of proper judicial review. The question here is whether the state law is so arbitrary or irrational as to violate the Equal Protection Clause. And that is a judicial, not legislative, determination. The majority has validated a legislative determination by Congress that a state law is violative of the Constitution. There is no record of any evidence secured by Congress to support this determination. The judiciary is the ultimate arbiter of constitutionality, not Congress.

▶ *ANALYSIS*

As has occurred before, there was a footnote to the decision that caused as much controversy as the decision

Continued on next page.

itself. In this footnote, the Court stated that Congress could enact legislation giving force to the Fourteenth Amendment that expanded the rights provided in the amendment, but could not dilute or restrict the amendment by legislation. In other words, Congress can make determinations of constitutionality so long as they expand rights but cannot make those determinations if they restrict rights. However, there is serious debate as to whether allowing Congress to take an independent role in interpreting the Constitution can be justified under any circumstances in view of *Marbury v. Madison*. Once loosed in this area, can any restraint be thereafter imposed? Congress has traditionally tried to stay within judicially circumscribed bounds of constitutionality. But if it has an "independent role" in this area, the restraints are removed. An example of this may be seen in the Omnibus Crime Control Act, wherein Congress made legislative inroads to judicially granted rights as expressed in the *Miranda* decision. The Court can always rule on these inroads, but is it not better that Congress not be encouraged to embark on them in the first instance?

■═■

Quicknotes

ENABLING CLAUSE OF FOURTEENTH AMENDMENT A constitutional provision giving the power to implement and enforce the law.

EQUAL PROTECTION CLAUSE A constitutional guarantee that no person should be denied the same protection of the laws enjoyed by other persons in like circumstances.

INVIDIOUS DISCRIMINATION Unequal treatment of a class of persons that is particularly malicious or hostile.

SUPREMACY CLAUSE Article VI, Section 2, of the Constitution, which provides that federal action must prevail over inconsistent state action.

■═■

Boerne v. Flores

[Parties not identified in casebook excerpt.]

521 U.S. 507 (1997).

NATURE OF CASE: Review of order overturning denial of building permit.

FACT SUMMARY: A church (P) that had been denied a building permit by local zoning authorities (D) challenged the denial under the Religious Freedom Restoration Act.

🏛 RULE OF LAW
The Religious Freedom Restoration Act is unconstitutional.

FACTS: In response to the case *Employment Division v. Smith*, 494 U.S. 872 (1990), Congress in 1993 enacted the Religious Freedom Restoration Act (RFRA). The *Smith* Court had held that religious belief was no defense to a state law or regulation of general application. The RFRA provided that when a law of general application was to be applied over a religious objection, the state had to show a compelling interest for application of the law. When a local church (P) was denied a zoning permit, the church (P) challenged the zoning board's action under the RFRA. The appeals court ruled in favor of the church (P), and the Supreme Court granted review.

ISSUE: Is the Religious Freedom Restoration Act unconstitutional?

HOLDING AND DECISION: (Kennedy, J.) Yes. The Religious Freedom Restoration Act is unconstitutional. The RFRA was passed under the supposed authority of § 5 of the Fourteenth Amendment, which gives Congress power to enforce the Amendment's guarantees of equal protection and due process by appropriate legislation. In this instance, the right of freedom of religion, made applicable to the states by the Due Process Clause, is the right being enforced. However, while Congress can enforce the rights protected by the Amendment, it cannot determine the extent of those rights. It is the province of the judiciary, not the legislative branch, to define those rights. This Court has the final say as to what a law means, not Congress. In *Smith*, this Court defined the limits of the extent of religious freedom under the First and Fourteenth Amendments. Congress can enforce those rights, but cannot expand them. While the distinction between enforcement and expansion may not always be clear, the RFRA clearly is an example of the latter, not the former. This was beyond Congress's power. Reversed.

CONCURRENCE: (Stevens, J.) The RFRA is a "law respecting the establishment of religion" that violates separation of church and state.

DISSENT: (O'Connor, J.) The Court should reexamine its jurisprudence as expressed in *Smith*.

DISSENT: (Souter, J.) As Justice O'Connor states, *Smith* should be reexamined. This case should be sent back for reargument on this issue.

▌ ANALYSIS

The present case is a good example of the Court defending its turf. *Smith* was widely criticized, and calls to legislatively overrule it began almost immediately. It is not at all uncommon for Congress to legislatively overrule Court decisions, but this is generally in cases that deal with statutory construction. Constitutional construction remains the province of the Court, one that it guards zealously.

■▬■

Quicknotes

FREEDOM OF RELIGION The guarantee of the First Amendment to the United States Constitution prohibiting Congress from enacting laws regarding the establishment of religion or prohibiting the free exercise thereof.

RELIGIOUS FREEDOM RESTORATION ACT Legislation enacted in 1993 that ensured the free exercise of religion as an unalienable right and restored the compelling interest test as a way of negotiating a balance between religious liberty and competing governmental interests; it also provides a defense to persons whose religious exercise is substantially burdened by government.

■▬■

Limitations on Judicial Power and Review

Quick Reference Rules of Law

Allen v. Wright

[Parties not identified in casebook excerpt.]

468 U.S. 737 (1984).

NATURE OF CASE: Appeal of order denying tax-exempt status to racially discriminatory private schools.

FACT SUMMARY: Parents (P) of black schoolchildren filed an action to compel the Internal Revenue Service (D) to deny tax-exempt status to racially discriminatory private schools, in conformity with the law.

RULE OF LAW
One does not have standing to sue in federal court unless he can allege the violation of a right personal to him.

FACTS: Parents (P) of black schoolchildren brought an action to compel the Internal Revenue Service (IRS) (D) to deny tax-exempt status to private schools that discriminate, an illegal practice. It was alleged that the practice promoted segregated schools and made desegregation more difficult. The court of appeals held in favor of the parents (P).

ISSUE: Does one have standing to sue in federal court if he cannot allege a violation of a right personal to him?

HOLDING AND DECISION: (O'Connor, J.) No. One does not have standing to sue in federal court if he cannot allege a violation of a right personal to him. Federal courts are not designed to air generalized grievances. A plaintiff must allege injury traceable to a defendant's conduct likely to be redressed by the requested relief. It has long been held that the "right" to have the Government act in accordance with the law will not confer standing; something more personal is required. To do this would constitute an excessive intrusion of the Judiciary into the Executive branch of government. In the area in question, a plaintiff must show that he himself has been denied equal treatment in order to have standing. This has not been shown here. The allegation that the conduct of the IRS (D) promotes segregation is purely speculative. No allegation is made that withdrawal of the funds would make a difference in public school integration. Since no personal injury traceable to the IRS' (D) conduct has been alleged, no standing exists. Reversed.

DISSENT: (Brennan, J.) Alleging that the IRS's (D) conduct hinders black schoolchildren's rights to a desegregated education is alleging a concrete injury.

DISSENT: (Stevens, J.) The plaintiffs allege that the conduct of the IRS (D) promotes the exodus of white children who would otherwise attend integrated schools. This is a sufficient concrete injury to confer standing.

ANALYSIS

The requirements of standing are based on both textual and nontextual concerns. The "case or controversy" requirement is a basis for standing requirements. Also forming a basis are prudential concerns such as not interfering with other branches unnecessarily.

Quicknotes

CASE OR CONTROVERSY Constitutional requirement in order to invoke federal court jurisdiction that the matter present a justiciable issue.

STANDING Whether a party possesses the right to commence suit against another party by having a personal stake in the resolution of the controversy.

Lujan v. Defenders of Wildlife

Secretary of Interior (D) v. Environmental organization (P)

504 U.S. 555 (1992).

NATURE OF CASE: Review of grant of standing to enforce the Department of the Interior to apply the Endangered Species Act to actions taken in foreign countries.

FACT SUMMARY: Defenders of Wildlife (P) brought suit based on procedural injury challenging the Department of the Interior's (D) reinterpretation of the Endangered Species Act.

🏛 RULE OF LAW
Only a person with a concrete stake in the substantive outcome of an agency decision has standing to challenge a procedural violation made by the agency in regard to the particular decision.

FACTS: The Endangered Species Act (ESA) of 1973, § 7(a)(2), required federal agencies to consult with the Secretary of the Interior (D) to insure that projects they funded did not threaten endangered species. Defenders of Wildlife (P), an environmental organization, sued the Secretary of the Interior (D) for reinterpreting regulations of the ESA to apply only to actions taken in the United States or on the high seas, but not extending to actions taken in foreign nations. Defenders of Wildlife (P) did not allege any direct injury, but two members testified that they had traveled abroad to observe endangered species and intended to do so again. The court of appeals held that Defenders of Wildlife (P) had standing to sue based on procedural injury. The Secretary of the Interior (D) appealed.

ISSUE: Does an individual without a concrete stake in the substantive outcome of an agency decision have standing to challenge based on a congressionally mandated procedural requirement?

HOLDING AND DECISION: (Scalia, J.) No. Only a person with a concrete stake in the substantive outcome of an agency decision has standing to challenge a procedural violation made by the agency in regards to the particular decision. Members of Defenders of Wildlife (P) have no concrete interest of their own at stake and therefore cannot base their claim solely on a procedural requirement. Traveling abroad to observe endangered species, or visiting a zoo, does not support a finding of actual injury. The court of appeals erred gravely in finding that a statutorily prescribed procedural requirement can be converted into an individual right permitting any citizen to sue. This view has always been rejected. Reversed.

CONCURRENCE: (Kennedy, J.) The requirement that an individual must show concrete and personal injury is not just an empty formality. It preserves the value of the adversary process and confines the Judicial Branch to its proper role in government.

CONCURRENCE: (Stevens, J.) Although the majority's judgment was correct because there is no evidence that Congress intended the consultation requirement to apply to activities in foreign countries, their conclusion that Defenders of Wildlife (P) lack standing because the threatened injury to their interest in protecting endangered species is not "imminent" or "redressable" was not justified.

DISSENT: (Blackmun, J.) Defenders of Wildlife (P) have raised sufficient issues of fact to survive summary judgment. Failing to follow procedural requirements of statutes can be equivalent to disregarding the substantive environmental issues at stake. The majority's blanket prohibition against procedural injuries is too broad an exclusion to set forth.

▶ ANALYSIS

Prior to this holding, the status of a party's ability to assert standing based on procedural injury was not as clear as Justice Scalia stated. Furthermore, Justice Scalia's opinion has been criticized for having the potential to limit standing under similar statutes even where actual injury has been alleged. Nonetheless, the Court seemed to maintain that individuals can enforce procedural rights so long as a concrete interest is also threatened.

Quicknotes

ENDANGERED SPECIES ACT Prohibits the destruction of the habitat of endangered species.

STANDING Whether a party possesses the right to commence suit against another party by having a personal stake in the resolution of the controversy.

DeFunis v. Odegaard

Law student (P) v. Law school (D)

416 U.S. 312 (1974).

NATURE OF CASE: Action challenging law school's special admissions policy based on equal protection violation.

FACT SUMMARY: DeFunis (P), an applicant to the University of Washington Law School (the Law School) (D), was admitted after a court sustained his claim that the Law School's (D) special admissions policy violated the Constitution's equal protection clause.

RULE OF LAW

A case is moot when the controversy between the parties ceases to be definite and concrete, or the underlying issue that generated the suit is resolved prior to adjudication.

FACTS: DeFunis (P) was admitted to the University of Washington Law School (Law School) (D) after a state trial court sustained his claim that the Law School's (D) special admission policy violated his right of equal protection. The Washington Supreme Court reversed, but its judgment was stayed. By the time the United States Supreme Court heard the claim, DeFunis (P) had registered for his final term of his third year and the Law School (D) stated that this would not be canceled. However, the Law School (D) also stated that if its admissions policy were upheld, Defunis (P) would be subject to it if he had to register for any additional terms.

ISSUE: Is a case moot when the controversy between the parties ceases to be definite and concrete, or the underlying issue that generated the suit is resolved prior to adjudication?

HOLDING AND DECISION: (Per curiam) Yes. A case is moot when the controversy between the parties ceases to be definite and concrete, or the underlying issue that generated the suit is resolved prior to adjudication. Here, because the Law School (D) has agreed to let DeFunis (P) complete his legal studies and receive his degree, a determination by the Court is no longer necessary to compel the result or prevent it. Furthermore, the case does not fall into the exception for cases that are "capable of repetition, yet evading review" because DeFunis (P) will never be required to apply to law schools again and another student is not prevented from bringing a similar claim if the admissions procedures remain the same. The Court cannot consider the substantive issues tendered by the parties.

DISSENT: (Brennan, J.) Several weeks remain until graduation and there are any number of unexpected events that might prevent DeFunis (P) from completing the term.

The Law School (D) did not admit any wrongdoing, so the case falls into the category of cases where "voluntary cessation of allegedly illegal conduct does not moot a case," according to *United States v. Concentrated Phosphate Export Assn.*, 393 U.S. 199 (1968). Not only is this case ripe for adjudication, but the issues concern vast numbers of people, colleges and universities and will not disappear.

▶ *ANALYSIS*

Although the dissent brings up the compelling point that the Law School's (D) admissions policy remains intact, the majority was correct in holding that the personal interest at stake to DeFunis (P) was no longer at issue. Courts have repeatedly held that the controversy must exist throughout the course of the suit, so any other verdict would have been inappropriate. Limiting the number of justiciable cases serves the important goal of efficiency, as court resources are already stretched beyond their means.

Quicknotes

EQUAL PROTECTION A constitutional provision that each person be guaranteed the same protection of the laws enjoyed by other persons in life circumstances.

MOOTNESS Judgment on the particular issue would not resolve the controversy.

RIPENESS A doctrine precluding a federal court from hearing or determining a matter, unless it constitutes an actual and present controversy warranting a determination by the court.

United Public Workers v. Mitchell

Civil service employees (P) v. Government (D)

330 U.S. 75 (1947).

NATURE OF CASE: Action seeking declaratory and injunctive relief based on a violation of First Amendment rights.

FACT SUMMARY: Poole (P) was the only member of United Public Workers (P) to actually violate the Hatch Act's prohibition against political campaigning, but all the members sought to have the Act declared unconstitutional.

🏛 RULE OF LAW
A case is ripe for review if the interests of the litigants require the use of judicial authority for protection against actual, imminent interference.

FACTS: The United Public Workers (P), federal civil service employees, sought a declaratory judgment and injunctive relief, alleging that the Hatch Act's prohibition against taking any active part in political management or in political campaigns violated their First Amendment rights. Only one member of the group, Poole (P), had actually violated the Act and faced dismissal from his job. The others stated that they desired to serve as party officials, write articles, circulate petitions, and participate in a number of ways, but had not yet done so.

ISSUE: Is a case ripe for review if the interests of the litigants require the use of judicial authority for protection against actual interference?

HOLDING AND DECISION: (Reed, J.) Yes. A case is ripe for review if the interests of the litigants require the use of judicial authority for protection against actual, imminent interference. Pursuant to Article III of the Constitution, the federal courts do not render advisory opinions. A hypothetical threat is not sufficient, and the existence of a law they have not yet violated is a hypothetical threat. The United Public Workers (P), with the exception of Poole (P), seek advisory opinions based upon broad claims. It would not accord with judicial responsibility to adjudge their cases until a definite right has been allegedly violated. Poole's (P) claim is rejected on the merits because he has not shown sufficient reason to grant the declaratory relief he seeks.

DISSENT: (Douglas, J.) If the United Public Workers (P) do what they want to do they will be discharged. Therefore the threat is real and immediate.

▶ ANALYSIS

Ripeness concerns the timing determining when a case is ready for adjudication. It is different from the issue of justiciability, which determines whether a court would be exceeding its authority in hearing a case. A case that is unripe may be eligible for adjudication as soon as a certain event occurs; however, there are many issues that will be nonjusticiable regardless of timing.

Quicknotes

FIRST AMENDMENT Prohibits Congress from enacting any law respecting an establishment of religion, prohibiting the free exercise of religion, abridging freedom of speech or the press, the right of peaceful assembly and the right to petition for a redress of grievances.

HATCH ACT Legislation enacted in 1887 that restricted the political activity of executive branch employees of the federal government, the District of Columbia government and certain state and local agencies. Subsequent amendments lessened restrictions on federal and D.C. employees, but some state and local agencies are still prohibited from engaging in partisan political activity.

JUSTICIABILITY An actual controversy that is capable of determination by the court.

RIPENESS A doctrine precluding a federal court from hearing or determining a matter, unless it constitutes an actual and present controversy warranting a determination by the court.

Common Latin Words and Phrases Encountered in the Law

A FORTIORI: Because one fact exists or has been proven, therefore a second fact that is related to the first fact must also exist.

A PRIORI: From the cause to the effect. A term of logic used to denote that when one generally accepted truth is shown to be a cause, another particular effect must necessarily follow.

AB INITIO: From the beginning; a condition which has existed throughout, as in a marriage which was void ab initio.

ACTUS REUS: The wrongful act; in criminal law, such action sufficient to trigger criminal liability.

AD VALOREM: According to value; an ad valorem tax is imposed upon an item located within the taxing jurisdiction calculated by the value of such item.

AMICUS CURIAE: Friend of the court. Its most common usage takes the form of an amicus curiae brief, filed by a person who is not a party to an action but is nonetheless allowed to offer an argument supporting his legal interests.

ARGUENDO: In arguing. A statement, possibly hypothetical, made for the purpose of argument, is one made arguendo.

BILL QUIA TIMET: A bill to quiet title (establish ownership) to real property.

BONA FIDE: True, honest, or genuine. May refer to a person's legal position based on good faith or lacking notice of fraud (such as a bona fide purchaser for value) or to the authenticity of a particular document (such as a bona fide last will and testament).

CAUSA MORTIS: With approaching death in mind. A gift causa mortis is a gift given by a party who feels certain that death is imminent.

CAVEAT EMPTOR: Let the buyer beware. This maxim is reflected in the rule of law that a buyer purchases at his own risk because it is his responsibility to examine, judge, test, and otherwise inspect what he is buying.

CERTIORARI: A writ of review. Petitions for review of a case by the United States Supreme Court are most often done by means of a writ of certiorari.

CONTRA: On the other hand. Opposite. Contrary to.

CORAM NOBIS: Before us; writs of error directed to the court that originally rendered the judgment.

CORAM VOBIS: Before you; writs of error directed by an appellate court to a lower court to correct a factual error.

CORPUS DELICTI: The body of the crime; the requisite elements of a crime amounting to objective proof that a crime has been committed.

CUM TESTAMENTO ANNEXO, ADMINISTRATOR (ADMINISTRATOR C.T.A.): With will annexed; an administrator c.t.a. settles an estate pursuant to a will in which he is not appointed.

DE BONIS NON, ADMINISTRATOR (ADMINISTRATOR D.B.N.): Of goods not administered; an administrator d.b.n. settles a partially settled estate.

DE FACTO: In fact; in reality; actually. Existing in fact but not officially approved or engendered.

DE JURE: By right; lawful. Describes a condition that is legitimate "as a matter of law," in contrast to the term "de facto," which connotes something existing in fact but not legally sanctioned or authorized. For example, de facto segregation refers to segregation brought about by housing patterns, etc., whereas de jure segregation refers to segregation created by law.

DE MINIMIS: Of minimal importance; insignificant; a trifle; not worth bothering about.

DE NOVO: Anew; a second time; afresh. A trial de novo is a new trial held at the appellate level as if the case originated there and the trial at a lower level had not taken place.

DICTA: Generally used as an abbreviated form of obiter dicta, a term describing those portions of a judicial opinion incidental or not necessary to resolution of the specific question before the court. Such nonessential statements and remarks are not considered to be binding precedent.

DUCES TECUM: Refers to a particular type of writ or subpoena requesting a party or organization to produce certain documents in their possession.

EN BANC: Full bench. Where a court sits with all justices present rather than the usual quorum.

EX PARTE: For one side or one party only. An ex parte proceeding is one undertaken for the benefit of only one party, without notice to, or an appearance by, an adverse party.

EX POST FACTO: After the fact. An ex post facto law is a law that retroactively changes the consequences of a prior act.

EX REL.: Abbreviated form of the term "ex relatione," meaning upon relation or information. When the state brings an action in which it has no interest against an individual at the instigation of one who has a private interest in the matter.

FORUM NON CONVENIENS: Inconvenient forum. Although a court may have jurisdiction over the case, the action should be tried in a more conveniently located court, one to which parties and witnesses may more easily travel, for example.

GUARDIAN AD LITEM: A guardian of an infant as to litigation, appointed to represent the infant and pursue his/her rights.

HABEAS CORPUS: You have the body. The modern writ of habeas corpus is a writ directing that a person (body) being detained (such as a prisoner) be brought before the court so that the legality of his detention can be judicially ascertained.

IN CAMERA: In private, in chambers. When a hearing is held before a judge in his chambers or when all spectators are excluded from the courtroom.

IN FORMA PAUPERIS: In the manner of a pauper. A party who proceeds in forma pauperis because of his poverty is one who is allowed to bring suit without liability for costs.

INFRA: Below, under. A word referring the reader to a later part of a book. (The opposite of supra.)

IN LOCO PARENTIS: In the place of a parent.

IN PARI DELICTO: Equally wrong; a court of equity will not grant requested relief to an applicant who is in pari delicto, or as much at fault in the transactions giving rise to the controversy as is the opponent of the applicant.

IN PARI MATERIA: On like subject matter or upon the same matter. Statutes relating to the same person or things are said to be in pari materia. It is a general rule of statutory construction that such statutes should be construed together, i.e., looked at as if they together constituted one law.

IN PERSONAM: Against the person. Jurisdiction over the person of an individual.

IN RE: In the matter of. Used to designate a proceeding involving an estate or other property.

IN REM: A term that signifies an action against the res, or thing. An action in rem is basically one that is taken directly against property, as distinguished from an action in personam, i.e., against the person.

INTER ALIA: Among other things. Used to show that the whole of a statement, pleading, list, statute, etc., has not been set forth in its entirety.

INTER PARTES: Between the parties. May refer to contracts, conveyances or other transactions having legal significance.

INTER VIVOS: Between the living. An inter vivos gift is a gift made by a living grantor, as distinguished from bequests contained in a will, which pass upon the death of the testator.

IPSO FACTO: By the mere fact itself.

JUS: Law or the entire body of law.

LEX LOCI: The law of the place; the notion that the rights of parties to a legal proceeding are governed by the law of the place where those rights arose.

MALUM IN SE: Evil or wrong in and of itself; inherently wrong. This term describes an act that is wrong by its very nature, as opposed to one which would not be wrong but for the fact that there is a specific legal prohibition against it (malum prohibitum).

MALUM PROHIBITUM: Wrong because prohibited, but not inherently evil. Used to describe something that is wrong because it is expressly forbidden by law but that is not in and of itself evil, e.g., speeding.

MANDAMUS: We command. A writ directing an official to take a certain action.

MENS REA: A guilty mind; a criminal intent. A term used to signify the mental state that accompanies a crime or other prohibited act. Some crimes require only a general mens rea (general intent to do the prohibited act), but others, like assault with intent to murder, require the existence of a specific mens rea.

MODUS OPERANDI: Method of operating; generally refers to the manner or style of a criminal in committing crimes, admissible in appropriate cases as evidence of the identity of a defendant.

NEXUS: A connection to.

NISI PRIUS: A court of first impression. A nisi prius court is one where issues of fact are tried before a judge or jury.

N.O.V. (NON OBSTANTE VEREDICTO): Notwithstanding the verdict. A judgment n.o.v. is a judgment given in favor of one party despite the fact that a verdict was returned in favor of the other party, the justification being that the verdict either had no reasonable support in fact or was contrary to law.

NUNC PRO TUNC: Now for then. This phrase refers to actions that may be taken and will then have full retroactive effect.

PENDENTE LITE: Pending the suit; pending litigation under way.

PER CAPITA: By head; beneficiaries of an estate, if they take in equal shares, take per capita.

PER CURIAM: By the court; signifies an opinion ostensibly written "by the whole court" and with no identified author.

PER SE: By itself, in itself; inherently.

PER STIRPES: By representation. Used primarily in the law of wills to describe the method of distribution where a person, generally because of death, is unable to take that which is left to him by the will of another, and therefore his heirs divide such property between them rather than take under the will individually.

PRIMA FACIE: On its face, at first sight. A prima facie case is one that is sufficient on its face, meaning that the evidence supporting it is adequate to establish the case until contradicted or overcome by other evidence.

PRO TANTO: For so much; as far as it goes. Often used in eminent domain cases when a property owner receives partial payment for his land without prejudice to his right to bring suit for the full amount he claims his land to be worth.

QUANTUM MERUIT: As much as he deserves. Refers to recovery based on the doctrine of unjust enrichment in those cases in which a party has rendered valuable services or furnished materials that were accepted and enjoyed by another under circumstances that would reasonably notify the recipient that the rendering party expected to be paid. In essence, the law implies a contract to pay the reasonable value of the services or materials furnished.

QUASI: Almost like; as if; nearly. This term is essentially used to signify that one subject or thing is almost analogous to another but that material differences between them do exist. For example, a quasi-criminal proceeding is one that is not strictly criminal but shares enough of the same characteristics to require some of the same safeguards (e.g., procedural due process must be followed in a parole hearing).

QUID PRO QUO: Something for something. In contract law, the consideration, something of value, passed between the parties to render the contract binding.

RES GESTAE: Things done; in evidence law, this principle justifies the admission of a statement that would otherwise be hearsay when it is made so closely to the event in question as to be said to be a part of it, or with such spontaneity as not to have the possibility of falsehood.

RES IPSA LOQUITUR: The thing speaks for itself. This doctrine gives rise to a rebuttable presumption of negligence when the instrumentality causing the injury was within the exclusive control of the defendant, and the injury was one that does not normally occur unless a person has been negligent.

RES JUDICATA: A matter adjudged. Doctrine which provides that once a court of competent jurisdiction has rendered a final judgment or decree on the merits, that judgment or decree is conclusive upon the parties to the case and prevents them from engaging in any other litigation on the points and issues determined therein.

RESPONDEAT SUPERIOR: Let the master reply. This doctrine holds the master liable for the wrongful acts of his servant (or the principal for his agent) in those cases in which the servant (or agent) was acting within the scope of his authority at the time of the injury.

STARE DECISIS: To stand by or adhere to that which has been decided. The common law doctrine of stare decisis attempts to give security and certainty to the law by following the policy that once a principle of law as applicable to a certain set of facts has been set forth in a decision, it forms a precedent which will subsequently be followed, even though a different decision might be made were it the first time the question had arisen. Of course, stare decisis is not an inviolable principle and is departed from in instances where there is good cause (e.g., considerations of public policy led the Supreme Court to disregard prior decisions sanctioning segregation).

SUPRA: Above. A word referring a reader to an earlier part of a book.

ULTRA VIRES: Beyond the power. This phrase is most commonly used to refer to actions taken by a corporation that are beyond the power or legal authority of the corporation.

Addendum of French Derivatives

IN PAIS: Not pursuant to legal proceedings.

CHATTEL: Tangible personal property.

CY PRES: Doctrine permitting courts to apply trust funds to purposes not expressed in the trust but necessary to carry out the settlor's intent.

PER AUTRE VIE: For another's life; during another's life. In property law, an estate may be granted that will terminate upon the death of someone other than the grantee.

PROFIT A PRENDRE: A license to remove minerals or other produce from land.

VOIR DIRE: Process of questioning jurors as to their predispositions about the case or parties to a proceeding in order to identify those jurors displaying bias or prejudice.

Casenote® Legal Briefs